Y0-DCH-829

THE ROMANTIC UNCONSCIOUS
A Study in Narcissism and Patriarchy

Previous books by David Punter:

The Literature of Terror: A History of Gothic Fictions from 1765 to the Present Day (1980)

Romanticism and Ideology: Studies in English Writing 1765–1830, with David Aers and Jonathan Cook (1981)

Blake, Hegel and Dialectic (1982)

The Hidden Script: Writing and the Unconscious (1985)

China and Glass (1985)

Introduction to Contemporary Cultural Studies (1986)

Lost in the Supermarket (1987)

William Blake: Selected Poetry and Prose (1988)

THE ROMANTIC UNCONSCIOUS

A Study in Narcissism and Patriarchy

David Punter

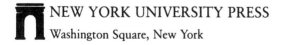

NEW YORK UNIVERSITY PRESS
Washington Square, New York

First published in the U.S.A. in 1990 by
New York University Press
Washington Square
New York, NY 10003

© 1989 David Punter

Printed and bound in Great Britain by
Billing and Sons Ltd, Worcester

Library of Congress Cataloging-in-Publication Data

Punter, David.
   The romantic unconscious
   Includes bibliographical references.
   1. English literature—History and criticism.
   2. Psychoanalysis and literature.   3. Subconsciousness in
   literature.   4. Narcissism in literature.   5. Patriarchy in
   literature.   6. Romanticism—English.   I. Title
   PR408.P8P8   1989   820.9'353   89–14014
   ISBN 0–8147–6612–9

1 2 3 4 5   93 92 91 90 89

The Song of the Demented Priest

I put those things there. – See them burn.
The emerald the azure and the gold
Hiss and crack, the blue & greens of the world
As if I were tired. Someone interferes
Everywhere with me. The clouds, the clouds are torn
In ways I do not understand or love.

Licking my long lips, I looked upon God
And he flamed and he was friendlier
Than you were, and he was small. Showing me
Serpents and thin flowers; these were cold.
Dominion waved and glittered like the glare
From ice under a small sun. I wonder.

Afterward the violent and formal dancers
Came out, shaking their pithless heads.
I would instruct them but I cannot now, –
Because of the elements. They rise and move,
I nod a dance and they dance in the rain
In my red coat. I am the king of the dead.

Sonnet 12

Mutinous armed & suicidal grind
Fears on desires, a clutter humps a track,
The body of expectation hangs down slack
Untidy black; my love sweats like a rind;
Parrots are yattering up the cagy mind,
Jerking their circles ... you stood, a week back,
By, I saw your foot with half my eye, I lack
You ... the damned female's yellow head swings blind.

Cageless they'd grapple. O where, whose Martini
Grows sweeter with my torment, wrung on toward
The insomnia of eternity, loud graves!
Hölderlin on his tower sang like the sea
More you adored that day than your harpsichord,
Troubled and drowning, tempted and empty waves.

John Berryman

CONTENTS

viii   *Contents*

PREFACE

It might seem from the title as though this book is about the many contacts which the romantic writers made with emergent concepts of the unconscious. There certainly is a book to be written about that; but this is not it, or not directly so. It is instead an attempt to grapple with the unconscious *of* romanticism; and I have seen this as a complex task which involves both the perception of romanticism as a historical phenomenon and a continuous awareness of the survival of romanticism as a mode of apprehension which still conditions much of our culture and much of our critical working. In particular, I have tried at points to dwell on notions of interpretation in general, and on the cross-connections between interpretation and romantic views of the world.

I have often tried to use psychoanalytic arguments; but the difficulty here is that I believe that the real gifts of psychoanalysis are of such a kind as to make writing itself very difficult. Certainly Freud's own writings throve on them; but then, his writing was so nearly always a set of records of the actual exchanges of individuals in all their complexity. When we try to think analytically about culture, we run, I think, in different ways into the inevitable problem of how to speak about that which is not known, and I do not think there are any straight lines through these quandaries.

Part 1 of this book might have been alternatively titled an 'optional introduction', except that this sounds rather coy; but it is true that the reflections which I have there tried to introduce on the nature of interpretation are largely imagistic, and I hope that, if they are read at all, they will be read as such. Readers wishing to proceed to a more identifiable topic of romanticism might be well advised to move straight to Part 2 and thereafter.

Several parts of the book contain reworkings of material which I have published earlier in other forms, and these will be found listed in the Bibliography. But it was not until writing this that I realised how thoroughly these materials were permeated by an unarticulated concept of narcissism, and in one sense this book is an attempt to articulate that concept in its romantic context; or, to follow through some common psychosocial root for narcissism and romanticism.

At some points in the book I have referred to certain activities, certain casts of mind, certain psychological shapings, as being under the rule of this or that god; I think Hephaestos is the most relevant. It has been suggested to me that this is a rather odd way of thinking, a trace of unaccommodated religiosity. I do not think that is quite the point. The gods, I suspect, are inhabitants of the dream-world, and in this sense more than in the historical one they ante-date us and will not go away if we wish them to; indeed, they have been noted for paying little heed to our conscious demands. The most extraordinary explorations into these realms are those conducted by James Hillman, to whose works I was introduced in the course of writing the present book, and I refer the reader to them. I was myself introduced to them by Caroline Case, and I should say that I feel deeply grateful.

You will have found in the preceding pages two poems by John Berryman; and I refer to them at several points in the book. I think they constitute a continuing underpinning to these reflections on narcissism. I also suspect that I cannot articulate what they are about, despite having tried to find out by tantalising several generations of students with the possibility of their exegesis. But I think that something is *at work* in them, perhaps performing some of that constant unregarded work which Hephaestos performs down in the deeps, to which I, for one, have felt it necessary to pay attention, and which I think is recognisable to romanticism; something of that inexplicable activity which sways the curtain, and which forces us towards the sometimes unwelcome explorations of unrest which romanticism also represents.

D.P.

ACKNOWLEDGEMENTS

Grateful acknowledgement is given to the following for permission to reprint material in copyright: reprinted by permission of Faber and Faber Ltd from *Homage to Mistress Bradstreet* and *Berryman's Sonnets* by John Berryman. "The Song of the Demented Priest" from *Short Poems* by John Berryman. Copyright © 1948 by John Berryman. Reprinted by permission of Farrar, Straus and Giroux, Inc. "Sonnet #12" from *Sonnets* by John Berryman. Copyright © 1952, 1967 by John Berryman. Reprinted by permission of Farrar, Straus and Giroux, Inc.

PART 1

ON THE NATURE OF INTERPRETATION

Interpretation

I think it is difficult, these days, to see literary history as simply linear; yet no more easy, despite Vico and Hegel, to turn to an imagery of circles and spheres, for there are many forces working against the sensing of the echo of a music which – and this especially in connection with romanticism – we may suspect not to have fled. The shapes of imagination of the late twentieth century, the metaphors which generate the illusions and gratifications of system, are other than that. Those shapes appear now in some relationship, however displaced, to other discourses, ones which lose their stability in the moment of utterance – the discourses, for example, of subnuclear physics and space exploration, which confound our precarious sense of geometry.

We have with us and in us – and with the overwhelming force added by media saturation – a world structured more in terms of ellipses, trajectories, orbits, spirals.[1] But as we describe these patterns, they are then deliberately forgotten by acts of the ordering will, which would otherwise be overwhelmed; yet thus they are simultaneously laid down in the objective realm of the unconscious, for this is where the shaping of our imagination cannot be evaded. From that embedded position they continue to produce puzzling effects of organisation, which startle with the readiness with which they rise to lips we had thought shaped to quite other sounds. I am suggesting that there are no longer any specific moments of historical recapture – revivals of classicism, neoplatonic moments, strenuous engagements with recuperable movements or schools; all that belongs to too simple a concept of sublation. Thus the problem, as I see it, with structuralism is that it is based on a modelling of the psyche which endlessly seeks a principle of equivalence between the will and that which is willed within and outside us. Instead we are being made aware of the possibility of instant information recall, and this is itself inflected with the cybernetic paradox: range and scope of choice simultaneously entail a quailing before the flexings of the machine.

And so I would like to try to see romanticism as both before our eyes and behind our averted gaze: the pantheon we know and love transmits itself to us no longer only as a set of comfortable, solid objectifications, but also as an orbiting of snippets, tyger and Abyssinian maid appropriated by the quite different lusts of advertising, a ragged army of images which might always be on the point of mobilisation, but which instead tends towards becoming a mercenary force thriving on the displacement of idealism.

My case about romanticism is, I think, both particular and emblematic. Any predominance of past cultural moments which we care to mention needs to be checked, in both senses, on its trajectory through the hall of distorting cultural mirrors, and within any of these accidental recaptures we find an intrinsic questioning abut the problematised nature of individual and group interest: what function is there to these moments of cultural recall, into what trap of debasement might the valued images fall if we even dare to call attention to them?

These questions are themselves widenings of the spiral. What is it that we see in romanticism? In seeing connnections, which themselves might be specifically focused on *irregularity*, on whose behalf are we speaking? In the fragmented and struggling self, there is always a multiplicity of sources: from which of these does the voice of the symbolic emerge? For the symbolic itself is now as never before the recognised site of a sardonic exploitation. To change the metaphor: we might talk of remixing the tapes, but where does the remastering skill come from, and therefore what as yet undreamed investments in the future are being furthered, resisted or retarded by each new dissemination of signifiers which occurs in the reinterpretation of culture?

This all sounds very grandiose; but it is of course very puny at the same time, in the same diastole/systole, the timings which are supposed to dictate our *jouissance*, our pleasure in the playful. It is as though the search is akin to the tarot: a search for the interpreter-king, although over his shoulder we are all the time aware of the voice of thunder, our own voices as critics drowned in the blare of exploitative multiplicity; as though we are trying to prefigure, and thereby avert, the bombers overhead with a saving deconstruction. This deconstruction might seem designed to protect us through the exercise of an unassailably remarkable intelligence; yet the activity itself seems merely jejune, because its power is only to interrogate the already discomposed self about its own preferred mode of vanishing.

Thus the act of *instituting* becomes a desperate necessity; we might say, before nightfall. And this can be seen as the beginning of another trajectory, whereon at some other time – on another scene, as Freud compellingly described it[2] – we shall not be able to avoid the impending forms of the millenial, for the desperation is that shown before the end of the world. I hope it is understood that I am talking, of course, about fantasies, and, I also hope, in their terms; and I mean to open up immediately a connection with romanticism, which was perennially haunted, in Britain, by the sense of a hovering across the waters of an invasive fate which bore, of course, a curious relation to the end of centuries, a relation compounded of fear and wish.

So I think that those states, those conditions of the word, with which we engage as we seek to recapture history resonate with a 'past' whose continuity we simultaneously need to deny, because it would remind us too strongly of the fantasy of apocalypse. Our relation to romanticism thus becomes of the nature of a parabola, its joining always receding; and how can you exert leverage on a parabola to make it yield meaning? Or does it thereby become a springboard, spinning our selves off towards the stars – or giving us thereby the privilege of further unavailability, a further avoidance of a threatened transmutation?

Behind what I am trying to say lies an acculturated fear of repetition. 'Absolute objectivity', says Jung in the days when such things could be uttered without irony, 'consists of nothing but exceptions to the rule', and 'has predominantly the character of *irregularity*';[3] and I take it that interpretation, which is the concept I am here trying to get at, is a way of coding that irregularity, and thus represents both our hopes of purchase or grasp and our fears of being dominated, our dual role as controller and controlled before whatever machine it is that we fear. The question of the utterer of the discourse is necessarily foregrounded in the boundaries of silence and speech which oscillate around the interpretative activity, and here I think we touch on a specifically romantic preoccupation (romantic also in so far as it continues into the contemporary world). Blake's troping of the Bible; the Coleridgean intimations of hidden voices; Scott's remaking of the past according to an overwhelming and shamelessly pragmatic moral law; the Gothic interrogation of the projections borne on the wind of silence and non-human motility, which may well remind us of the preternatural motility of the infant stuck before the mirror; Keats's questioning of the mask of the chthonic goddess; and indeed all the strickennesses into silence – Nietzsche, Hölderlin and their avatars, John Berryman among them[4] – which ensue from the confrontation with perceived irregularity and the unjust cosmos; all these are movements of interpretation seeking purchase on the power against which Jung's Job and Blake's variously impotent deities never cease to rail.

These, then, are some of the cogs in the ensemble, and I see no harm in reusing the romantic armoury of terms and perceptions to try to focus on this notion of interpretation attempted and repulsed. What, then, can we bring to this reconstituted discourse? I want to try to touch on a quaternary model of interpretation, situated somewhere between ourselves and the body of romantic imagery, a quaternary which might act as a map; although our sailors, like Lewis Carroll's, might well throw up their hands in delight to discover that, in another time and space, the map is perfectly blank, and the habit of inscription is only the site of an intense and prized relativity.

Psychoanalysis

> Interpretation becomes a sort of phlogiston: manifest in everything that is understood rightly or wrongly; providing it feeds the flame of the imaginary, of that pure display, which, under the name of aggressivity, flourishes in the technique of the period.[5]

We are talking, then, about the inscribing of the blank sheet, which simultaneously raises a question about priorisation, for the blank might itself be a delighted, romantic apprehension of the failure of all constricting systems. And the inscription has also to be a negation, and we can therefore place it within the 'fundamental negations described', according to Lacan, 'by Freud as the three delusions of jealousy, erotomania, and interpretation'.[6] I shall try to describe the internalities of this scheme later;[7] but for the moment, I want to interrogate this now conventional urge to bring Lacan, whose main work, after all, was to bring the revelations of structural linguistics *to* the analytic process, back into a different correlation with those literary demands and habits which themselves, in a sense, underlie the drive towards explanation.

One of the obvious connections can be made through Gothic fiction. The fragmented body, according to Lacan

> usually manifests itself in dreams when the movement of the analysis encounters a certain level of aggressive disintegration in the individual. It then appears in the form of disjointed limbs, or of those organs represented in exoscopy, growing wings and taking up arms for intestinal persecutions – the very same that the visionary Hieronymus Bosch has fixed, for all time, in painting, in their ascent from the fifteenth century to the imaginary zenith of

modern man. But this form is even tangibly revealed at the organic level, in the lines of 'fragilisation' that define the anatomy of fantasy, as exhibited in the schizoid and spasmodic symptoms of hysteria.[8]

A deconstructionist approach to this passage would begin from that 'for all time', and would examine the underside of this submerged worship of the transcendental power of the visual arts, those arts and skills so vigorously debased in all non-Jungian analytic schools. We would then be thinking about the power-effects of the word from a certain angle: as an uneven contract, as a metaphor for the death of affect, as guarantor against the disruptions of discourse; so that the real deificatory power can be reserved for the sacerdotal investment of the analytic institution itself, with its emphatic schismaticism, its delight in heresy, and its occasional discourse of ethical responsibility in which it tries to recuperate the dishonesty of its bargains in the market-place.

But the point I want to make is about a duality of reading. The relevance of the content here is obvious: all the severed organs in Horace Walpole's *Castle of Otranto* (1764), the floating part-objects in Blake's prophetic books, the mark of Geraldine's curse and blessing, which is nothing less than the mark on the shoulder which designates the ambiguity of the gift of tongues, for which the wilderness is the reward and the punishment. But the questions left are the familiar ones about aetiology: what, then, in the case of romanticism are we to designate in historical terms as correlative with 'a certain level of aggressive disintegration in the individual'? The industrial revolution? The breakdown of social order consequent on and anterior to the events in France? A certain isolation of the intelligentsia? Some specific fate of the feminine as refracted through the body and work of the male poet? A trajectory through the canons of word and value? And how are we to take – and reinterpret – the notion of 'fragilisation', now that we can no longer recognise a quarantined duality of form and content?

I hope to make some suggestions about these points; but we can be in little doubt about the existence of this encounter along the spiral, between romantic accounts of alienation and analytic versions of the disintegrating self:

> Correlatively, the formation of the *I* is symbolised in dreams by a fortress, or a stadium – its inner arena and enclosure, surrounded by marshes and rubbish-tips, dividing it into two opposed fields of contest where the subject flounders in quest of the lofty, remote inner castle whose form (sometimes juxtaposed in the same scenario) symbolises the id in a quite startling way.[9]

A terrain of a terrain; and it is the terrain of Frankenstein's castle, or ('stadium') of the castle which hosts the man-eating game of neoromantic movies like *The Hounds of Zaroff* (1932) – which is also known as *The Most Dangerous Game*, which spirals us back to the life-and-death, negating encounters of psychoanalysis itself.[10] In these myths, however, we have a substitution for the 'rubbish-tips': an anthropomorphic revision producing the sullen peasantry whose anti-aristocratic and anti-miscegenative feelings are aroused by the lure of latent Puritanism (the 'ghost-hunters') to remit torture with torture, and thus to bear an ambiguous and unconscious witness to the brutalising power of Frankenstein's misogyny made flesh. 'The unconscious is that chapter of my history that is marked by a blank or occupied by a falsehood: it is the censored chapter. But the truth can be rediscovered; usually it has been written down elsewhere'.[11] Yes; but because we are continually rereading it is not going too far to say that it has been written down, among other places, in the future, in the long chain of looping iterations through which we articulate our mistrusts. The name-of-Frankenstein can be managed no more effectively by the processes of rational chronology than by the equally significant determinations of the commercial cinema.

What I want to pick out from psychoanalysis is the ambiguity of the goal of interpretation, 'in the dialectical discussion between the conscious mind and the unconscious',[12] a discussion in which there is no assurance of parity, or regularity, between the poles. 'The unconscious does not simply act *contrary* to the conscious mind but *modifies* it more in the manner of an opponent or partner'.[13] This mapping, however, of the interpreter/patient dyad onto the conscious/unconscious is at best the beginning of the situation, at worst a nest of fallacies and the very haunt of irregularity; indeed it is in the very disguising of these irregularities, the notion of a fixed analytic schemea, that we can trace the connections between interpretation and paranoia, connections which Coleridge saw only too inescapably.

The crucial category here has often been phrased as desire. We could say that within the establishment of power-relations, or within the forms which historically transmit those relations through the media of professionalisation, or asceticism (the adequation of analysis to Zen Buddhism), or the removal of the self behind a protective veil, what we come across is in fact a yearned-for reversal of roles. There should be no question here of cover-stories, of a simple interpretation of the repression of drives: the structures are too closely interwound, for 'in its symbolising function speech is moving towards nothing less than a transformation of the subject to whom it is addressed by means of the link that it establishes with the one who emits it – in other words, by introducing the effect of a signifier'.[14] Following this metaphor, for the analyst the experience of the interpretative encounter can be read as a putting into motion, although this is an attention to the unconscious which always simultaneously draws upon myths of the strengths of containment, so that it is in fact the *real* world outside the window which is in the end experienced as the feared and protected realm from which the patient's attention must be withdrawn. This, I think, is an exemplary experience of deferral, which distributes itself down both sides of our pyramid of irregularities and manifests itself emblematically in the symbolism of absence from the session. For that absence grotesquely signifies (as do romanticism's ghosts) the absence of the central subject, and thus the redistribution of core into a refined notion of interpretation as a continual marking of abstract boundaries. The poles of the experience, as Lacan says, are not acceptance and rejection but recognition and abolition;[15] the reality status of the phantom is truly at stake here, in the impress on the couch, where the conditions of speech always teeter on the brink of an inexpressible inequality which touches also on a possible remaking of the conceptualisations of power and the pressure of the always-already existence of language.

And it is that 'always-already', that power which threatens the will, which is at stake in interpretation and which is also, I shall argue, a prime romantic preoccupation. 'Everyone recognises in his own way that to confirm that an interpretation is well founded, it is not the conviction with which it is received that matters, since the criterion of conviction will be found rather in the material that will emerge as a result of the interpretation'.[16] In the psychoanalytic interpretation, time itself loops through a vast outward trajectory, encompassing whole biographies which must nevertheless be bracketed or denied. What is at stake is nothing less than the continued efficacy of metaphor itself, yet the proof of effectivity is constantly deferred in the act of marking the boundary of the future, whether it be through the ending of the session or the termination of the analysis; or, indeed, the ability of the profession to live with the prospect of its own supersession, another intelligentsia, like the the romantic one, in possession of quasi-magical power yet simultaneously imprisoned in the group defences erected against ellipsis.[17]

The group

The belief that reality is or could be known is mistaken because reality is not something which lends itself to being known. It is impossible to know reality for the same reason that makes it impossible to sing potatoes; they may be grown, or pulled, or eaten, but not sung.

And so a locking into the binary as a protection against dispersion inflects psychoanalysis no less than it does other realms: international relations, gender roles, the freedom struggles (so meagre) of literary criticism. 'The analyst has to establish a relationship with *both* halves of the patient's personality, because only from them can he put together a whole and complete man, and not merely from one half by suppression of the other half'.[18] The longing-to-be-half can itself be deconstructed in many ways, some of which can be described in terms of Plato's texts, others in feminist criticism.

To explore this binary further, we have to turn to Jung. His system is built on a massive working through of number and quantity symbolism, and its bedrock, enacted in religious texts, is the femininity of even numbers and the masculinity of odd ones. Thus the Trinity caps the act of reproduction with an ineffable third, which in its power is unavailable for questioning; Jung's welcome for the Virgin Mary as an inhabitant of the Kingdom of Heaven seemed to him to revolve on the possible entry into the age of Aquarius, but other interpretations are possible.[19] At all events, one way of looking at what we find in the theorising of the classic analytic interpretative situation is by observing the continual marks of a spinning out from duality into the quaternary, although in different ways. We can take two polar examples. One is lodged in Jung's mandalas. His theory of archetypes maintains, against popular understanding, the primacy of shape: the archetypes are shapes, forms, the evidence of the effects of the stamp of the unconscious always having been pressed onto the underside of conscious experience; so that when we turn it over (in our minds) we discover a hallmark, a signature which we did not produce but which has been fitting our experience more snugly against the underneath, the less we felt at home in it. The shape of this impress is fourfold,[20] the split binary which forms for the first time a grid of evaluation and thus provides, paradoxically, a saving grace of organisation at the same time as it reveals our mortality in the form of the intrusion of that which is not ourself, and yet has its habitation on and across every boundary we encounter.

Lacan's most accessible diagram, which I think comes closer to romantic intimations of the unconscious, represents the fourfold in a *Z* shape,[21] along which we can plot no direct addressing, since the act of utterance already presupposes a two-way traffic along the lines of deflection. The engagement of the analyst's practice with that of the patient, we might say, is refracted back through the imago of the analyst in such a way as to represent in itself, and thus to permit, an entering of the imaginary of the patient into (but also by) a dialogue which is, always, a tetralogue, but which, except in professional circles, dares not admit its name; and thus partakes of sin. This complication of Others, modelled on a freeing of unowned voices, matches many other modellings of the psyche – for example, the imagery of the four Celestial Kings;[22] and the occupancy, in the position of dominance, of an affect rolls down the bagatelle board to disturb from their dust those prior responses which have been laid down in childhood as responses to the anger of the father which dare not be challenged, but which survived in the child's mind as he or she, for example, assessed the weather the following morning.

We shall see later that these quaternaries have their counterparts in literary interpretation, and that the struggle towards the different shape of the parabola can also be relativised against this guarded inclusiveness (which is, always, a turning away from the open window); but for the moment we might think about the nature of interpretation where the mere duality of analyst/analysand has been deflected, and where what is at stake is the kind of life a *group* might have, and where the keynote is thus representation in a wider sense; in other words, where reinforcements of the real might be available outside the interpreter's discourse.

> There are times when I think that the group has an attitude to me, and that I can state in words what the attitude is; there are times when another individual acts as if he also thought the group had an attitude to him, and I believe I can deduce what his belief is; there are times when I think that the group has an attitude to an individual, and that I can say what it is. These occasions provide the raw material on which interpretations are based, but the interpretation itself is an attempt to translate into precise speech what I suppose to be the attitude of the group to me or to some other individual, and of the individual to the group.[23]

The issue here is a clash of signifiers: interpretation/intervention, observation/speech, attitude/will; or a discourse of powers. The functions of interpretation in the life of a group – whether it be 'artificially' constituted in a small bare room, or 'naturally occurring' in the shapes of institution, profession, canon – can be variously described, but always they abut onto our everyday efforts to make sense of the world.

For what is at stake in group interpretation, I take it, is a parabola of attention. What is conceived as contained within the inner world of each individual is not simply to be conceived in terms of presence: among the contents of that inner world, however precariously manifested, however contaminated in its effects by setting and 'presentation', will be shaped fantasies of the other worlds, intimations of what lies beyond the curtain. The cleric or the managing director, for instance, manifesting his or her acceptance/resistance of the difficulties of attending to the here-and-now, are not in that context less members of external echelons; their efforts will take place along the difficult path of squaring and understanding a spread of experiences of membership.

And from the point of view of expression, what happens is a multiple checking of contents, so that the limits of the acceptable will be defined along the boundary of these various memberships, and their internal images: and it is also an inner power struggle, as the 'self-as-confused-member' seeks purchase against the 'self-as-writer', or as literary critic; so that, most of the time, it is unclear on whose behalf we are speaking, as our various self-constructions jostle for supremacy and, in doing so, engage in an inner discourse of values. What, in this context as we apprehend it, can we sacrifice and still remain human? What do we find we emphasise as we build precarious walls against uncertainty and the threat of dissolution?

In group situations, therefore, the flow of interpretation passes through the constitution of the subject: the ways in which we receive projections from the Other will be filtered through, resurrected by, the institutions in our minds. What seems often to happen in groups is a fantasy reincarnation of the family,[24] which is where the analysis of the group, with its apparatus of basic assumptions and subgroupings, parts company with psychoanalytic interpretation: because the primacy of the historic, the familial, is never the to-be-taken-for-granted, but is rather the model which has always already been invaded by our attempts at maturation and the external props we use in guaranteeing that difficult maturity. Speech thus becomes more desperate, in so far as there is less hiddenness than in the windowless room: less hiddenness, certainly, from the present Others, but less hiddenness from the strategies we have adopted to cover over vulnerability, less hiddenness from the multifariousness of the assaults on the ego; and less hiddenness from our own self-interpretations of how we might be constructing those assaults themselves in order to justify an internal psychic economy.

The question which is foregrounded is, 'On whose behalf we do speak?' Behind this there lies a range of shadowy movements, as each utterance shifts the weight of alliance in ways which are partially unforeseen by us. We know who we might want as our allies, and our various stabbings in the dark have the effect of a validation of this necessary line-up. Interpretation, in this diffuse field, thus becomes more processual: by a curious contradiction, the superflux of introjected externalities becomes that onto which we thought we could cling for safety, but also that in which we are lost; and the here-and-now moment which we approached with fear becomes simultaneously the unrepeatable moment which the life of the group might, with luck, forget, as we ourselves wish to forget past humiliation, past allegiance.

The relevance, then, to the ways in which we might want to support romanticism lies in the notion of representation; just as the analytic model corresponds to the comparatively illuminated area of speaking to others, or at least being overheard by them, so the group model might correspond to the far more shadowy question of the others' voices which we might find from time to time incarnated within us. We can see this second realm as haunting the first, providing the reservoir of instability which gives so many romantic voices the sense of an echo. And echo and Narcissus thus become a principal theme of romanticism, a myth of soaring individuality and a myth of inseparability from a punitive background bound back to back, isolation constantly reminded of the lure of the crowd, companionability troubled by the pride of selfhood.

The object

But these two types of interpretation, psychoanalytic and group, are in a sense parallel: in their dealings, they insist upon an element of presence, even if that presence is only the hook which secures some attention to primary process. In this room, we might say, there are at least bodies, two or more; and in this pressing world there is a simultaneous privileging and disparaging of the mode of speech which ensures that we are in the world of the spoken at all points. And here lies the strength and the doom of interpretation: that in its pressings towards the absent, there comes a duplicity towards evidence: that which is said is the only chain, yet its significance derives purely from the continual and multiple sliding of signifieds under signifier, a drilling for oil the success of which can only result in a lowering of the price.

Interpretation has to do with a discourse of human value. To interpret in the mode of the present is to confer value and to remove it: to grant the pleasure of attention while directing one's attention over the shoulder to see who this fascinating but unowned person may be to whom the comments are directed, and for whom – who knows? – they may even be valid. The company of the unconscious at such times resembles turning up at a party with a dubious friend, and finding that they become the centre of attention. Much as we may then wish to own to them, with an abashed pride, we may also suspect a deeper plot. Perhaps there are webs of communication, prior histories here of which we know nothing. Perhaps it is the ego which is the wallflower, and these deeper levels have already known each other all along.

When we instead look toward object and system, one of the things we find is the comforting presence of structuralism, in which 'attention is shifted away ... from the ways in which human beings have altered and do alter and may yet alter their objectifications; in consequence, structuralism finds nothing to investigate but order, the codes of order, reflections upon order, and the experience of order'.[25] The world of the bounded diagram stamps itself with a sigh of salvation on those puzzling arcs of the subject which might otherwise elude interpretation. We may forget the task of integration, may comment cheerfully on the fictionality of wholeness, while mapping the dotted lines which connect us onto the systems which possess the true agencies of the world.

It is a comforting set of fictions in the service of a power-strategy; the strategy of withdrawal coupled with a pricing of the individual out of the market. If I can have no effect on the way of the world, then at least I may find a sense in becoming, in my own psyche, the shape *of* the effects of the world. The problem of value – which is, in the end, the problem of how, and whether, it is possible to attend to experience – can be sublated in a world where all value is relativised and where, as an apparently minor consequence, interpretation becomes reduced to assessment, a judicious appraisal of the beauty and symmetry of form. In the service of this reduction, it is, as Baudrillard has pointed out, necessary to construct a substitute conceptualisation of the unconscious, a tamed and lethargic beast which will quail before a different kind of objectivity:

> The 'rediscovered' unconscious, generally exalted from the beginning, runs directly counter to its original meaning: initially structure and labour, it is transformed into a sign function ... The revolution of the unconscious becomes the avatar of a new humanism of the subject of consciousness; and through the individualist ideology of the unconscious, fetishised and reduced by signs ... to a calculus of pleasure and consumed satisfaction, each subject itself drains and monitors the movement and the dangerous labour of the unconscious for the benefit of the social order.

The domestication of the unconscious eventuates in the ideology of the bargain basement, the glittery underworld where the poverty of capitalism can be evidenced but which nonetheless sustains a belief in the inevitability of system and a consequent massive disenfranchising of hope. Interpretation, in a parallel move, becomes a cottage industry, satisfyingly removed from the nexi of power and commercial transaction.

It could thus also be said that there is a loop here back to romanticism. The profusion of a world of objects, accompanied by an increase in the mystification and invisibility of system, creates a world in which we clasp an unconscious life close to our bosom: because it serves to give us a sense of inner depth with which we can match the profundities of an ever more intricate economy; because, paradoxically, it validates our claims to an emotionality which, we sense, is being exiled by the blast furnaces outside the windows of our fantasies; because, even more peculiarly, it gives us the belief that, if we have nothing else to call our own, at least we are privileged with an inalienable and individual set of fantasies which cannot be taken away from us, even if, in the inner world, neither can they ever be fully disclosed. Certainly there would thus be an assumed immunity from competitivity: the interpretation of dreams becomes the paradigm of an area wherein there can be no comparative assessment and where, indeed, the question of value can finally be squeezed out under the barricaded door.

Thus hound becomes watchdog:

> we believe in a real subject, motivated by needs and confronted by real objects as sources of satisfaction. It is a thoroughly vulgar metaphysic. And contemporary psychology, sociology and economic science are all complicit in the fiasco. So the time has come to deconstruct all the assumptive notions involved – object, need, aspiration, *consumption* itself – for it would make as little sense to theorise the quotidian from surface evidence as to interpret the manifest discourse of a dream: it is rather the dream-work and the dream-processes that must be analysed in order to recover the unconscious logic of a more profound discourse.

But this is far from clear. It is one thing to see how object and system meet along the trajectories of commodification and fetishisation; another to interpret the muteness of the goods on supermarket shelves *as if* in terms of *parole* and *langue*.

The obscure object of desire is nowadays part of our everyday reckoning: the redoubling of the term 'object' to denote the element of *Trieb* within the objectification. What remains, however, problematic is the function behind this of the body as organising and sedimented metaphor; not, that is, in terms of the phallic emblems distributed through commerce, but in terms of attachment and loss, bereavement, alliance, the invested feelings which provide objects with life; or which, as Hegel and Blake would have said, provide intimations of the infinite at the heart of the product.

But this in-finite – this facility for releasing the unbounded – will itself have a dialectical relation to the shaping of the product, and not all our enjoyments are the same.

In appearance, or rather, according to the mask it bears, historical consciousness is neutral, devoid of passions, and committed solely to truth. But if it examines itself and if, more generally, it interrogates the various forms of scientific consciousness in its history, it finds that all these forms and transformations are aspects of the will to knowledge: instinct, passion, the inquisitor's devotion, cruel subtlety, and malice.[26]

We are thus returned to the dialectic of interpretation and paranoia as a variant of power/knowledge. Within the analyst's craft, within the activities of the group consultant, within the systematisations of the great interpreters of structure – Lévi-Strauss, Foucault, Barthes – lies a moment which itself must be amenable to historical deconstruction, and a moment which, therefore, inflects the willed moments of our interpretative activities. Interpretation may occur on the site of fear; there can, as Bion says, be no co-operation when there is simply identification with an idea, with a leader, with a group, and similarly the impulses towards power which we feel in the presence of speech, in the attempted bringing-under-the-sign of muteness, will be coded according to the inner attitudes towards institution which form the overarching shapes of the archetypes.

We may refer back to Jung's mandalas as a principle of design, again in a double sense of the term. The unwilled, in interpretation, is confronted by the willed: as we work with the rereading of literature, the weaknesses, the unknown knots of language, the attributed resistance of discourse to the intentions of the practitioner – all these are made available for 'interrogation'; and the results will be the display which we hold as a cure for a feared hiddenness. There is, to put it simply, a listening to and a listening for, and the attempt to bridge this gap with science, system, an armoury of protective devices, informs the interpretative with its meanings – the meanings, that is, of the act itself, which inevitably gives shape to the 'results' for which we may conceive ourselves to be striving.

The rule of the father is striated with an ambivalence. The 'because' clause is always double: you must do as I say because the way of things is such-and-such, but also, and in the identical breath, you must do as I say because I say so. *Explication du texte*, hermeneutics, attempts to codify interpretation as a practice in which there is a non-reflexive dialogue, become transmuted in the very act into strategies for silencing. Don't answer back; and more to the point, if you answer back you are simply showing your unawareness of the dangers. Don't swing on the banisters because they will break; but also, don't answer back because you will be excluded from the canon – of literary texts, but also of case histories, of available proofs, of signs which can be comfortably habilitated within a system.

The act of remastering, to revert to an earlier metaphor, is therefore always fraught with attendant doubts about the authenticity of the original, perhaps especially in the West, where that term carries a trailing freight of value with it. As you accept the interpretation, as you overcome resistance, thus in the act of disbelieving all you hold most dear, so you come to hold to yourself that which you hold most dear, the imago of the father, the authority which predetermines your objects of attention. Nurture, bear love to, all the filaments of being; but while you do so, remember that it is at the ends of those filaments that the tiny capillaries touch the outer, in ways we have not yet explained, and so to concentrate on the centripetal force of interpretation is to drain attention away from the wound, from the continuing possibility of pain; and it is the resistance to pain, as H.G. Wells says, which guarantees your membership in the élite, in patriarchy, in the white races, in the rule of knowledge over sympathy.[27]

Here again, I think, there is a romantic implication: the extreme investment of the poeticised object with feeling and meaning can promote not enrichment but impoverishment of the already unhappy self. And behind that, as I shall try to suggest, lies a deeper concept of the object, a Kleinian notion of the relation of part-objects to projection, according to which the very formation of these objects – and our own continued investment in them – must be seen under the sign of guilt and reparation.

Literature

> Critical theory is always threatened by the temptation to puff itself up into a kind of gigantic version of the sign, replete with its strategy of abstraction and reduction. This pitfall is implicit in the very activity of constructing a critical model of the 'object', which in its claim to avoid passivity, must paradoxically stress its adequacy and therefore its identity with what it claims to transcend. But even the most aggressive model must in principle fall short of its object.

What a great deal of criticism ignores, perhaps unavoidably, is that in the process of interpretation there is a double look, outward and inward; and even that enters a more complex hall of mirrors. What are we to say of this complexity? Who, indeed, are the participants in it? The interpreter utters to the (silenced) interpreted; but in this communication two other things occur. Along Lacan's non-directional model – or a slightly different non-directional model which I would prefer to construct from it – there is a seepage back along the thin line of conscious interchange; so that in association with our topic we become variously romantic critics, neoclassical critics, New Critics. And also the intervention which is the silent shadow of the interpretation – as the grasping of the elbow underscores and takes over the words of companionship and simultaneously marks cultural and historical difference – releases, somewhere in this unclosed system which leads off into the realms of the unbounded, a reconceptualisation of the subjectivity of the addresser, which in turn becomes the imago which, alone, can connect with the unspoken of the text.

This leads us, I think, to a necessary question about deconstruction. 'The 'hermeneutic' tradition . . . takes account of the interpreter's puzzles and perplexities by *including* them within the terms of a full and generous response. Such a style is 'answerable' in its sense of the constant provisional adjustments the critic has to make between theory and text'.[28] We can gloss the 'answerable' from Krishnamurti,[29] and establish its connections with notions of responsibility; but the crucial terms here are 'taking account of' and 'including'. The interpreter's puzzles are thus not integral: they are additional 'perplexities', invisible earnings, the profits, perhaps, of service industries – shipping insurance for example, by means of which the essential traffic is kept under weigh while we have the commercial common sense to include in our accounts the invisible detriment, the barely perceptible erosion of objectivity – or 'standards' – which, in these hard times, must inevitably but unfortunately accompany the driving of a commercial trade.[30]

As capitalism winds down, we sense the social cost emerging, rocks left behind by the tide; we wish there were no reefs out there, no interpolations, no interjections (of pain) between ourselves and our empire of understanding; but that hope having passed, we had better reckon with difficulty. An ignorant metaphysic: but behind it, a deeper difficulty, a deeper sandbank. Because, of course, all the discourse of presence and absence – as Derrida tells us – is a coding of writing and speech; and, as Derrida does not often appear to recognise, an excrescence of the development of communities, of human groups. Largely exiled from speech (although victimised by speeches) and cast afloat on a habit of writing which has only a 'prestige' audience (we need now to use publishers' terms), the exploration of real interpretation is hardly available. Interpretation, in that sense, belongs only to the utopias; and now only to the feminist ones, where ritual can be practised and interpreted to the full, and where the penalty for adriftness from the communal can be real exile.[31]

We, however, are exiled to the printed page; which, as Ian Watt said years ago, is the confrontation with the black hole. Not, however, in the sense of depression; rather, in accordance with certain dictates of aristocratic pride. And here we are again on terrain which is already inhabited, already redolent of romanticism: inhabited, for instance, by a woman wailing for her demon lover, by that side of romanticism which existed and wrote, above all, to establish that there was an available audience. Behind all the posturing, and alongside the desperation (and perhaps only in Coleridge can the full dialectic be seen) lies a simpler address: is there anybody out there? Among the readers of the *Morning Chronicle*, against the odds of a fossilised and, in any case, overdetermined party politics, is there some kind of small unimaginable consensus which will hear; or rather, in whom there exists a set of connections which can be mobilised by a certain speech?

And of course, it goes without saying that we are that listener. Not, to go back to my original argument, because of some unique conjunction of events which might be explained in terms of a neat sociological circle to do with the parallelisms between industrialisation and the advent of the new technology; but because we have, in a way which was foretold, become promiscuous in our dealings with the sign, and that is itself not a choice. We wish to trace avatars, the patterns of a past promised promiscuity; an avatar was the 1960s, but that was itself precursor to the promiscuity of information which is itself the underground – and to-be-suppressed – accompaniment to the gathering of power into a single set of hands in time of war.[32]

To know that one lives under the shadow of disaster is one thing; to exile that knowledge is to pass it into the symbolic, and thus to ignore the present threats of radioactivity in the milk. 'To commit one's thoughts to writing is to yield them up to the public domain, to risk being miscon-strued by all the promiscuous wiles of interpretation'.[33] Not so, I would say; the promiscuity lies not in the activity of interpretation, but already in the defence mechanisms which inhabit the various poles among which interpretation might move. In engaging, then, with the interpretation of literature, one is, I take it, trying to bring something into being: a moment of contact, within which is enfolded a historical trajectory, itself not available merely as the traces of the past but simultaneously as the hallmark which runs through the interpreter's own subjectivity. In the act of writing, in the bringing to articulation, what is also dredged up is our own self-formation, the many inscriptions which, in turn, have come to determine how we attend, listen, read. So, at least, romanticism would say.

And the nature of interpretation is that it also brings about a reshaping, however minute: the urge to be comprehensive is itself also available for deconstruction, emblematically in Derrida's work on Husserl, where the act of bracketing stands revealed as the underside of the rage for the comprehensive, the need to establish origins as also the need to find a firm foothold whence one may embrace the world.[34] I shall not try to be comprehensive; the patterns which may emerge in the course of this book will not pretend to be the 'patterns of romanticism', but they will be part of an attempt to realise a pattern which romanticism may have for present culture.

In the course of this attempt, it will seem reasonable to present moments where the concerns and shapes of romanticism appear to resonate across the highly populated void of history; and this, I think, need not be an approach which descends into random subjectivity. It follows from what we now know of the psyche that the effects of the unconscious partake also of the pressings of objective knowledge – the inescapable – on our attempts at individual ordering; and that it will be worth interrogating the resistances which make us regard the unconscious as the *unknowable*. It was, of course, during the romantic period that precisely this kind of thinking began to occur in English culture, most notably in Coleridge's writings, where the encounter between a willed comprehensive consciousness and the eruption of that which is already known becomes dramatised as a conflict between different assessments of the limits of knowledge, best evidenced in Thomas McFarland's outstanding critical psychodrama of the 'I am' and the 'it is'.[35] The 'it is', I shall contend, is the speech mode of the unconscious; the 'I am' the speech mode of the embattled ego seeking to downgrade precisely the insights which threaten to subvert the pettier ordering which we seek as a way of blanking out patriarchal or parental dictate.

But simultaneously, in the drama of the 'I am' and the 'it is', there is also codified the problem of historical agency, and typically here in the form of definitions of what it is to be British in a situation of international turmoil, under the ever-present threat of invasion – from across the Channel, from below the bar of the sign, from the effects of the unconscious; and it is to this knot that we need first to turn, bearing in mind Freud's admonition that, in the end, all analysis confronts us only, but clearly, with the moment when all the threads and chains disappear below the floorboards, in an intricate wiring, the pattern and patent of which is held only 'on another scene'.

PART 2

ROMANTICISM AND HISTORY

Narcissism and contamination: 'Christabel'

Let us begin from a hypothesis. It is the function of the ego to construct: to construct for itself a series of defences, and simultaneously to construct in the world a specular image of itself, which turns out to be an image of the defences themselves, inscribed with the markings of evasion, which figure in the world as the mystery to be explored, the tiger face peering from the suspected unconscious. Both of these inseparable activities are represented in the search for the comprehensive, the bridge over the chasm, which is also the search for the originary. The outered shapes which the ego builds can take many forms; but typically, they are philosophical systems, the specular losing sight of its own (reflected) origins and turning into the speculative in a continuing falsification of the significance of reflection.

These processes are those of primary narcissism,[1] wherein the ego, in its inattention to the noises off which might betray the relativity of its own existence, forms a coded version of world and self which articulates an apparently inalienable centrality for consciousness; this narcissistic system is, of course, constantly subverted by the unquenchable activities of the unconscious, which emerge in the various forms which Freud describes,[2] but which also take on the contours of the symptom, the translation into bodily form of features of psychic life which are unowned by the defended consciousness. That there is a relationship between this bodily form and the 'material' form of the text is an assertion which can only be justified in its articulated detail; such that the investigation of the 'body' of romanticism encounters precisely the issue of 'murdering to dissect'. The critical problem then takes on its old shape; how to negotiate the body without producing a corpse, how to reanimate that which is consigned to the charnel-house; how, in a different field, to continue to deal with (the patient's) experience by conferring a new meaning on the *symptomale*. If we can trace this pattern of narcissism also in culture – and the theoretical abutment of ego-defences onto systems of rational and speculative thought suggests that this is an already-given in the analytic approach – then we might here have the beginnings of a characterisation of romanticism. We would begin to gather evidence from, for instance, the phenomenon of the philosophical poem, with all the psychological ambiguity that enterprise entails, both at a theoretical level and in the inner experiences of those writers who try to fabricate it.[3]

And here we come up against a crucial ambiguity of cognition, which is also one of control. Is the philosophical poem an articulation of a strategy for bringing non-rational areas of response and experience under the sign of metaphysical speculation; or is it a key which might unlock the door of the unconscious and demonstrate the limits of system? At all events, it clearly bears an important relation to Blake's speculations on the connections between 'system', organisation and the self; and also to Coleridge's explorations of the psychological purposes and effects of speculative enquiry, and the form of the agon which shows through his writings.

And behind these thoughts and speculations, there is the continuing theme of subversion, accompanied by the doubts about agency which we would expect to find attached to the narcissistic ego encountering the irrepressibility of the symptom. We can find it in Shelley's ambivalence about poetic responsibility; in, of course, the numerous supernatural hauntings of Gothic fiction but also of Coleridge and Keats; in the tones of subversion and transgression, partly owned and partly unowned by the authorial self (the authority of the self), which permeate Byron's work. The specific dealing with system which runs through the romantic period thus opens itself as a central object for enquiry.[4]

And the problem which is thus thrown up is indeed about the author and authority. The radical decentring of the self which goes on in analytic thought, and which (and this is essential for our trajectory) exists in trace in romanticism,[5] ceaselessly threatens to erode the ground on which we stand by demonstrating that the solidity of that ground is a fiction of the ego's own desire to be the exclusive centre of consciousness. It is therefore not clear on what basis we can continue to speculate, let alone theorise, about the world; and it is this difficulty of focus which, again, romanticism brings to light.

In Coleridge's 'Christabel' (1797),[6] we may find a model for parts of this dilemma. The motifs of sleeping and waking are curiously intertwined, figuring the rebus along which inscriptions are ceaselessly changing as the dreams squirm through the processes of primary and secondary revision.

These forms of revision are, of course, elided in textual terms with the notion of re-presentation and the 'grounding' of the interpretative. Sir Leoline – the lion, the straight clear line of tradition, blood, all that is known along the fictional path of the ego's secure integrity – is 'weak in health,/And may not well awakened be',[7] while Christabel and Geraldine explore together the realm of the specular other, the curiosity of symbiosis. He has for his defence only the 'toothless mastiff bitch' who lies 'fast asleep' as, on another scene, the narrative of the 'mark' is played out, a narrative which Sir Leoline and his last remaining defender can know only in and as dream, as that which produces the 'angry moan' of disturbance and impotence in the sleep of the unguarding dog.

Yet, as Coleridge points out, who can 'know' the source of this disturbance: 'what can ail the mastiff bitch'[8] (as, of course, it also ails Keats's pale knight)? Who, indeed, is the more 'asleep' here – as Christabel and Geraldine pass the father's room, the space of a linear history freighted with armorial bearings, the sleep as in a Crusader's death with the dog at the lion's feet; as they bypass the threshold of a weakened consciousness, it is *they* who are (also, but yet as a 'difference' from Sir Leoline's waking sleep) as 'still as death, with stifled breath';[9] and so the problem of cognition enters into the hall of mirrors and generates a redoubled unconsciousness. The twined images of sickness and guarding are then also redoubled: Geraldine is she who 'ails' as she sees the ghost of Christabel's dead mother, who comes in dream to 'guard' Christabel against that which we must name as contamination, the Typhoid Mary of dream. It is the unlocation, the decentredness, of the danger, the 'sickness unto death', which is here forced upon us in these tremors of the disordered psyche, and which, of course, prefigures symptomatically the coming break, which is a break in the ordering of the ego's defences but also, as elsewhere in Coleridge's work, the break in textuality derived from the pressure of the unassimilable 'Other' of the text, where the sheet of paper and experience is cut inexplicably against our (readerly) will.[10]

And the break is not long in coming, for Christabel has passed under a double sign. The arrangements of patriarchy, the passing down of the name-of-the-Father, are already, we may surmise, disrupted at the site of Christabel's absent mother, at the threshold of maturity, in her semi-orphanage, as these lines of tradition and clarity are also broken and subsequently rewoven in Gothic narrative. But the advent of Geraldine comes as an intimation of the half-world into which the supremacy of the ego is passing, and thus it is that Christabel lies down to thoughts 'of weal and woe', and cannot sleep: 'So half-way from the bed she rose',[11] prefiguring in turn the 'half-ness' which will be the vision of uncertainty offered by Geraldine.

> Her silken robe, and inner vest,
> Dropt to her feet, and full in view,
> Behold! her bosom and half her side –
> A sight to dream of, not to tell!
> O shield her! shield sweet Christabel!
>
> Yet Geraldine nor speaks nor stirs;
> Ah! what a stricken look was hers! [112]

Within this bedroom, which is itself disputed territory, the property of the old knight and also Christabel's sanctuary, what occurs across this crucial textual juncture which is also a hiatus is a complexity of regard, of the look, in which is coded the problem of cognition. And this complexity interweaves further the theme of guarding, through a knot in which the term 'guardianship' may be entered as the signifier of the 'holding for' and the 'being held in thrall' which become key motifs in romanticism, and have also to do with the notion of passing down, in continuity, against a background of change.

For who is looking at Geraldine? The author, clearly, since he seizes this opportunity to apostrophise and to share his 'guardianship' of Christabel, and thus of a presumed innocence, with the reader. And yet in doing so, and in thrusting Christabel away from the contaminated heart of the poem, it is of course he who takes on the sacred task, stands within the forbidden circle on our behalf, and who guarantees our immunity by risking the effects of contact with the images welling from repressed contents. And yet again in this imperative address, this call to arms, this changing of the guard, there is a further interweaving in the readerly position, for clearly the role on offer to us is one which is already filled, by the ghost of Christabel's mother; and we are thereby confronted proleptically with a banishment in the course of which we shall be made to feel Geraldine's power, and to experience also a dealing with this question of contamination. How shall Geraldine pass on her mark? Can these 'effects of the unconscious' be controlled and consigned to the abyss which brought them forth, or will they, in their pressings up against us, mark us also? And behind this again, there are questions about the mode of agency of the unconscious; for the 'stricken look' is Geraldine's as she speculates on whether (or how) to 'lift some weight' onto Christabel, which is also to shift the weight of the exile of desire and to reintroduce it to the bloodline, despite the 'massive' mastiff and the castle walls, which have been in any case thoroughly penetrated in the sickness of Sir Leoline's fitful sleep.

What is at stake here is a hovering on the brink of a palace revolution. It is indeed under an oak that Geraldine claims to have been set by her unknown assailants, as a preparation for her encounter, all too easy, with the tameable force of the lion; as it is in a world of solid English emblems and heraldry that the disturbances of Keats's narrative poems enact their forebodings of a rotting away of the foundations. The question for us becomes one of the boundary, in a redoubled sense: the contested boundary between ego and its self-created enemies, but mapped within a wider structure of invasion which takes on an orbit which necessarily crosses the English Channel and confronts us with the 'majesty' of a different revolution, and with the input of uncertainty which dictates the inflections of these dramas of desire and bereavement.

1789: Rhetoric and hyperbole

The events in and around 1789 resulted in the developing of specific rhetorical and textual strategies in English writing;[13] and thus in the establishment of a new discursive and ideological field which, however, is inevitably marked with the illusions of its own mysterious origins, as the ego searches for a form of narrative which will centre itself as agent in an arena where it wishes to drown the ceaseless reminders of the voice which speaks over the shoulder. It is therefore necessary to offer some hypotheses about socio-economic conditions; and this should not be regarded as a stepping away, but as a working further into the defiles of the signifier as it performs its acrobatic trajectories through the subject.

The basic formation of the English historical conjuncture in this part of the late eighteenth century, we may suggest, comprised, in the lineaments of an imagined project as well as in the specific instances of labour and change, the potential for alliance between agrarian, mercantile, colonialist, and nascent industrialist socio-economic fractions, this tension being manifest in the complex manoeuvrings of Tories, Old Whigs, New Whigs; of aristocratic radicals and dissenting radicals; of proponents of society as a stable organism versus proponents of the natural market. The complexity of the social formation, a far from unfamiliar complexity, was such that these positions mapped themselves ambiguously over several sets of divisions and oppositions; and yet we undoubtedly see a situation in which, over the course of a few years, this society produced a set of homogeneous discourses which systematically elided certain features of the French Revolution, foregrounding some and negating others. In effect, for all its diversity, it produced a myth of the Revolution that allowed for specific selective representations, even when a pro-revolutionary stance was being affected.

One way of working with the homogeneity of this response would be to say that by 1789 the various economic interests which had access to discourse in Britain had already resolved their differences to such an extent that there was no social base onto which a different view, a view of difference, could fasten itself. As opposed to France, with its more backward and divided bourgeoisie, and powerful if contradictorily articulated agrarian interests, Britain, through colonial expansion, was able to promote manufacture at the same time as capitalising agriculture. Thus in Britain, radical positions, already heavily repressed, were further eroded by the fundamentally expansive nature of the economy, in a series of movements which needs to be related to the urge towards comprehensivity which characterises the ego under threat; and which may in turn help with the analysis of the model of colonialism in the mind.

The distinguishing achievement might be seen as that of Burke, who orchestrated discourses taken from Britain's differing ideological fractions into a form in which a putative majority could recognise their common interest, and thus performed a massive act of representation. At the suasive level, and with no lack of rhetorical ingenuity, Burke was able to use the 'threat' of the French Revolution to urge the mutual interdependence and compatibility of two socio-economic paradigms, that of landed property and that of the market economy. It would be on grounds such as these that one might see Burke as the representative figure of the political moment; but representative in a multiple sense. Representation clearly signifies the relation of language to event, of signifer to signified, of enunciation to enunciated. But also and inseparably, in its bourgeois–political sense, it involves 'speaking-for-others', in the area which opens up the questions of in the name of whom or what (on whose behalf) the speaker is taking up language and, in the process, constructing his/her own subjectivity and that of others. And *re-presentation* clearly also connects with the complex fields of primary and secondary revision, with the operation of devices for removing and 'forgetting' contradiction; and thus with the mechanisms which enable the ego to pursue its chosen course as articulator of a narrowed and expurgated version of history.

The problematic nature of the events of the French Revolution – which have not ceased to be problematic – for British writers took many forms. There was a need to confront, and in some fashion to represent, events for which there appeared to be no precedent – events which could only by a great deal of twisting be referred back to imaginary source. There were consequent strains on the conventions of representation, which during the Augustan period had evolved into a system which can be named: resemblance, analogy, sympathy, imitation, emulation, order, degree, would form the boundary markers of that process of naming.

The question now becomes, however, about the potential usefulness of these revisionary devices in the representation or covering over of an interruption, a discontinuity in the ordering procedures productive of a 'cover' of naturalisation (one of the ego's main labours of productivity). And of course, associated with this comes the problem to which we have already alluded, which contextualises itself as nothing less than the formation of a mode of cognition which can find ways of dealing with the 'new' without positing an 'extra-ordinary' source beyond the knowledge or comprehensiveness of the ego's self-fictionalising narratives – an epistemological endeavour which would take us to the boundary of the definitions of the imaginary, and of that inheritance through which the conceptualisation of fantasy passes from Coleridge to Freud.

We can look at some of the resources which were developed, staying with Coleridge. In 'To a Young Lady with a Poem on the French Revolution' (1794)[14] – not a particularly remarkable piece, and for that reason among others usefully indicative of a genre – is discovered a massive weight of personification: 'Freedom', 'Disdain', 'Fury', become the giant forms who 'slumber', are 'roused', 'burst' their chains; in this respect there is little difference between the personifying habits of the 1790s and 1720s. But here the personifications, because adorning a commentary on contemporary political events, serve also a specific set of misattributions of agency: especially they work to attribute to unchanging, ahistoric forms – the forms in which the past remains concealed at every level – the powers of action which belong to individuals, groups, classes.

We may refer here to a particular variant of anthropomorphism which oscillates between gigantism and miniaturisation. The complicated and muddled processes of social change are simplified in a series of acts of projection, and purified into cosmic battle, relying on an ideological use of hyperbole: 'high', 'giant', 'burst', 'fierce', 'yelling' and so forth become simultaneously a way of distancing events from possible experience and a justification for the withdrawal of the subject. Since the poet cannot make himself heard in this war-torn arena, where the voice of integration is torn apart on the winds blowing from nowhere, the only course becomes a mournful retreat, a lapse into a discontented solipsism 'where peaceful Virtue weaves the Myrtle braid'. In the inequity between massive dehumanised forces and the impotent individual we can, of course, sense the contours of a massive set of unrealised projections; and we can also observe the shade of persecution, a major theme in so much of the contemporary fiction. We can also explore the harried consciousness and its responses as, insecure now in its own narcissistic fantasies and suspecting a potential bereftness, it finds itself unseated from its majesty by events beyond its control or explanation, events which, in rubbing roughly against the edges of the particular system, no less produce the forms of unease about the notion of system itself which will come to inflect romanticism as it agonises about the identity of the 'royal road'.

Here Coleridge finds himself holding the ends of a complex projected mediation between the megalomania of 'strode in joy the reeking plains of France' and the self-pity of 'heart aches' and 'wearied thought'. The subject of the poem moves between extremes of private and public voice, from the soothing of the breast to the shaking of the lance, with all the associated implications of passivity and agency, themselves verging on the distribution of male and female roles.

As we might expect, we can find this sense of disruption and the attempts to find the rhetorical figures to cover it more strongly in evidence in the cruder poetry of the time. 'Freedom and Peace' (1801), by George Dyer,[15] is one example among many, and one which serves also to demonstrate a further purpose of this particular figure of personification:

> The Wars of ages thus decided,
>   Commerce shall bless each smiling Land;
> And Man from Man no more divided,
>   In Peace shall live, a friendly band!
> But Tyrants, with their glare of pow'r,
> Like Meteors fall – to rise no more!

In view of the complexities of the look which we uncovered in 'Christabel', and which increasingly come to relate to a contested notion of the possession of the 'theatre' of history, we might wish to pause on the participular structure of this 'glare'; but what also stands out in the tissue of personifications is the sliding of commerce under the sign of peace, in a curious and motivated reversal of the realities of commercial warfare and capitalist competing.

The prevalence of hyperbole and its attendant forms may be variously interpreted. One pole would have to do with the prevalent implications of the pressure on language to give shape and representation to a 'new' reality. Another would speak of 'new' functions which language might have to carry when a classical unity of discourse – which is also a falsely unified distribution of power – is being shattered; namely, in this case, the ways in which to assume a burden of anxiety, of fear and ambivalence. Is hyperbole an indication that simile and resemblance, like so many of the 'castles' of the texts, are under siege, and are to be rescued by replacement with a rhetorical figure which, in its very (apparent) abstraction from a discourse of accommodation, stands for the limit of analogical thinking, and is in fact under the sign of incommensurability *per se*? Have we to do here with the prevalent concern with the sublime, with falls into place as a reticulation of the search, in all available directions, for a 'ground' to underpin a renewed and energetic effort to mark out a comprehensiveness for the embattled ego?[16]

We might characterise these peculiar hybrids of hyperbole as a series of immense Gothic bridges thrown between the universe of discourse and the forces of history, standing like Atlas (or fallen, like Ozymandias) in the gap at the heart of the newly disrupted world, that heart which, as we saw in 'Christabel', has for a time to be in quarantine to quell the danger that this opening in the fabric of history might permit some unqualified contamination. Yet in that very ideological gesture, we can also sense a reversed contour: of the sublime as precisely that rearguard code which is necessary to neutralise, through a 'pricing out of the market', the threat to the universe of what can be said among classically educated men and women.

The unification of the text

One general issue raised by this reflection on hyperbole concerns the extent to which the French Revolution marks a point at which politics begins to striate the form of non-political texts in a systematic way, in a ubiquitous politicisation of literary and aesthetic discourses; and one of the signs of this process can be found in the romantic revolt against genre, because hyperbole is the figure which exceeds expectation, and it is precisely a dialectic of expectancy and bereavement which these 'torn' shapes seek to enact, over and above the scenario of justice and judgement which now slides into a discredited past – as such hopes of fulfilment quail in the face of the obstacle represented in the 'shades of the prison-house'.

Here we find the figuration of a difficult and thwarted transition to maturity, to which we shall return. But thinking still about genre, we need to have reference to that notion of genre which bases itself in formal contract, a contract which the speaker assumes to obtain between a discourse and its receptions. Within this are also involved assumptions about historical and narrative agency, masked as they may be by mythologisation. The representing of a feared and discontinuous history, then, we can figure as a tearing up of the contract, in pattern with the tearing up of authority in France; and simultaneously as the torn fabric, the ripped curtain through which leakage of contaminating repressed contents might occur.

This dissolution can be cited in a host of examples: the tonal uncertainties and oscillations of Gothic fiction; the agential vacillations of Shelley's epic poems; the structure of Blake's Prophetic Books; the already alluded to yearnings after a philosophical poetry; and so on to Scott and the first attempts at the historical novel, and indeed to Carlyle, and *Sartor Resartus* (1833–4) as the 'other side' of the *History of the French Revolution* (1837), the reverse text which is simultaneously the impossible discourse. A striking instance of this emphasis on political and subjective malleability occurs in a precursor of the Revolution, Cowper's 'The Flatting Mill' (1781),[17] in which, after describing the process of making gold ingots, the text moves to outline the procedure of poetry in terms which suggest the enfolding of the subject within the poetic act, and raise all the necessary questions of agency:

> Alas for the poet! who dares undertake
> To urge reformation of national ill,
> His head and his heart are both likely to ache
> With the double employment of mallet and mill.
>
> If he wish to instruct, he must learn to delight,
> Smooth ductile and even his fancy must flow,
> Must tinkle and glitter, like gold to the sight,
> And catch in its progress a sensible glow.
>
> After all, he must beat it as thin and as fine
> As the leaf that enfolds what an invalid swallows,
> For truth is unwelcome however divine,
> And unless you adorn it, a nausea follows.

The key term here is 'employment', which straddles a doubt about who, or what, is the worked-upon material; and undoubtedly the conditon of the invalid which then ensues brackets the poet's diluted strength with a conventional critique of the receptive powers – and, indeed, recuperative potential – of the audience. The poet becomes his own material, a linkage which is signified in the apparent objectification of the 'fancy'; and what also appears here is a strange connection between dissimulation and truth, in which we are left unsure about the 'sources' of poetic inspiration, and, above all, about the relations between nature and artifice which might inhere in this 'new' world where even the processes of labour and change are obscured at the service of an unknown set of interests.

This state of perplexity can also be referred to the well-known problematic around the relation between public and private writing: in Wordsworth and Coleridge cardinally, where we find the journalistic and the pamphleteering back-to-back, as Cowper hints, with the private and the meditative, as the invasion of privacy proceeds apace. What we are dealing with here, I suggest, cannot best be considered in the terms of a unitary 'emergence of a new phase of the subject', of which the structuralists might wish to convince us. It is more a matter of a multiplicity of discourses in search of a new fiction of unity to set against the experience of disruption, a new source to place in the gap left by the defection of the mother. The hybrid genres of the romantics would then figure as the index of a concern with an uncontrollable multiplicity, an index on which are also registered the pressure of unaccommodated fear and the pressure to build new boundaries to contain experience which threatens secure assumptions.

It seems, then, especially important, in approaching the romantic response, to conceive of a textuality which does not speak from a unified position, and to interrogate that textuality as to the strategies by which it maintains itself in being in contested discursive space, against, for instance, the background of Orders in Council and repressive parliamentary Acts – a space to which no unitary truth corresponds, and *therefore* within which Burke's juncture of interests can function effectively as a holding operation. Such non-unified texts, their lack of unity passing indeed down to the present day as the very living mark of the 'literary' in its modern phases, characterised as the ensemble of discourses which resist instrumentalisation, are certainly symptomatic of the crisis of political representation of which the French Revolution is the first major modern manifestation.

Who or what utters in history? Who speaks in the mode of interpretation, where the meanings of historical experience are at stake? And on whose behalf are these primary and interpretative manoeuvres accomplished? It is in attempting to respond to these questions that the paucity of the elaborated conceptions of ideology may be revealed, in the impossibility of attributions to single 'unitary' classes; instead we may wish to conceptualise sets of processes which effect transmutations between discourse and action, but if so this cannot be along the thin line, for it is here, at the points where there is a threatened emergence into historical agency, that the processes of revision take place and the desires are revealed to be unamenable to exposure to the light of day. What we can, and indeed have to, engage with are the processes which limit, regulate, define and put into circulation the possible and permissible discourses of a world; and in thus defining an object of attention, we are also describing a primary ego-activity and opening the way to a consideration of the mobilisation of the unconscious along the trajectories of language.[18]

And it is here too that we need to begin to elaborate the concept of the group, for it is in the 'guardianship' to which we have already alluded that we find the roles which alone describe an intelligentsia. To return to Burke, and to precisely the position in cultural history which is filled by his body of text, we find an orthodox historical account which casts him as Goliath against Paine's failing David; yet we find also an attractive image of struggle which is clearly belied by the fact that in Britain no real struggle ever took place. Thinking of the activities of representation, we might say instead that Paine spoke for the intelligent artisans who were about to benefit from an unrestricted market; and that Burke spoke for the established landed gentry who stood also to benefit, provided only that the rate of transformation was held back to the rate of agricultural improvement. Alongside their much-vaunted disagreement subsists a unanimity which we can only see as arising from the intellectual's need to negotiate the terms of assent with the class to whom/for whom he speaks. In so far as these classes may be economically allied, so are their spokesmen.

In the paradox of these radical conservative figures we can see how the French Revolution marks a convenient point from which to study a new formation of discourse and power, in the sense that it confronted society with an immense task of representation, and substantial parts of this task devolved directly on the intellectual, the spokesman, the apologist. The society which was emerging from the Revolution was, indeed, prepared to yield part of its political power to those who were able to represent the world in discourses which both defined and opened up the channels of power. So the devices of evasion which we may find in the writing need to be related not only to 'external' fears of contagion, subversion, invasion, or to 'internal' anxieties about the collapse of narcissistic constructs, but also to specific worries about the weight of representation attaching itself to the intellectual stratum. These worries figure themselves to us now as the romantic insistence on the 'social role of the poet'; they also resulted in a need for a type of group security which we may describe as collusion, although this would not be to suggest that this collusion, forged under a pressure of real or imagined persecution, took its place in consciousness.

The armoury of resultant devices includes not only hyperbole and gigantism, but also, then, a shifting of agency, typically in demonisation and animalisation. What is happening here is an actual reinscription of the Revolution, a 'forging' in Blake's resonant term;[19] an investment of events with significance by mapping them onto already existing matrices, already authenticated discourses, a type of naturalisation proceeding by the perverse means of caricature and disjunction. Thus already-given power-relationships are altered, in so far as the processes of transcription and reinscription allow both the writing and reading subject to place him/herself *in* representation. The collusion of strategies springs from the set of those texts which permitted the placing of the writing and reading subjects in positions of unification, positions corresponding perhaps most closely to the class positions they occupied – or, as in the manner of advertising today, hoped, or imagined, or desired themselves to occupy.[20] Or, to put it another way, what becomes important is the set of those texts to be troped – Milton is only the most obvious and pertinent example – and the consequent arrangement of the supplement.

John Sterling was later to complain that Carlyle's style was 'as amazing as if the Pythia on her tripod had struck up a drinking song, or Thersites had caught the prophetic strain of Cassandra'; to which Carlyle replied that 'the whole structure of our Johnsonian English [is] breaking up from its foundation, [and] revolution there [i.e., in language] is visible as everywhere else';[21] as we look back from this comment, we see also the labours of Blake's character Los to build a new language from the foundations up.[22] And we trace there the modes of appropriation and loss (and also that violence that secures possession of self and discourse) experienced by writers and intellectuals in England during the events of the Revolution. As we perform this tracing we encounter a central hollow, a lack of concrete engagement between discourse and action; which, of course, serves only as a timely reminder of the inadequacy of the ego's self-comforting stories, and signifies a leading towards a distrust of narrative, which takes us again on the line to Carlylean bombast. In that hollow exist the outlines of a repressed fear, and alongside it an envy: constantly it is the French who are portrayed as the carriers of desire, as those who are capable of taking up active, aggressive roles *vis-à-vis* the forces of history.

The discursive devices used frequently reinforce inexorability, and in doing so they ward off, or act as guards against, the possibility of change, as something too dangerous for the beleaguered ego to contemplate. No individual or group is left with the power to act; spectatorial commentary, the literary equivalent of a certain kind of withdrawal, with its concomitant devices of caricature and misrepresentation, the phenomena precisely of *méconnaissance*, becomes the means of collusive identity. And it is, again, this spectatorial (or specular) subject-positioning which becomes codified in the aesthetic of the sublime: what you can see but you just cannot touch. The Gothic picks up on the ultimately regressive content of this mesmerised staring up at the mountain, the mainland of Europe, the 'Montagnards'; and presses through to consider precisely this element of exiled desire.

Desire and representation: Burke

> Into the purpose: or out.
> There is only, without a tune,
> timelessness of desire.
>
> Don't open up the way
> this town shines in through glass
> and the days darken;
> there's nothing better,
> not one thing better to do –
>
> What's now only disproved
> was once imagined.[23]

> ... desire is always outside of time, outside of narrative: it has no content, it is always the same in its cyclical moments of emergence, and the event in question takes on historicity only to the degree that the context of the explosion, the nature of that particular and historical repressive apparatus, knows specification.[24]

Text gives body to desire; the body which, in Berryman's poem, otherwise 'hangs down slack', in some formless and unimaginable prehistory.[25] Formation, we may also take it, comprises repression among its moments, and the sudden release into the realm of transcendence. All this renders, for us, romanticism as quintessential; around the romantics, in their continuing incarnation, hangs an aura of what writing is 'really' about, the closest condition, as even Paul de Man puts it, of the merging of language with the world being found in Wordsworth's long poems.[26] And it would be there, of course, that we would look primarily to examine the reticulations of narrative, its own story of difficulty as it strives to maintain its shimmering coherence within the cage of the ego.

The reception of the events of 1789 is caught in a dialectic of fact and fantasy; and that 'body' of fantasy is trans-individual, and is marked with something which we are beginning to see as 'group narcissism'.[27] We do not need to 'side' with Freud and against Jung's protestations to claim that, within this dialectic, we shall be able to discover a sexual shape; this is not to revert to a theory of origins, but rather to search among the paradoxical mists of historical specificity for a libidinal content; which, in turn, will prove to be responsive to the ceaseless and unrewarded sensitivity of the unconscious to the modifications of time.

Narcissism as containment is integrally bound to an exiling of desire; and to try to demonstrate this point we can begin from a specific 'exemplum', which is Isaac Kramnick's argument about the nature of desire as evidenced in Burke's *Reflections on the Revolution in France* (1790).[28] 'Throughout the *Reflections* Burke suggestively links the Jacobins with sexuality',[29] says Kramnick, and he gives various instances of what seems to be the unconscious project, the unowned agenda, behind the 'political' judgements.

The vivid description of the attack on the French Queen bears little relation to eye-witness accounts, which make no mention of the slaughter of her guard or of her 'almost' nakedness.[30] Yet these are, of course, the very terms – the relaxing of guardianship, the 'undress' which reveals the mark of shame and the problems of transmission and responsibility, the verging on an inquiry about orphanage – which we have already noted in 'Christabel' as materials which hover on the brink of the break, which signify the approach of historical and psychic hiatus; the averting of the glance, and the need to mobilise a specific representation of readership behind this twisting of fantasy.

To place in question a national constitution is likened by Burke, Kramnick reminds us, to 'taking periodical doses of mercury sublimate, and swallowing down repeated provocatives of cantharides to our love of liberty',[31] and so forth. We do not need to pick up on the curiously displaced intensities of 'mercury' and 'sublimate', with their multiple connotations centring around material which cannot be pinned down, which reaches to the heights in its extravagant strivings to conceal the forbidden recourse to the depths, to allow these metaphoric chains to bear a full weight of purgation and exile. In sum, says Kramnick, 'the extent to which Burke described the Jacobins in sexual language is striking, and always in terms of aggressive masculine conquerors bent on violating and possessing passive women';[32] Burke 'could not escape the linkage of social and political aggression with sexual energy',[33] and that of a specific kind.

This argument about Burke is quite familiar, and tends to move towards an analysis of personal neurosis. 'Had not', Kramnick asks rhetorically, his own writing inflected with the tones of already-answered questioning which pervade Burke's own texts, 'Burke himself marshalled his own internal resources to meet and defeat the urgings of sexual passion in order to keep them in their proper subordinate place',[34] and is he not, therefore, using his own experience as a model for the political situation? Yet what this argument appears to underplay is precisely the question of representation. The *Reflections* is, first and foremost, a public document, an intervention in an arena of actual and potential action. Yet in the very lines of this public-ness we discern a contradictorily articulated engagement with the private: a bringing onto the stage of a private obsession which is simultaneously a prurient evasion of the sources and consequences of that obsession. But in this act of personal disclosure/concealment, in connection with which we do not have to worry about the level of consciousness, there is also a 'speaking to' and a 'speaking on behalf of'.

This 'giving voice', with all its ambiguities, is retained in the contemporary and continuing fame of the *Reflections*, a fame in the constitution of which the title and short title of the text are not unimportant. We can explore it further in one of the other Burke passages which Kramnick quotes:

> When the fence from the gallantry of preceptors is broken down, and your families are no longer protected by decent pride, and salutary domestick prejudice, there is but one step to a frightful corruption. The rulers in the National Assembly are in good hopes that the females of the first families in France may become an easy prey to dancing-masters, fiddlers, pattern-drawers, friseurs, and valets de chambre, and other active citizens of that description, who having the entry into your houses, and being half domesticated by their situation, may be blended with you by regular and irregular relations. By a law they have made these people their equals. By adopting the sentiments of Rousseau they have made them your rivals.[35]

There are two terminological points we may pick out here. One centres on 'corruption', which we can link onto the chain of contamination, a chain which, of course, itself crosses and recrosses the boundaries of the 'public' as the politicians warn those citizens who may be tempted to be 'active' that they are picking up the 'French infection', an infection which, indeed, mercury sublimate and its cognates will only inflame. The second is the set of linkages which take us from the 'domestick', the antique sanctuaries of Sir Leoline and the Whig squirearchy, through to the 'half domesticated', at which point we are again in the territory of Christabel and Geraldine, and, indeed, of the mastiff whose allegiances are, of course, deeply swayed by the problematic of territory, the question of who properly holds the threads which bind the 'house', the nation, the tradition.

But more important is the deployment of the second-person pronoun. In his usages Burke here places himself in a boundary position which needs detailed description. It is a position which establishes the site for a doubling of the interpretative. On grounds which we may identify as a suffusion of ripe, worldly experience, he feels enabled to interpret the unconscious meanings of the Jacobin phenomenon 'outside' to an audience to whose own less than conscious fears he, in turn, aspires to speak, his grounds now being a combination of 'English-ness' and quasi-aristocratic pastoral care. We are indeed entwined in this address, in the very sense of the Lacanian diagram:[36] it is to the Other over our shoulder that Burke aspires to speak, and of course the concept of aspiration reveals a further twist, for it is only by responding at the unconscious level that we might sense the appropriateness of his carefully repressed personal experience to the matter apparently in hand. Yet the consequence of this complex engagement will be precisely a renunciation of the suspect materials which might thus be brought to light.

Burke's voice is, in these strictly rhetorical senses, the voice of privilege, the voice of one who is peculiarly 'privileged' to perceive approaching danger, rivers of blood whose biblical origin serves simultaneously as a unifying code for those who have ears to hear, or, rather, eyes to see the contours revealed in the panorama of dishevelment and flight which is conjured. The 're-presentation' may be summarised as the transformation of resistance into protection; such that we may indeed be inoculated by a small 'dose' of the excitement which, taken more repeatedly, would overwhelm these defences which Burke, after all, considered very much more frail than, at least in the early years, did his patrons.

Burke manipulates the power which necessarily derives from a boundary position with consummate skill: there is an exhilaration present in this gigantised and magnificent, 'dressed in purple', view of the dangers, of the tide which, heroically, only the man of destiny can roll back – a position which, of course, the reader is invited to share, as within his master's protective cloak. The articulacy is itself in the service of this role as 'guardian' of a boundary; the purple passages are neither accident nor nervous habit, but are a prolonged demonstration of the credentials appropriately brought to the appointed task of moral defender. For, as a literary man and a member of a specifically literary intelligentsia, Burke's wish is to be seen pre-eminently as a 'namer' of the unnameable, as one who, through mastery of image and rhetorical figure, possesses access to the hidden of language and action. And in this respect, we can see by looking further at the contemporary writing what is being held by Burke for the group of which he is a part, and some of the other interlinked stances by which the unconscious self-conceptions of that group become manifest.

Excesses

> When Luxury opens wide her arms,
> And smiling wooes thee to those charms,
> Whose fascination thousands own,
> Shall thy brows wear the stoic frown?
> And when her goblet she extends
> Which maddening myriads press around,
> What power divine thy soul befriends
> That thou should'st dash it to the ground? –
> No, thou shalt drink, and thou shalt know
> Her transient bliss, her lasting woe,
> Her maniac joys, that know no measure,
> And Riot rude and painted Pleasure; –
> Till (sad reverse!) the Enchantress vile
> To frowns converts her magic smile;
> Her train impatient to destroy,
> Observe her frown with gloomy joy;
> On thee with harpy fangs they seize
> The hideous offspring of Disease,
> Swoln Dropsy ignorant of Rest,
> And Fever garb'd in scarlet vest.
> Consumption driving the quick hearse,
> And gout that howls the frequent curse,
> With Apoplex of heavy head
> That surely aims his dart of lead.[37]

Thus, in the oddly titled 'Happiness' (1791), Coleridge represents the fate of unbridled desire, the inscription on the other side of Blake's 'wine presses'.[38] The terms are too close to other accounts of the Revolution for us to miss the analogy. Again the speaker is warning a second person; again the key fear is of excess, the dropping of the guard, which is also the relaxation of the ego's patrol around his sliding domain.

The position offered here for the addressed is, however, different, specifically in terms of the 'familial' model which now shows through the texts. With Burke our (masculine) fathering is alerted, as Sir Leoline's was not, to the possible fate of our daughters, at the mercy of an invasion of vigour which replicates the lineaments of a class fear. Here it is an image of the inexperienced (male) youth which is mobilised, and the projected defence is against the blandishments of a contaminated female experience. In both cases the problem of knowledge is transformed into the carnal; yet the ambivalence centres on the valuing of experience.

The condemnation of that experience is simultaneously the condemnation of a popular 'aspiration' to a happiness greater than that which is permitted by convention (analogy, order, degree . . .); and thus we find the gigantism circling back on itself in the twinned form of aspiration/transcendence and guilt, the quintessence through which the image of Coleridge precipitates the romantic condition. This structure can be usefully compared with the 'riven oak' imagery which is frequent in the poetry of the time; not now the oak under which Geraldine was offered the possibility of recuperation and, in the same breath, an identification of the 'target' for her own blandishments, but the oak which is in an odd specular relationship with the meteor:

> Britannia needs no Bulwark,
>   No Tow'rs along the Steep;
> Her march is o'er the mountain-waves,
>   Her home is on the Deep: –
> With thunders from her native Oak
>   She quells the floods below,
> As they roar on the shore
>   When the stormy Tempests blow –
> When the Battle rages loud and long
>   And the stormy Tempests blow!
>
> The Meteor Flag of England
>   Must yet terrific burn,
> Till Danger's troubled Night depart
>   And the Star of Peace return!
> Then, then, ye Ocean Warriors,
>   Our Song and Feast shall flow
> To the fame of your name,
>   When the Tempests cease to blow –
> When the fiery fight is heard no more
>   And the Tempests cease to blow![39]

It is indeed the matching of the sublime 'Tow'rs along the Steep' (which are also the defensive ramparts) with the search to 'remaster' the depths which is here at stake, but this chain of imagery is crossed by the uncertainty of oak and meteor. Spinning out the meteoric thread, we uncover a millenialism which, we might wish, is laughable but can still conspire to produce a hollow at the heart of the oak, in 'Ye Gentlemen of England'

(1801), the 'Old Ballad' of which this is said to be an 'Alteration ... composed on the Prospect of a Russian War'.

It is, perhaps, the conventional phrasing '*on* the Deep' which signifies most strongly here; the facilitation of progress (shipping, rapidity of commercial movement, effective international intervention) elided with the keeping down of that which properly belongs in an underworld, from which the divine sign of 'thunders' might, in a fearful way, call down an answering burst of meteoric lightning; in which, at the same time, we might see illumined the corruption in the heart of the oak and the very fate which will befall us as the tree topples, sacrificing its own integrity in the composite act of 'quelling'.

This imagery of the precariousness of dealing with danger – of exercising our recognisable cognitions on material which might, in itself, 'know' more than we do – is taken further in Byron's later, and startling 'Ode to Napoleon Buonaparte' (1814):

> He who of old would rend the oak,
>   Dream'd not of the rebound:
> Chain'd by the trunk he vainly broke –
>   Alone – how look'd he round?
> Thou, in the sternness of thy strength,
> An equal deed hast done at length,
>   And darker fate hast found:
> He fell, the forest prowlers' prey:
> But thou must eat thy heart away![40]

There is a massive condensation operating here around the oak, which we need to spell out. The oak is the aristocracy and the entire *ancien régime*, with all the ambivalence which attaches to a source of power the toppling of which will signify both our liberation and also, in its enactment of the death of the father, our fears of succession and a calling to take up the guardianship in the very moment of our unfittedness, our welling suspicions about our manhood. It is also a peculiarly English mytheme of passive strength; and it is the ordering phallus, under attack from the disorderly corruption in France. It is, of course, also the oak from which warships are built, and which thus guarantees mastery of the deeps.

But here also, and intertwined with this condensed signification, there is an emphasis on a permanent enmeshing of desire: the force of resistance, the 'stout' protection, is deployed to keep the desiring in a state of continuing non-satisfaction, and this is perhaps less surprising when we consider the versions of the consequences of violent revolution which were being peddled by many of the sensational novelists of the time, and which were serving to reinforce the equation between Englishness and passivity, a waiting out of the storm.

Matthew Lewis's *The Monk* (1796) is typical here. The wicked abbess is ambushed by popular 'justice' before she can be smuggled to the regular courts, an important cross between official and unofficial, public and private:

> All representations were fruitless; the disturbance grew still more violent, and the populace more exasperated. In vain did Ramirez attempt to convey his prisoner out of the throng: wherever he turned, a band of rioters barred his passage, and demanded her being delivered over to them more loudly than before. Ramirez ordered his attendants to cut their way through the multitude. Oppressed by numbers, it was impossible to draw their swords. He threatened the mob with the vengeance of the Inquisition: but in this moment of popular frenzy, even this dreadful name had lost its effect. ... The rioters heeded nothing but the gratification of their barbarous vengeance. They refused to listen to her: they showed her every sort of insult, loaded her with mud and filth, and called her by the most opprobrious appellations. ... At length, a flint, aimed by some well-directing hand, struck her full upon the temple. She sank upon the ground bathed in blood, and in a few minutes terminated her miserable existence. Yet, though she no longer felt their insults, the rioters still exercised their impotent rage upon her lifeless body. They beat it, trod upon it, and ill-used it, till it became no more than a mass of flesh, unsightly, shapeless, and disgusting.[41]

There is here a curious reversal and doubling of the signification of justice; more to the point, there is also a picture of the fate of 'representation', in the political sense, and considered as an act of giving voice through naming. The 'dreadful name had lost its effect'; and in that draining of ordering power (through terror), the form which makes the body over into text becomes unsustainable. On the one hand, the naming process itself retreats to a ludicrous and perceptibly inappropriate level of formality ('opprobrious appellations'); on the other, the body again hangs down slack, the distinction between life and death, the word and the mutation, impossible to draw, and the rage, Burke's rage and the 'representative' rage of a nation bypassed by history, becomes impotent as the consequences of the draining of desire make themselves felt.

Thus this passage fleshes out, in a literal way, the 'darker fate' to which Byron alludes, and which might be figured, by a displacement, as punishment for an agential role in history (the punishment of Cain, of the Ancient Mariner); and it represents a stream of imagery quite close to Burke's but significantly 'tipped' in both senses, revealing how readily the tones of admiration can be reinscribed as an ambiguous yearning for a postpone violation. And indeed, Lewis points up this connection in a way which demonstrates again that the boundary to be traversed is that between public and private:

> All this while Ambrosio was unconscious of the dreadful scenes which were passing so near. The execution of his designs upon Antonia employed his every thought. Hitherto he was satisfied with the success of his plans. Antonia had drunk the opiate, was buried in the vaults of St Clare, and absolutely in his disposal.[42]

In this dream of absolute power free from all the uncertainties and perils of 're-presentation', Ambrosio is not only 'unconscious' of the scene 'above ground'; he is, in the depths of his crypt, *the* unconscious of that scene.

Fathering the orphan

If these responses are to be interpreted in terms wider than those which, in the act of pursuing an untenable diagnosis of the individual symptom in the text, merely serve to reinforce the ego's determination to separate out the different worlds so as to establish its own jurisdiction, then we again need to refer back to the sense of the group; to the literary intelligentsia of the period.

The encounter between this group and the events of 1789 needs to be seen as a process of boundary establishment, wherein a sense of political identity, of communality of values, involving a complex network of inclusions and exclusions, is drawn up against the possible intrusion of chaos. There remains, as we have seen, the problem of inoculation, and from one aspect we could say that the intensity of romantic love provides the necessary *internal* release of libido which can, in its turn, prevent a destructive tangling with the wider forces abroad. 'It appears', to Wordsworth, 'that the most calamitous effect, which has followed the measures which have been lately pursued in this country, is a rapid decay of the domestic affections among the lower orders of society';[43] and in this displaced echo of Burke's fears of class miscegenation we can again trace the shape of a familial model, and of a notion of the group of the intelligentsia as conceiving itself in a specific role within an imagined wider constellation.

The 'lower orders' to which Wordsworth refers are 'small' proprietors, the owners of 'small' estates and 'little' tracts of land; the stance is one of quasi-paternal protectiveness, and indeed – and perhaps more importantly – of the frustration of the feelings which, we are led to suppose, should go by rights with that inherited paternal position.[44] It is indeed a name-of-the-

Father which is being handed down, and is being mobilised as an internal moral law to wield against the intrusion of threatened lawlessness. The model of the group on offer is that of a well-ordered family, at just the time when under the pressures of massive social change, accompanied later by war, the ability of the family to sustain itself in 'traditional' form – and, indeed, the power of the father to make his writ run against the changes in employment patterns and in the connections between life and work – was under severe threat; the transgression of boundaries which might be happening across the Channel was also happening in the well-ordered domestic sanctuaries of Britain – and not only, of course, in the countryside whereto many of these imaginings were to be displaced.[45]

We can, significantly, see a similar structure of defence repeating itself in the conflicting work of later commentators. An example would be the argument offered by M.I. Thomis and P. Holt against E.P. Thompson:

> In the 1790s ... working men were much more inclined to form Church/King mobs and display their xenophobia in wild celebrations of victories over the enemy than they were to form revolutionary mobs. Popular sentiment, such as it was, was crudely patriotic and anti-French, and reform was identified with the foreign cause. Where riots occurred they concerned food, wages and unpopular recruiting methods, and there were even mutinies in the fleet and militia over conditions of service, but all these grievances were ends in themselves, not indicative of a common ideological position or able to be co-ordinated for protest against something bigger than the immediate target, the system of government, for instance, rather than a local baker.[46]

One of the things which seems to be going on in the debate which this passage represents is an argument about child-rearing: will we be able to justify the activities of our 'children', the working classes, by claiming that at least they strove very hard for 'enlightenment', or by saying that enlightenment would in any case have been unavailable to them? Thomis and Holt appear to be concerned with the 'difficulty' of adolescence, which returns us again to some shadowily glimpsed obstacle on the path to maturity, some block of signification which resists learning; the convenient ending on the 'local baker' is again belittling, has a toy-town feel.

The Thompsonian alternative is, of course, that these people were splendid, grand, a hidden nobility with all the associated connotations of 'natural' inheritance from the dying powers of the past;[47] it seems very hard still to identify the group and its membership without either removing the sense of individuality or constructing an image of a collection of raw individuals incapable of ideological (unconscious) commitment – and in this oscillation we feel once more the problems of scale behind the coining of the rhetorical figures. The realities of grouping and classing are, of course, more complex than this, as are the relations between active political process and the induced passivity of industrial labour; it seems to be the threat of independent adult action on the part of the working classes which feeds the insecurities of the group which was taking on responsibility for 'representing' the English plight in the context of external change.

This oscillation in the representation of the people is, then, in continuity with an oscillation within the contemporary texts themselves; and many of the romantic and Gothic writers supply us with evidence that all was not well with the 'family' conception, even though it was supposed to be strong enough to deflect the threat of change. The hero/villain of John Moore's *Zeluco* (1789) emerges typically from a family background which obviously symbolises loss of 'natural' authority in a more political sense:

> In the tenth year of his age he lost his father, and was left under the guidance of a mother, whose darling he had ever been, and who had often blamed her husband for too great severity to a son, whom, in her fond opinion, nature had endowed with every good quality.
>
> A short time after the death of his father, Zeluco began to betray strong symptoms of that violent and overbearing disposition to which he had always had a propensity, though he had hitherto been obliged to restrain it. Had that gentleman lived a few years longer, the violence of Zeluco's temper would, it is probable, have been weakened, or entirely annihilated, by the continued influence of this habit of restraint, and the rest of his life might have exhibited a very different character; for he shewed sufficient command of himself as long as his father lived: but very soon after his death, he indulged, without control, every humour and caprice; and his mistaken mother applauding the blusterings of petulance and pride as indications of spirit, his temper became more and more ungovernable, and at length seemed as inflammable as gunpowder, bursting into flashes of rage at the slightest touch of provocation.[48]

Here the 'premature' death of the father is important enough to be textually doubled, and to be attached at root to the manifestation of the symptom. It is a remarkably prescient account of how one might narrate revolution if one is polemically restricting the channels of thought to a locus around de-politicised individual indulgence; and clearly it contains within it the fear of contamination in the absence of properly constituted parental authority.

Anna Laetitia Barbauld points to the revealing hiatus, in her later Preface, saying on the one hand that 'Zeluco is painted as radically vicious, without the intermixture of any one good quality', but adding a few lines later that what this amounts to is that 'the whole character has a darker tinge of villainy than is usually found in this country';[49] thus suggesting, along with a whole subgenre of Gothic novelists, that it is quite possible for an undifferentiated total evil (or rather, perhaps, an 'evil' absence of differentiation) to exist outside the secure boundaries of English moderation.

What is thus demonstrated is a lack of purchase on the outside, a failure of reality-testing, as if the hyperbolic moment has turned back on itself and prised loose the grip of consciousness on judgement. Clearly also, historical and geographical displacements come increasingly massively to serve as codes for the displacement of feared material from sources *within* – the psyche, but also the English class structure – onto the shocking events in Europe. It is worth noting that William Godwin's *Caleb Williams* (1794) gives a substantially similar account of primary process. Caleb spends the whole novel trying precisely to reverse this activity of undifferentiation by distinguishing between degrees of good and evil, in the service of an attempt to establish his own personal authority; but he ends up unable at the last minute to shed the imago of the father, and is left with an appalling residue of guilt. Anxiety about loss of faith in the father thus appears in a new guise as the motive for a kind of childlike jealousy of the 'freedom' to be enjoyed in France, although even within that equation appear the stigmata of anarchy.

It is the case that at certain moments when the experience of a group becomes radically painful – and here we seem to be dealing with a vertiginous vacuum of authority – an impulse is manifested to tell stories; among other reasons, because narrative stands as the sign for the covering of the gap and for the establishment of a version of 'how we got to this' in which the ego can find its feet on the precipice. The Gothic novelists, and Scott and his followers, provide us with one variant of these stories, the ones which move the group away into the distance, so that we may abandon the 'domestic' site where we have already made a mess of things which nobody is going to come and clean up.

With other 'narratives of revolution', the action is different, and consists in recounting the history itself in a displaced form: Shelley's *Revolt of Islam* (1817) is very much a case in point, with its transformation of public into private and its condensation of sources of terror into polished images of idealistic hope. But what lies behind this is the fact that what the writers are carrying is the responsibility for an evasion of desire: an evasion of the threat that the French revelation – which is that father-figures are removable, although that, of course, only begins to open up a series of consequent questions – may actually allow some specific manifestation of desire, both within the self and at other social levels. And it is towards this exile of desire, this refusal to accept that, within England itself, there might be an active striving towards fulfilment and away from parental control, that the endeavour among the literary intelligentsia, in all its various forms, is crucially geared.

Adolescence and transition

What evolves in this spread of symbolisation is a system: in the strong sense. That is to say, it is a system as we consider system to be the extension of the ego's narcissistic activities into the world, the 'system' which Blake suspected to be the 'metaphysical' equivalent of slavery. And since slavery was precisely the inexcusable base on which the myth of continuous expansion was founded – and, perhaps, still is – it is worth emphasising the strength of the work of forgetting which was necessary to conceal the inequities and human misery which were embedded at the root of the mythologisation of Englishness at this, one of its most significant formative stages.

But system is also inevitably the sign under which we bring process as we attempt activities – like criticism – which entail the freezing into product; and it is at this point that I would like to return to the question of the quaternary, the mandala, the polar 'system' which seeks to arrest the turning globe.[50] In what follows, I shall be trying to use a model to interrogate a text; but also to be pursuing the work of interpretation along the line which takes us further towards the heart of the modelling, in order to reveal the impulses behind it. The model I shall use is A.J. Greimas's semic rectangle,[51] which readily falls into place as part of a structuralist series, and which also neatly reflects the assumed replacement of hierarchical quaternaries (best exemplified in the long tradition of biblical interpretation) by democratic quaternaries, where the potential supremacy of terms is replaced by the supposedly equitable emphasis on relations. Whether this implicit structuralist polemic partakes of the same duplicity as its overt political model is a matter I propose for the moment to leave hanging.

The pivotal representing of experience on which I want to concentrate is this exile of desire and the problem of its location 'elsewhere'; and the rectangle will serve to demonstrate for us a way of approaching some of the strategies used to remove the problematic manifestation from British shores; or in other words to deny the connection between manifest and latent, such that the dream need never come dragging into view, the chain of signifiers will be broken at the crucial point of transition into/from the unconscious. My instance is one we have come across before, Coleridge's

'To a Young Lady with a Poem on the French Revolution'; which now may come to seem, in its stance and address, a type for the 'supplementarity' proclaimed in its own title.

It is also, at a simpler level, an evidence of the 'change of heart' to emerge from the romantic disillusion:

> Thus to sad sympathies I sooth'd my breast,
> Calm, as the rainbow in the weeping West:
> When slumbering Freedom roused by high Disdain
> With giant Fury burst her triple chain!
> Fierce on her front the blasting Dog-star glow'd;
> Her banners, like a midnight meteor, flow'd;
> Amid the yelling of the storm-rent skies!
> She came, and scatter'd battles from her eyes!
> Then Exultation waked the patriot fire
> And swept with wild hand the Tyrtaean lyre:
> Red from the Tyrant's wound I shook the lance,
> And strode in joy the reeking plains of France![52]

By now the meteor requires some attention. As a figure it stands in relation to a *deus ex machina*, but scientised and randomised to cope with the problematic combination of enlightenment and millenarianism with which the British were confronted. The force of the image, here, is far from obvious: what are we to make of this apparent transience of 'banners', when the whole polemical force is towards making a thing of permanence of these 'British' virtues, except by having recourse to Derridean arguments about the resistances inherent in language – arguments which are themselves only a rhetorical updating of Hegel's formative encounters with the *List der Vernunft*?

Here we have also the 'storm-rent' skies, the rip of history through which might come ... the meteor? Perhaps, but there we might be encountering the form of the stopgap, and thus, of course, a continuing British mytheme about the necessity of an island race as a God-given inbuilt frustration of the designs of tyrants – those tyrants across whom we have already come as reaping their just deserts in the 'crash and ruin of their grand designs'. We may represent the material carried by the stanza in the diagram overleaf.

A crucial trajectory here is through adolescence. A world of brute power is invoked as a negative sanction for the achievement of some kind of real authority (which may also be the root of the power of the analyst, through his/her naming of the brute, raw emotions – envy, fear, lust, the signifiers which claim an extralinguistic power, a power which is reinforced by the actual silence of the inscribing). The path to adulthood appears to depend

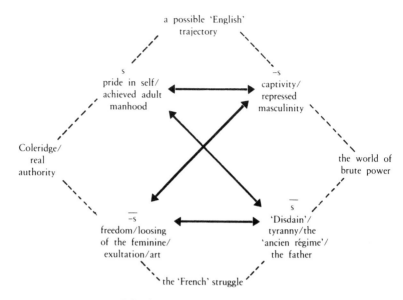

on an acceptance of the feminine, which will then guarantee the real force of the phallic 'lance'; a force which, after all, is barely freed from the castration imagery of the tyrant's wound, the rent in the hollow tree, the fear and envy lying in the 'enfolding', and the chain which, in its paths through the recesses of the signifier, eventually leads us to the content, frequently repressed in the process of psychoanalysis, of womb envy, and of the wish to convert this unacceptable wound into the productive wound whose only, suppressed, emblem is Hephaestos, foster-child of the unfathering and unrelenting gods.[53]

The need is to enable the poet to act as prophet of an English struggle which will both parallel and supersede the French emergence into a putative adulthood; and this quite clearly takes on the contours of a sibling rivalry which now begins to explain the problems of gigantism and miniaturism which beset the representing of internal/external conflict. The scene is set for the onrush of the primal horde; but what is not set is the alleged supremacy of access to experience, because the suspicion is that, when this is owned to, it will simply count as another disqualification from a (military) version of power which has no time for the activity of reflection which may 'represent' the feminine in this dialogue of the lads.

The passivity of 'sad sympathies' figures as a ground on which a passage may be described to a fullness of action present in embryo in the striding of the last line. The key factor thus becomes 'Disdain', giant among terms, an ignoring of the feminine sources of power represented in art, and at the same time a signifier readily translatable into the 'contempt' which stands as the sign under which impotence must muster itself in the armies of the night, hoping against hope to evade detection. The path to be followed will involve a recognition of others, so it is ambiguously hoped, and an active participation in a trans-individual struggle; but in the next stanza, all this has altered:

> Fallen is the Oppressor, friendless, ghastly, low,
> And my heart aches, though Mercy struck the blow.
> With wearied thought once more I seek the shade,
> Where peaceful Virtue weaves the Myrtle braid.
> And O! if Eyes whose holy glances roll,
> Swift messengers, and eloquent of soul;
> If Smiles more winning, and a gentler Mien
> Than the love-wilder'd Maniac's brain hath seen
> Shaping celestial forms in vacant air,
> If these demand the empassion'd Poet's care –
> If Mirth and soften'd Sense and Wit refined,
> The blameless features of a lovely mind;
> Then haply shall my trembling hand assign
> No fading wreath to Beauty's saintly shrine.
> Nor, Sara! thou these early flowers refuse –
> Ne'er lurk'd the snake beneath their simple hues;
> No purple bloom the Child of Nature brings
> From Flattery's night-shade: as he feels he sings.[54]

Beneath the detail of the change of stance, we can glimpse a substitution of basic categories, (see diagram overleaf).

Here the passage from adolescence is portrayed in terms of internalisation: freedom can exist only *within*, and is represented in the context of a peculiar 'monologic interchange', in which the feminine figures only as addressee, although imbued with a reserved power (figure itself for an absent aristocracy) which requires a continual effort of convincing.

The suppressed category, evidenced partially in sexual metaphor, is action: the lance has become the 'snake', whose very existence or whose relation to cognition, like the possibility of the 'purple bloom' (the purple of Burke's protecting cloak) and the ambiguous 'night-shade', is denied in its re-presentation. Power and authority have become grouped together as manifestations of a feared involvement with the world, in the double sense of involvement which also implies the lingering of re-enfolding within the 'mastering' womb.

The 'oppressive' figure has been caught up in the entire masculine trajectory which had previously seemed to show the possibility of

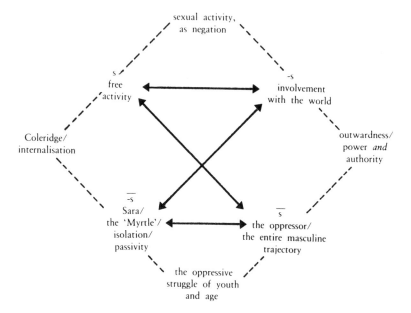

transcendence; or, at least, of a movement forward along the thin line of maturation. Coleridge's guilt assimilates itself to that of Caleb Williams: the collapse of the father–imago does not move the (male) child forward, but locks him into a predicted circle of guilt and remorse. Desire is exiled and replaced by a series of obsessive and repetitive struggles, in which the free individual (Sara) can be manifested only in silence and in the receipt of the placatory gift, which is also what poetry has become, doubtless having recoiled from the sound of the 'Tyrtaean lyre'. To replace the possibility of actual conflict with the forces of oppression, therefore, no matter where they may be located, we have a continuous tension, as Coleridge tries to hold together the possibility of a liberation of the 'feminine' which will be totally absorbed in the power of his own writing: the poem represents a self-enclosing of the sexual, as a key to the repulse of the forces of invasion.

Humiliation and the oak

We have seen that some of the fears that appear through these responses are of violation, which is hardly surprising; yet I would want to contend that, within the unconscious process generating and holding in tension these literary surfaces, certain further and more expressive peculiarities about maturation and gender role may be observed. It is true that much of the popular poetry of the period refers to Britain as female, and suggests that the unloosed virility of the Jacobins is about to pose a threat to social and sexual integrity;[55] and within this occurs a constellation in which the imagining of the French Queen becomes the basis for the establishment of the character of the Gothic heroine.

Similarly, we can find references to France itself as a female in the process of being violated by her own 'sons';[56] and these fears, of course, were ones on which Pitt was happy to play in the interests of building up a national defence and an ideology which would countenance such concomitant repression as might be deemed necessary. But behind this there lie more twists in the route through the processes of revision; and one form which we there encounter is indeed of an assault on a precariously maintained masculinity. The myth of 'Englishness' during these troubled years sustains itself on the acceptance of the idea that the English State has already achieved a stable maturity; that it has already survived the traumas of republicanism and the punishment due on the murder of the monarch.

The revolutionary disturbances of adolescence are thus already over, and need not be recapitulated. And this is a myth which repeats itself in the very texture of literary history, whereby enthusiasm for the French Revolution is attached to the 'adolescent' phase of romanticism, in Coleridge and Wordsworth before their 'adult' renunciations; in Shelley under the sign of a permanent postponement of maturity, confirmed by death; and perhaps in Hazlitt, linked and sanitised by its connection with different sorts of forbidden and laughable enthusiasm.

Romanticism has been characterised as 'a process that, on the one hand, consolidates the domestic sphere as private – a privacy haunted by fears of its own violation – and, on the other, sees the emergence of a form of confessional literature which gives an unprecedented publicity to the life history of "private" individuals';[57] and here we see the knot of issues around public and private brought together with domestication/violation, and attached correctly to an arena within which writing as self-disclosure and writing as self-concealment becomes a contradiction in the service of a double standard: a hope for liberation which is simultaneously a refusal to renounce the stable State. Three possible reasons are offered for the emergence of this structure: 'a process of retreat . . . ; a means of coming to terms with sexual humiliation . . . ; a form of self-advertisement'.[58] The first and third of these reasons are joined in the rebus: whereby the withdrawal and absenting of the self entails also its replacement by a series of 'advertisements for myself',[59] in patrolling the chain of which we draw no closer to the 'reality behind the language'. Thus the self can continue to advertise its own seclusion in a double twist of power.

Sexual humiliation fits into this structure in terms of a set of attitudes towards the possibility of competitive failure, a set which cannot fail to be informed by the 'new world' of labour and domesticity which is being constructed. In Shelley we find an attempt, not unique to him, to comprehend the two genders within the self, which would obviously be one way of avoiding the possibility of defeat in this 'new' struggle for survival and accumulation. Coleridge and Southey in the pantisocratic experiment appear to be experimenting with the possibility of cloning, which would in turn entail a denial of the individuality of women; and this clearly connects with the many difficulties which Blake has with the identification of the 'Female Will', to which we shall return later. We might hypothesise that this fear of potential humiliation is linked to a particular weak point in masculine identification, the failure of 'Mother Security', and that some of the evidence for this might be found in the pathology of pre-maturity which inflects Blake's invocation of the 'girls of mild silver, or of furious gold', and which of course supplies the crucial audience position for Hazlitt's *Liber Amoris* (1823) in a completing of the circle of parental abdication.[60]

In a sense, 1789 signified to an English intelligentsia a lifting of constraints on self-disclosure, connected with the imagined removal of a possibly condemnatory parent. But the reactions of the key writers to this putative adulthood are fraught with ambivalence: the attempt to accept what Hazlitt is aware of as a (female) 'softness' becomes indissolubly linked to suicide and early death. We can see some of the roots of this problem of cathexis in a poem like Cowper's 'Yardley Oak' (1791), which, in terms of much of the imagery we have come across before, accurately diagnoses the 'hollowness' of the myth of maturity:

> At thy firmest age
> Thou hadst within thy bole solid contents
> That might have ribb'd the sides or plank'd the deck
> Of some flagg'd admiral; and tortuous arms,
> The ship-wright's darling treasure, didst present
> To the four-quarter'd winds, robust and bold,
> Warp'd into tough knee-timber, many a load.[61]

In that invented past, then, there was a (mythical) possibility that the phallus might be linked to some principle of action, connected with the mastery of the deeps, and with all the imagery which would imply a revaluation of the hollow as the location for fertility and a kind of productivity for ever immune from the distortions of industrialisation; a possibility that 'arms' might reach out to the world, and isolation might emerge and intervene or embrace.

> Embowell'd now, and of thy ancient self
> Possessing nought but the scoop'd rind, that seems
> A huge throat calling to the clouds for drink,
> Which it would give in rivulets to thy root,
> Thou temptest none, but rather much forbidd'st
> The feller's toil, which thou couldst ill requite.

The image is one of senility; but within that there rests the baby bird, weak and desperate, crying out in need, to an absent mother. No longer is there the possibility of a 'natural' fusion of tree and rain, phallus and female principle; by sheer demand this tree has priced itself out of the market, become too vast, too 'gigantised' to enter into any kind of equitable relationship – or even into any commercial travesty.

In this context, we might suggest some new forms for the psychopathology of romanticism:[62] we may see romanticism as a moment when, under the pressure of massive external change, the layer of doubts constructed by narrative to convince the ego of its own maturity became lifted, and a fear of adolescent powerlessness becomes the dominant sexual figure. 'Yardley Oak' continues:

> Yet is thy root sincere, sound as the rock,
> A quarry of stout spurs and knotted fangs.
> Which, crook'd into a thousand whimsies, clasp
> The stubborn soil, and hold thee still erect.

Running up against difficult material, as he so often did, Cowper resorts here to a rhetoric which sounds very much like an exercise in cheering oneself up. The external face may be pitted with acne, but down below, in the secret places of heart and loins, some kind of strength still exists in reserve, in hiding, folded into the hollow, and alongside it is the implied threat of 'knotted fangs', which returns us to the uncertainties of the serpent. Whether this purely private strength will in fact be sufficient to move the 'erect' phallus into the public sphere of action seems, however, doubtful, as do the possibilities of resurrection prefigured in the transformation of the Cross. What is present here is a 'hugging to the self', which prefigures the consolidation of the dominant characterisation of England in 1789: as that realm in which the movement of desire must not be felt, because it is tainted with an adolescent sense of guilt.

Many strategies of containment are used to reinforce the distancing which is thus needed. In particular, we may refer now to the dialectic of maturity and childhood as indeed represented in the urges to present revolution as a Promethean struggle between 'Giant forms';[63] and folded within this is an evasion of the possibility that the struggle in France might involve human beings and might, as such, be open to a realistic imaginative participation. And here we touch upon a whole constituting of romanticism in Britain as the outcrop of an unconscious project which, in its emphasis on individualism as protective isolation, continues into the literary and social history of the twentieth century.

As far as representation was concerned, the writers found themselves in a complex position, in which the very act of 'penetrating' the fabric of history, in the French manner, becomes a metaphor although its force slides away from violation into an impotent exposure, related to the fear that adult life might actually invade the adolescent's bedroom and reveal the inadequacy which it was the 'articulate' intelligentsia's duty to *guard*. Returning to Burke, we may see his portrayal of the French Queen less now as an incitement to violence than as an image with the ambiguity of a pin-up; and suspect that, within his resonant imagery, wrapped in the purple cloak (which is a transformation of the serpent), what he is holding for the 'literati' is the fear that contamination by the real (the objective, the unconscious) might expose and destroy the fantasies on which the mythical structure of Englishness was based.

Myths of war

It is still too easy, despite the efforts of David Erdman among others, to forget that for many British people the major constituent of experience in the years between 1793 and 1815 was war.[64] Such is the regularity with which the Revolutionary and Napoleonic Wars are treated as experiences peripheral to British culture that behind this blurring of memory there appears the shadow of a more deliberate evasion, and an evasion of greater dimensions even than those characteristic of a national criticism which has traditionally preferred its historical 'contexts' to be presented severely diluted, and preferably bent into the service of moral instruction.

The reasons for this evasion are complex, and some of them bear a particular relation to the contemporary: this is not an economic or political phase in which intra-European warfare presents itself as a privileged object of attention, nor is it one, indeed, in which military history can be happily seen as free from political partiality.

In referring to the experience of war I do not mean to effect a simple contentual connection. War, certainly, produces its own hierarchies of signification, and it is the wars of the romantic age which provide, for instance, a shape for particular connections between aggressivity and commerce, ones which have not been lost through the unrolling generations. But those hierarchies are themselves dependent on deeper arrangements of social life. In economic terms, the seemingly interminable years of conflict with the French can most fairly be seen, after the processes of revision, as an era of interrupted potential, of hanging on the brink for some new and unprecedented 'at-home-ness' of the psyche. The exploitation of the colonies, the bitter taint of slavery, and the steady progress of expansion attendant on that exploitation, did not cease to proceed, but they did so under uneasy conditions, constantly dependent on the next round of commercial sabre-rattling; and thus the war effort comes increasingly to be seen as something to be undertaken *in order for something else to begin*,[65] as an increasingly burdensome impediment to the birth of a new age. The fiction of newness is thus visibly textually tied to the notion of obstacle: the possibility of interpreting change read through the blockage which (perhaps thankfully) prevents the plumbing of the depths of anxiety.

And so we find this element within the popular imagination, this prolonged 'labour' so graphically presented in its hope and its sterility in *Frankenstein* (1818), which is both the production of munitions, and thus tied to the hierarchies of weaponry which signify the levels of divinity, and simultaneously validate a certain important complexity of myth, carried through now on *Dungeons and Dragons*, and also the delayed attempt to give birth to a mythically stable Britain of the future, the transference of a mytheme of gold, now rendered pregnable by the pregnancy, into a future where no validation can be threatened. Otherwise all those difficult births which punctuate Blake's Prophetic Books would have been less bloody, and their place within a formal textuality less prominent.[66]

Equally, without the thunder of firearms, and of accusations of treason *pour encourager les autres*, the thunderings of a harvest of romantic demiurges would seem part of a quite different vocabulary: the foregrounding of war as a fact of social life is the essential prerequisite for relevant and operable definitions of clarity, opacity and volume. For the Tories, this clamour of the guns contains a double danger, to be offset in the mythic constructions of the inviolable State: that hearing it might spark a corresponding rebellious clamour at home, in the space of domesticity which is in any case under a different kind of siege, and/or that continental furore (the raging voices of Gothic heroes, now being heard again in their full, ancestral Jacobean grandeur – Jacobite? Jacobin?) might obscure the sounds of an underground unrest when they occur. Against the first – and thinking still in the armoury – there is always the weapon of repression of communication, so that dissent is squeezed along the thin, stoppable, predictably rhythmic line, the setting up of resistances which will prevent the rapid electric flow of revolutionary thought, the galvanic charge; against the second, the quieter resource of spying, the ear which Pitt had always to keep uncomfortably close to the ground, however grand an international posture he might seek to assume.

In the context of this search we would want to transform the implications of the romantic longing for a plainer 'language of men'. Some of the major romantics may find their way to pockets of silence, which we may now characterise as 'safe houses', with all the intensifications of the *oikos* which the assumed classical education should bring us. They may be able to test subtle tuning-forks on the mountains and the winds; but alongside this refinement there was, in the writing of the period, a great deal of stentorian bellowing, from which indeed Coleridge, Byron, Shelley are not immune – and as a legacy of which Landor tries to re-create the suppressed linkages back to a traditionally violent statecraft.[67]

This bellowing, as we read the popular poetry of the time, the condensation of argument into ritual cries of 'liberty', 'freedom', 'justice', appears at first glance to come from a realm of anonymity: from anonymous, or merely initialised, poets, a writing devoid of its signature, where the evidence is strangely dead on the issue of fear of reprisal; and from the newspaper editors, a realm of perpetual willed anonymity. But of course this anonymity is puppetry, what Russell Hoban refers to in *Riddley Walker* (1980) as the 'Eusa show', the retelling of myths of power under the guise of lapsed memory; a phenomenon which is indeed not totally distinct from interpretation, as we are trying to articulate its ambiguities.

Neither Tory nor Whig felt happy with freedom of speech. Too much was at stake; the unpredictable outcome, in particular, of a massive social ambivalence, the breaking apart of this collusion which, like a chemical compound, formed the very air to be breathed. We are not talking about suppression; certainly politicians manipulated, and editors were under no misapprehension about their national responsibilities, but it would be inane to argue for some variant of 'poesy' which could see through chauvinism to chauvinism's psychological operations. The operations of hegemony are more all-embracing than that, and this could best be evidenced from the example of Robert Bloomfield, from the representation of the working-class 'view',[68] which is that view which the psyche might take of its long exploitation were it not too always-already wedded – in a curiously common-law marriage – to its own myth of emancipation.

Such popular poets tended towards formal and ideological traditionalism; but in any case, as Betty Bennett puts it, 'poets who supported the war as well as those who opposed it use the same terms'.[69] It is the consolidation of rhetoric which is at stake; partly because the issues of revolution, war and national unity are close (and closed), and generate, or relay, an enormous power to absorb contradiction and represent it as confirmation. In a poem of 1807 called 'Britain's Genius Triumphant',[70] Britain is referred to as 'freedom-fost'ring' and 'coop'd up' in successive lines; and what we thus need to wonder about is the pressure on the individual voice to survive under fear, a fear clearly related to invasion but more to the problems of change and the destruction of stability, which are really the phenomena responsible for the familiar myth of the 'resistance of language' so beloved, for ideological reasons, of the deconstructionists.

There is a terror of chaos: 'confusion whelms all forms, all properties;/ And chaos reigns among the sons of men,/Till God's avenging arm restores fair Peace again';[71] and thus a root of romantic transcendentalism. There are the shapes of disorder to be found in the Gothic; and lost in their inception. Within this, there is the military and nationalistic Gothic absorption recognisable in the mode of the 'Ossianic', with so many imitators during these two decades. But that discourse itself enters into relation with the imagery of a rousing battle hymn like 'Stop to a Stride', written in 1803,[72] which has Napoleon (Byron's necessarily bounded victim of a preternaturally prolonged vengeance) violating each European country in turn, a rhetorical flourish which also commanded the contemporary reportage of the early stages of Hitler's war, and where, significantly, greater concreteness is invested.

But it is not rhetorically simple to achieve a consensus around the images of France as savage aggressor and France as the victim of a pseudo-egalitarian conspiracy. One way in which it is attempted is by a separation (quarantining, inoculation, decontamination) of masculine and feminine characteristics. In a 1794 'Ode' from the *Scots Magazine*,[73] the male French are conjured away completely, so that the stalwart, 'hearts of oak' British can perform the ideologically necessary function of protecting French virgins – who are also, of course, virgin minds free from the taint of Jacobinism.

Frederick Atkinson's 'The Emigrée' (1799)[74] can stand for a genre in which French womanhood is reduced to penury and – again – orphanage, British commerce (commercialism, carnal invasion, counter-revolution) being therefore her only means of survival. Helen Maria Williams, in her 'Ode to Peace' of 1801,[75] entertains hopes that all might yet indeed come right with a marriage between France and England, but for the most part the benignity is such that a solution to the quandary of the relation between 'innocence' and 'experience' remains very distant. Scott, in 1811, also wrote a 'Bonaparte',[76] where, after a first verse in which the poet waxes rude about Napoleon's low birth in a 'suburb hovel', we learn that 'before that Leader strode a shadowy form,/Her limbs like mist, her torch like meteor show'd'. Leaving the meteor on one side to be connected to the earlier signifying chains, we note that this 'shadow' turns out, conventionally, to be 'Ambition'; yet what is significant is that it should be this phallic quality which serves to obscure real historical connection, and thus to do duty to a different obscuring.

Historical narrative is not simple, especially at times of emergency; and the confident celebrations of old English beer and pudding bear the constant marks of a system of linkages from which the sustenance is gradually leaking. An effort of mainstream poetry in these years was to generate a connection between simplicity of structure and deliberate (shadowed) opacity of image, whereby the representation of physical action could be turned into schematised psychic conflict – inoculation again. And thus the hierarchy of the State is represented in the formal limitations of poetry: while outwardly professing them to be made of oak, the poets portray 'the people' as cowering beneath the feet of mighty semi-invisible contestants, the grandiloquent representatives of a less than fascinating conflict between the schools of rhetoric.

Myth is not genuinely susceptible of opposition, nor even can it be destroyed or modified by the construction of counter-myth; since its realm is contradiction, it is capable of remaining unaffected by weapons intellectual, modifying its contours only in a complex and variable dialectic with changes in the real. A poem of 1813 entitled 'National Discord' is revealing. The poet regrets the lack of a 'Thracian Lyrist ... gifted with skill/To humble the Tiger to crouch at his will', and bemoans the collapse of the world into discord, rather than the harmony which, of course, once prevailed:

> ... the Genius of bright intuition is fled;
> And harmony passed from the heart to the head;
> No rapt inspiration now succours the brave!
> No sounds of the lyre are effectual to save!

> The reign is establish'd of Discord; delight
> Exults in narration of siege and of flight;

Where losses confuse in the flames spreading-far,
And distresses in pageants and tumults of war.[77]

The crucial terms are 'narration' and 'siege'; the crucial juxtaposition 'Discord; delight'. While the martial is criticised, 'delight' and 'exults' are attached precisely to this condemned narration. And for 'condemned narration', we could substitute all the romantic usages of the Bible and Milton, and be at the same time enquiring about the limits of 'representative collusion' at the root of the romantic psyche.

Keats and the wound

It is the collapse into discord against which the narcissistic root, the root of the 'Tree of Mystery', grows.[78] Or we may turn to a different mythic structure and incarnate (incarnadine) the wound which must not be admitted, the trace of the umbilical cord which forever betrays the ego into the necessity of disowning its own origins, but which simultaneously requires the crying for mother which, it knows, can only betray it further into an admission of that lack of autonomy which threatens and beckons with the voice of the Other.

Poetry is the form of the wound.[79] We may place this as a historical judgement, and one which itself refers to the tracing of romanticism as the quintessential poetic mode and stance from the eighteenth century to the present day. It situates itself across the limits of narrative, at the point where questions begin to be raised about the vaunted self-sufficiency of the ego, about the possibility of tracing tenable histories of the psyche or of the world. Thus narrative poetry is engaged in a continuous and oscillating process of story and rebuttal, of sinking down the metaphoric chains while struggling to keep an eye on the distant forward and backward horizons which would convert these complex trajectories into the safe story of the linear. The wound can be admitted and denied, in a far realm from the certainties of novelistic realism. And thus also the forces of commerce, in their presence but also in their sinking backwards into the all-absorbing structures of objectivity which are the unconscious, come to figure in this constellation: this 'social role for the poet' is structured, then as now, on the awareness of its paradoxical status as a 'junior branch', without the appeal and access to validating circulating consumption of its more profitable scions; while this is conjoined with the opposite awareness, of the claims to antiquity which shade back to pre-written forms, the unknowable history which is also the hazing around the origins of the individual consciousness in the womb.

Narcissus ignores and covers his wounds in the specular moves of perfection; against him again we may range Hephaestos, whose wound is the emblematic guarantor of creative power, as the romantic myths of the construction of the pearl attain predominance. The wound of the pale knight, who is also the grounded pale rider, is the outcome and recognition of the impossibility of the search for sources, the knowledge, coded as it is, of the fantasies which prevail in and around the 'elfin grot', which is the substantial and mythic retreat which covers the perpetually unacceptable absence of the womb. And this leads us to Keats's reflexivity about the effects of narcissism in 'Lamia' (1819), where indeed the touch of 'cold philosophy'

> will clip an angel's wings,
> Conquer all mysteries by rule and line,
> Empty the haunted air, and gnomed mine –
> Unweave a rainbow, as it erewhile made
> The tender-person'd Lamia melt into a shade.[80]

Philosophy has no power to heal, as Keats the putative healer knew too well:

> On the high couch he lay! his friends came round –
> Supported him – no pulse, or breath they found,
> And, in its marriage robe, the heavy body wound.[81]

It is not necessary to pun on 'wound' and 'wound' to notice that this death is a death unrepresented by a mark; a causeless and, more to the point, symptomless death which, we are invited to believe here and elsewhere in Keats, owes as much to satiation as to the gift of the serpent. The fear of narcissism in Keats is transmuted into a series of myths about a superflux of perfection, sorrow glutted 'on a morning rose', so that the wounded and tubercular body can suffuse the shaft of poison with ease, restfulness, comfort, a version of death in which the body remains sufficiently perfect to 'be among her cloudy trophies hung'.[82]

It is Saturn, among others, who does battle with the elemental emotions and enters into the circle of encounters which prove and disprove his own problematic mortality:

> the supreme God
> At war with all the frailty of grief,
> Or rage, of fear, anxiety, revenge,
> Remorse, spleen, hope, but most of all despair.

Against these plagues he strove in vain; for Fate
Had pour'd a mortal oil upon his head,
A disanointing poison ...[83]

So that the devouring of the children passes into a curious relation with the romantic myths of creativity, whereby fathering, the fathering which Hephaestos was denied, through its displacement to the wombless reproduction which is poetry, then becomes freighted also with the possibilities of re-ingestion whereby the fruits of the world have to be absorbed in order to facilitate the achievement of a perfect, nerveless birth.

Keats's unfinished poems are then in relation to the notions of 'glutting', greed, satiation: they attempt to meet around the break, the break in the psyche which ensures that the wealth of conscious experience will always stand in the shadow of a greater and inaccessible wealth which threatens to dwarf the accumulations which might otherwise guarantee the ego a richness of content, the content of riches. Via the wound, however bound, this richness seeps away, and the greatest intensities of creativity peter out on the desert sands: even, as the ending of 'Hyperion' has it, 'from all his [Apollo's] limbs/Celestial'.[84]

The substitutive aping of the riches of commerce runs throughout Keats's work: there are the landings from the rich Levant, the 'ancestral merchandise' for which 'the Ceylon diver held his breath,/And went all naked to the hungry shark;/For them his ears gush'd blood'.[85] Here the orbit of the ego storing up treasures where moth and rust, we hope, doth not corrupt meets the trajectory of a genre which holds to its own priority while fearing its sense of an ending, poetry itself aping the ending of prophecy which might have come with millenarian fulfilments. The question is of a magical infusion of power, such as might be performed at a dinner which reverses Timon's stones and water, love in a hut becoming dust and ashes; in this luxury the ego might forget its lowly birth, the humble origins, for instance, of Napoleon, and revel in a perfect cushioning without a stain.

That the impulse towards perfection is thanatic is something we can evidence from the Grecian urn and also from the life of groups, where the myth of perfection emerges as a bulwark against the flux which threatens stable identity.[86] Where the possibility of a communicative interchange which smacks of interpretation becomes too strong, the self resigns itself to gilded cushions, enacting Oscar Wilde's world of substitutive grandeur, again at root an economic aping, and attempts to build a perfected pattern on shifting sands, tries to write indelibly in the water.

In 'The Human Seasons' (1818), Winter gets short shrift, summarised in 'pale misfeature':[87] this pallor which runs through and through Keats's writing has affinities with a dawn in which we shall awake, all revelry now present only in the 'heavy body', the heavy head, to find that the wound which had seemed all too gaudily concealed now stands out, like the lines of erased tattooing under the skin which are re-revealed only under emotional stress, or under a relaxing of the narcissistic guards which will demonstrate how far from satiation is the Other who dwells within us and who ceaselessly proves the capacity to absorb all possible ingestion without coming any nearer to an ending of desire.

We need to deal at greater length with the knot of womb-envy, fear and satiation which invades 'Endymion' (1817) at a crucial point; and to read this passage as an account of the genesis of the wound and of the process of its overcoming, which is the ego's (mature, masculine) response to the threatened self-awareness:

> There lies a den,
> Beyond the seeming confines of the space
> Made for the soul to wander in and trace
> Its own existence, of remotest glooms.
> Dark regions are around it, where the tombs
> Of buried griefs the spirit sees, but scarce
> One hour doth linger weeping, for the pierce
> Of new-born woe it feels more inly smart:
> And in these regions many a venom'd dart
> At random flies; they are the proper home
> Of every ill: the man is yet to come
> Who hath not journeyed in this native hell.[88]

This 'den', perhaps does 'lie'; or perhaps we lie about it, but at all events the awareness of its presence undermines the secure boundaries of this space which is 'made' for us, made by the ceaseless activity of the spidery ego. And perhaps we do sense that there, in this unhurried and unhurriable realm, there are memories which cannot be forgotten under the suffocating weight of satiation, memories on which, however, we will hardly choose to dwell, an endless river 'with a mazy motion'[89] but by which we shall not 'choose' (if choice we have) to pitch our tents. And then, of course, in the straining of syntax around the 'new-born woe' we find all the pain of the unknowing of origins, a pain which unseats language in the same breath as its realisation of the perpetual inaccessibility of the truly inward, no matter how much we feed it, no matter how we try to propitiate Sir Leoline's ageing mastiff. It would be comforting to believe that the darts which here flow, evidencing the fears which accompany restfulness, are 'at random'; yet the evidence of some (other) design is here everywhere, and particularly

in the grasping at 'hell' to provide an ethical explanation of this condition
of ambivalence, which is also the condition of an interrupted and unsustainable metonymic chain.

> But few have ever felt how calm and well
> Sleep may be had in that deep den of all.
> There anguish does not sting; nor pleasure pall:
> Woe-hurricanes beat ever at the gate,
> Yet all is still within and desolate.
> Beset with painful gusts, within ye hear
> No sound so loud as when on curtain'd bier
> The death-watch tick is stifled. Enter none
> Who strive therefor: on the sudden it is won.
> Just when the sufferer begins to burn,
> Then it is free to him; and from an urn,
> Still fed by melting ice, he takes a draught –
> Young Semele such richness never quaft
> In her maternal longing. Happy gloom!
> Dark Paradise! where pale becomes the bloom
> Of health by due; where silence dreariest
> Is most articulate; where hopes infest;
> Where those eyes are the brightest far that keep
> Their lids shut longest in a dreamless sleep.
> O happy spirit-home! O wondrous soul!
> Pregnant with such a den to save the whole
> In thine own depth.[90]

Let us first connect the rhetorical figure of the invocation, here taking the
form of a spell on the absent 'happiness', as so frequently in Keats, with the
'maternal' and the pregnancy. Here, surely, we have an invocation which
might condition the future; such that the inextricability of the past, the
serpent, the windings of the night-sea journey, might be forever banished,
with Auden's 'faceless insect' and Keats's own 'death-moth',[91] and will
never have the chance again to knock on the outside of this protected
channel.

   Here is the putative pallor of pleasure, 'where pale becomes the bloom/
Of health by due', with its punning on 'dew' and all the connotations of
the robbed fruit, where its seeming absence of sweetness may be
moralistically referred back to its 'getting', to its origins outside the
(paternal) law. And this returns us via 'La Belle Dame sans Merci' (1820)
to the 'loitering' on the scene of the crime, the awareness that the cord will
not be broken and that we are condemned to a blank sea-shore which is the
desert through which trickle the thin streams of the ego's puncturing.
Narcissus hovers over the pool as a prelude; his image threatens, invites,

beckons, confronts him with all the ambiguity of the specular, which here becomes only seepage, the absence of the solid content which belongs only 'on another scene'.[92]

Interpretative work falls under the sign of a wrong-headed 'striving', which is itself inextricably wedded to a movement which cannot result in entry. Penetration is beyond the control of consciousness; and the nervous system referred to, as well as being one which will not heal the wound – because the wound is, after all and in one of its guises, a symptom, a warning, and to heal it would be to complete a perfection of defences which, paradoxically, could result only in an unforetold and unwarned death – is also the new nervous system of commerce alongside which the poetic pursuit can only haul up at the mercy of the tides and attempt the *jouissance* of forgetting, which converges on those very thanatic rocks which have wrecked many a narcissistic enterprise.

The thrice-repeated 'den', then, becomes the study from which all these hopes and fears are absent. As in the repeated, obsessive motif of M.R. James's late-romantic ghost stories,[93] it is outside the circle of the study light that the bushes themselves start to shift in their alignment and to creep up the walls, signs for an experiential component which cannot respond to the demand for ingestion, because, quietly and without benefit of consciousness, it is also ingesting, and every attempt we make to banish it brings us closer to the cycle, 'red in tooth and claw', from which we, with our romantic heritage, can only plead an aesthetic exemption, and against which we can only mount in evidence precisely that attribute which we are most at pains to deny, the wound which renders us vulnerable but which provides the grounds on which we, as individuals, claim against our fellow-humans (and thus our siblings) the right to a privileged feeding.

The Wordsworthian family

It is less than surprising that the interrogation of the romantic unconscious has skirted Wordsworth, the supreme articulator of a consciousness which appears sufficient in its *own* interrogations, from the staring up at the mountain to the profounder starings into the pool, or lake. Although that is not the main reason, which has more to do with the insistent validation of a moral order to which we have free access; a fictional direct route to our better judgement which does not need to enter into the defiles of the signifier, because the valleys are already laid out for inspection from the fresh air of the isolated peak. None of which is to talk of the familiar red herring of a 'darker side' of Wordsworth; the question must rather be about containment and owning, and in these terms at least one aspect of the poetry and the programme springs to life. For in terms of the complexities and interrelatedness of social change, the element of containment is overt: and it is the means of effecting a separation between country and city, wilderness and civilisation, literality and irony, a multilevelled mapping which attempts to isolate the straight line and assert that no recircling can prejudice the clarity of effect.

Owning, ownership, possession are terms which Wordsworth's texts serve to connect with a deeper-laid chain of signification which has to do with 'prior' grip on language: prior to commercial blandishment and social amelioration, but also prior to the reverse contamination of philosophy and the expedient – which we can here correctly bracket, because the metaphysical thrives on the excuse of pragmatic necessity. It is, of course, an environmental dialectic: the old Cumberland beggar has to be assumed to be in a state of confusion, medically and economically, for the mutuality of possession which characterises Wordsworthian rural life to separate itself sufficiently from the notion of the destroying, eating, ingesting spiral which is thus usefully exiled to the city, and separated from that 'organic' of which it is, in fact, the beating heart.

Thus Wordsworth sterilises nature and potentiates the city in a set of displacements which enjoin our constant attention to these forbidden pleasures which would provide an alternative escape from the claustrophobia paradoxically entailed in the emptying of the countryside. Only 'on another scene' could the truth of these utterances about libido be taken seriously, or, to put it another way, with their full latent irony; out here, although also in a heartland which simultaneously claims the privileges of a fringe, such contortions cannot occur, and it is thus that Coleridge picks up the tab for a type of contamination which continued to exercise its effects through the impotence infecting his exercises in the theorising of creativity.[94]

Between what interlocutor and what potential respondent, then, does the Wordsworthian text interpose itself, remaining as it does within a fiction of muteness which is simultaneously the standard-bearer of a type of response which can carry itself proudly beyond the limits of language? What is the arrangement of the self which is distributed by these texts which have come to stand for a supremely undefined achievement, because within this voice is available every conceivable voice which has not itself been contaminated by an assumed urban restriction of freedom – a freedom which is itself the object of an envy of movement which is forever to be denied in favour of a locking into an eternally unresolved sibling rivalry?

> What could I do, unaided and unblest?
> My father! gone was every friend of thine:
> And kindred of dead husband are at best
> Small help; and, after marriage such as mine,
> With little kindness would to me incline.
> Nor was I then for toil or service fit;
> My deep-drawn sighs no effort could confine;
> In open air forgetful would I sit
> Whole hours, with idle arms in moping sorrow knit.[95]

The kinship of the father has passed on down the line, proud of exhortation and command; here remains, as ever, only the 'small', the 'little', the paradoxical move into a childhood which, 'unaided' and deliberately so, must establish a shape for the world which is unrevised by the complications of familial bonding. This is the knot of escape: pursuit by the flood of recollection which remains 'after marriage such as mine', a marriage which is destroyed in its inception and yet which serves as an inoculation against the instrumental ('toil or service'), as the apprenticeship to poetry is delineated as the summation of redundancy, the inhabitancy only of the blank space from which we may wrest only those meanings which are immanent to an arching meaninglessness.

'My deep-drawn sighs no effort could confine' is a reversible syntactic structure, which may be paralleled many times in Wordsworth's 'oeuvre', and which demonstrates a lock on the limits of design, a prolonged and reflexive meditation on impotence – which fits well with the issues of surpassing which themselves suit a commercial context, but also the fate of the child launched on a hitherto unforeseen market-place, the market, perhaps, of a surpassed rural town, but inflected with the connotations of slavery, which is after all the living of the Cumberland beggar, as also of the leach-gatherer held in thrall, if not to anyone else, at least to the poet as the new colonialist of those abandoned spaces now growing from the root of a societal transformation which is beginning to set new internal and external boundaries of family life.

For, precisely as old Matthew says,

> No check, no stay, this Streamlet fears;
> How merrily it goes!
> 'Twill murmur on a thousand years,
> And flow as now it flows.
>
> And here, on this delightful day,
> I cannot choose but think

How oft, a vigorous man, I lay
Beside this fountain's brink.

My eyes are dim with childish tears,
My heart is idly stirred,
For the same sound is in my ears
Which in those days I heard.[96]

The dialectic is between lack of choice and vigour; and in that dialectic there is evidenced a new problem of determinism, which carries in its wake a connotation for the interpretative. Wordsworth's authorial presence in the face of the leach-gatherer and his numerous *confrères* is poised on the brink of an eliciting through silence, which *generates* silence as the modality of response; and thus we construe a reversal of the analytic process, where cognition flows up the line and offers us the 'readerliness' of the unreadable text, an activity in which there is a problematic sapping of vigour which leaves us prostrate beside the meaningless stream, the flow of uninterpreted speech. And what is constrained here is a passage to maturity which is undercut in the 'childish' passage of 'a thousand years'; there is a fierce undertow to this stream, which will unravel the work of democratic change in Europe. What it will also undermine in a pretence of support is the passage of the generations; as now the sign of Wordsworth conjures the few remaining bookshelves where, alongside Scott, Byron and Mrs Hemans, 'Wordsworth' stands as a name for an unattainable freedom of reference, a contradictory allowing in to an 'enclosure' where the remains of freedom lurk beneath the forbidding thorn.

We may return ourselves to the outward, European forces which were generating psychic shaping by recalling Wordsworth's 1815 Ode:

But if the valiant of this land
In reverential modesty demand,
That all observance, due to them, be paid
Where their serene progenitors are laid;
Kings, warriors, high-souled poets, saintlike sages,
England's illustrious sons of long, long ages;
Be it not unordained that solemn rites,
Within the circuits of those Gothic walls,
Shall be performed at pregnant intervals;
Commemoration holy that unites
The living generations with the dead;
By the deep soul-moving sense
Of religious eloquence, –
By visual pomp, and by the tie
Of sweet and threatening harmony;
Soft notes, awful as the omen

> Of destructive tempests coming,
> And escaping from that sadness
> Into elevated gladness;
> While the white-robed choir attendant,
> Under mouldering banners pendant,
> Provoke all potent sympathies to raise
>   Songs of victory and praise,
> For them who bravely stood unhurt, or bled
> With medicable wounds, or found their graves
> Upon the battlefield, or under ocean's waves;
> Or were conducted home in single state,
> And long procession – there to lie,
> Where their sons' sons, and all posterity,
> Unheard by them, their deeds shall celebrate![97]

Here the fathers (the 'progenitors') and the sons are aligned in an unbreakable chain of masculine protection, whose literality is nonetheless bracketed by the 'Gothic' walls, as the familiar translation of human beings into emblems is undertaken in the tying of the living and the dead. These, then, may be the difficulties at the root of the 'pregnant intervals': now in 1815, more than at any other time, perhaps there may be a moment for 'mature' contemplation of those gaps in nature between the living and the dead; or of those gaps in history which have so recently and demandingly returned to disturb the smooth flow of the uninterpretable stream.

What may come to birth in the hiatus, as Yeats was later to meditate, may again be signified in the tempest, here the 'destructive tempests' which are in a curious but presumably essential relation with the 'white-robed choir', unsullied by the contortions of history and the possessor of a named potency which is, however, also of the nature of a response. Perhaps it is indeed only under the threat of bad weather, or of an invasion by the scudding clouds which signify uncertainty, that this British potency can be 'provoked'; and here again we touch upon a long-standing mytheme about the island race, and one which, in its reminder of the national anthem, finds its place also in the very rhythms of the ode.

These 'medicable' wounds of war occupy the midpoint between the 'unhurt' and the dead, a position of mediation which has been carried in the charge and responsibility of the wound for millenia. The wounded are the evidence – in a highly practical sense – and are also those who bear the marking of experience; as does the poet, who alone enters into the play of metaphor from which there is no unscathed return. The peculiar position of the war poet is strung between an unmatchable accuracy, a primary reportage, and the need to serve a set of interests which might be, from time to time, but dimly glimpsed as the national self-image sways, a torn curtain, in the tempest.

And this dilemma is translated into the position of strength which holds together the generations, which strives for a seamless version of history, the 'long procession', while recognising that the power to heal the break, a power enacted only and always in language, is both totalising in the name of the father, and thus has the effect of rebuilding the ego's defences; while in the name of the mother it signifies the long but interrupted memory of the break, the survival of the myths of source which in turn refers us to an insoluble problem of origins, of originality, so that the solemnity which surrounds the beds of birth and death can become once again fused and the disruption can be made whole again in thought, whole in the abandon to the moving stream which signifies also the tamed waters which have once again proved our salvation.

Thus we may say that the apparent shifts in the political orientation of romanticism constitute an adventure of discourse where different positions are mobilised to remove, in time of war, threats to stable identity through the battling of the giants; and are then reknit together as the enduring evidence of language's status as protector, a role where familial models must be drawn upon and indeed intensified as that microstructure of the State which guarantees continuity: against all odds.

PART 3

ROMANTICISM AND THE SELF: AN ENGAGEMENT WITH BLAKE

Problems of gender

The problems of origin and continuity which generate the central structures of romanticism; the issue of the break and the attempt to circumambulate the break through a mobilisation of the processes of narcissism; familial modelling and its role in the production of language: all of these centre on the specific productions of gender, as we have seen across several different romantic trajectories.

It is in an engagement with gender, also, that we can get at the 'median term', the constant negotiation between outer and inner worlds; between history and the unconscious; between the 'real' and the imaginary: for gender has a primary relation to the symbolic. And I propose to interrogate this relation by selecting a single writer, Blake; for it is in the fictions of authorial integrity which underlie such a critical procedure, and in their bearing on our own handlings of the text, conditioned as *they* are by the various legacies of romanticism, that we can most closely observe the processes of revision and interpretation which have a dialectical relation to narcissistic structures.

Blake's writings also have a peculiar relevance for our purposes, because of the central hiatuses which occur around the terminology and syntax of the 'Female Will', the anguished treatment of which cannot be separated from the anguish produced in the politically radical reading of Blake by what is taken to be a signal lapse from progressive vision.[1] I will also pay close attention to a particular group of Blake texts, especially some passages from *Visions of the Daughters of Albion*; and will touch on some limits of literary discourse in the area of gender, suggesting an interpretation of those limits located in the concept of trauma, which should thus enter into relation with the historical concept of the hiatus.

One of the most widely known details about Blake-the-poet is that he was once observed in his garden with his wife, both of them naked.[2] Explanations of this incident, or rather of its cultural persistence since it is clearly lodged in the general memory in such a way as to require continuous efforts of interpretation, as also of the sexual libertarianism which can undoubtedly be found at many points in Blake's writings, are usually cast as adaptations from readings in a certain tradition of radical thought. In particular Blake was, so conventional interpretation very reasonably runs, heavily influenced by certain kinds of Christian sectarian radicalism, which in turn derive from a historical reversal of the Pauline condemnation of physicality.[3]

That a kind of libertarianism is present in Blake's texts is not, however, what is most distinctive about the relevant attitudes towards gendering. Certainly Blake says that social and institutional structures restrain our bodily development; but that is hardly new. It is also more fundamentally incorrect – and, indeed, a specifically neoromantic misreading – to suppose that Blake preached free love as a solution to, or palliation of, wider sociocultural problems.

The parts of the corpus which I take to contribute to the limiting instance are the prose fragment 'Then she bore pale desire' and the lyric 'How sweet I roam'd', from the early *Poetical Sketches*; and parts of the *Daughters of Albion*. The dates are the 1770s for the fragement and the lyric, 1793 for *Daughters of Albion*; and I would like to adopt as a horizon the heartland of the eighteenth century, the period which Blake so savagely parodies and attacks in the *Sketches*. There is a celebrated passage from Fielding's *Joseph Andrews* (1742) where the author digresses into a set of what he calls 'Philosophical Reflections, the like not to be found in any light French Romance' which may be taken as setting up the specific, central play of signifiers in terms of which Blake's marginality may be defined:

As the Passion generally called Love, exercises most of the Talents of the Female or fair World; so in this they now and then discover a small Inclination to Deceit; for which thou wilt not be angry with the beautiful Creatures, when thou hast considered, that at the Age of seven or something earlier, Miss is instructed by her Mother, that Master is a very monstrous kind of Animal, who will, if she suffers him to come too near her, infallibly eat her up, and grind her to pieces. That so far from kissing or toying with him of her own accord, she must not admit him to kiss or toy with her. And lastly, that she must never have any Affection towards him; for if she should, all her Friends in Petticoats would esteem her a Traitress, point at her, and hunt her out of their Society. These Impressions being first received, are further and deeper inculcated by their School-mistresses and Companions; so that by the Age of Ten they have contracted such a Dread and Abhorrence of the above named Monster, that whenever they see him, they fly from him as the innocent Hare doth from the greyhound. Hence to the Age of fourteen or fifteeen, they entertain a mighty Antipathy to master; they resolve and frequently profess that they will never have any Commerce with him, and entertain fond Hopes of passing their lives out of his reach, of the Possibility of which they have so visible an Example in their good Maiden Aunt. But when they arrive at this Period, and have now passed their second Climacteric, when their Wisdom grown riper, begins to see a little farther; and from almost daily falling in Master's way, to apprehend the great Difficulty of keeping out of it; and when they observe him look often at them, and sometimes very eagerly and earnestly too, (for the Monster seldom takes any notice of them till at this Age) they then begin to think of their Danger; and as they perceive they cannot easily avoid him, the wiser Part bethink themselves of providing by other Means for their Security. They endeavour by all the Methods they can invent to render themselves so amiable in his Eyes, that he may have no Inclination to hurt them; in which they generally succeed so well, that his Eyes, by frequent languishing, soon lessen their Idea of his Fierceness, and so far abate their Fears, that they venture to parley with him; and when they perceive him so different from what he hath been described, all Gentleness, Softness, Kindness, Tenderness, Fondness, their dreadful Apprehensions vanish in a moment; and now (it being usual with the human Mind to skip from one Extreme to its Opposite, as easily, and almost as suddenly, as a Bird from one Bough to another;) Love instantly succeeds to Fear: But as it happens to Persons, who have in their Infancy been thoroughly frightened with certain no Persons called Ghosts, that they retain their Dread of those Beings, after they are convinced that there are no such things; so these young Ladies, tho' they shake off all that hath been instilled into them; they still entertain the Idea of that Censure which was so strongly imprinted on their tender Minds, to which the Declarations of Abhorrence they every day hear from their Companions greatly contribute. To avoid this Censure therefore, is now their only care; for which purpose they still pretend the same Aversion to the Monster: And the more they love him, the more ardently they counterfeit their Antipathy. By the continual and constant Practice of which Deceit on others, they at length impose on themselves, and really believe they hate what they love.[4]

Rather, obviously, than trying for some direct connection with social pressure, we should see this as a discourse which seeks to set up a particular space bounded by love and deceit. What is frightening is the description of the implanting, through upbringing and education, of an ideology which bears a distorted relation to some fiction of 'natural' gender behaviour; but the point is more complex.

Fielding says that it is 'usual with the human Mind to skip from one Extreme to its Opposite' (while implicitly connecting this tendency with women), and thus notes a difficulty of escape from an indoctrination which operates on an Althusserian level of thoroughness and reproductive circularity. The aspect of upbringing which consists in the defining and precluding of monsters is less disturbing than the suggestion that, once such postulates have been set up effectively in the field of melodrama, even such changes of stance as may occur in dialectic with experience will still be interpreted within the same melodramatic problematic.

Monster (like giant) may be transformed into deity or saint, but not into human being;[5] and Fielding points near the end of the passage to the economically purposive relation between this inculcation of an ambiguous fear and the isolation of the subject. Where the discursive field is bounded by these markers of extremes, the result is to remove from the developing individual the means of triangulating experience in such a way as to gain purchase upon difference. The language of deceit, which is inextricably directed inward and outward, becomes bound back to back with the language of the affections, and relationships thus become fixed, enstellated, into a calculable and quantifiable system, in a process of narcissistic by-product by now familiar to us.

The basic terms of this system reject difference, and a reading of almost any eighteenth-century novel gives us further evidence. The key metaphors are military: emotional encounters are represented under the guise of warfare: attack, defence and force become the central terms, and thus a concept of violation is implantable at the heart of the feelings. Sterne, of course, is parodying this conflation of categories in *Tristram Shandy* (1760), in terms of Uncle Toby and the Widow Wadman; yet in *Sentimental Journey* (1768) he too is content to bask in the air of nervous excitement generated by this assimilation of affection and violence.

These imaginings of violation reveal to us then the pattern onto which the anxieties of the Revolution became mapped, and they run, as a doubled absence at and of the heart, through from Richardson to Smollett and Sterne himself.[6] As the century progresses, however, this central imagining is increasingly disclosed under the agency of the Gothic, bringing us back to Lewis's *The Monk* and its dealings in the discourse of melodrama. We could say that this monstrous focus of the imagination, which is also the violating father and thus the dead weight of tradition attempting to pre-impregnate the future with a seed which will tie it to a sterile circularity, is realised in the shape of Ambrosio, who achieves the 'honour' of violating his virgin victim in a sepulchre magnificently surrounded with graves, winding worms, skeletons. That Ambrosio is a monk makes the essential connection, which has been hovering with us since 'Christabel', between this internalised attack and the process of guardianship, in that here is coupled a shielding *from* the world and a shielding *of* the world from the monstrousness of the denied flesh.

Ambrosio's lack of experience represents, while safely evading, the more general question of the isolation of the sexes, and the discursive fracture through which this isolation operates. Here deceit reaches a point of climax in ecclesiastical garb, a deceit which is simultaneously visited upon the readerly position, and a reconflation with a devalued and inverted language of the affections:

> 'Why these terrors, Antonia?' rejoined the abbot, folding her in his arms, and covered her bosom with kisses which she in vain struggled to avoid. 'What fear you from me – from one who adores you? What matters it where you are? This sepulchre seems to me love's bower. This gloom is the friendly night of mystery, which he spreads over our delights! Such do I think it, and such must my Antonia. Yes, my sweet girl, yes! Your veins shall glow with the fire which circles in mine, and my transports shall be doubled by your sharing them!'[7]

This is a particularly unpleasant form of pornography, in which a dominance of the male imagination, which can be vindicated by no means other than hidden violence, engages with the discursive and institutional limits in ways which entail a denial that what is being constructed is merely an eccentric subjective narrative. The implication in which the authorial position revels is that Ambrosio's experience of women, such as it is, has brought to his attention that it is a socially accepted fact that women's discourse has nothing to do with the truth of the feelings, and that all he is dealing with is a resistance born of the thinned signifiers of convention.

We need also to note the words which are then 'forced' on Antonia by the author:

> 'Unhand me, father!' she cried, her honest indignation tempered by alarm at her unprotected position. 'Why have you brought me to this place? Its appearance freezes me with terror! Convey me from hence, if you have the least sense of pity and humanity! Let me return to the house, which I have quitted I know not how; but stay here one moment longer, I neither will nor ought.'[8]

It is the formality of this disclaimer which sparks off the next interaction, in which Ambrosio rejoins in terms which combine the military with a discourse which precisely assimilates itself to a parody of women's 'education':

> 'Compose yourself, Antonia. Resistance is unavailing, and I need disavow my passion for you no longer. You are imagined dead; society is for ever lost to you. I possess you here alone; you are absolutely in my power ... My adorable Antonia! Let me instruct you in joys to which you are still a stranger, and teach you to feel those pleasures in my arms which I must soon enjoy in yours.'[9]

The author leaves Ambrosio filled with self-disgust and revulsion; yet late eighteenth-century fiction remains a melodramatic fulfilment of a discursive representation already ratified in the behavioural code. If it is seen as part of female education to dissimulate under a pressure of fear, then the dominant ideology renders it impossible to attach meaning to respect for the continual expression of that fear, despite Pamela; all sexual experience falls under the sign of violation, and difference becomes unjudgeable. Gothic fiction is, as we know, the fruit of a society in which moral codes have been set up which are impossible of attainment, and in which virtue and repression are thus perceived as identical, as they are by the narcissistic ego, which is aware of, even if cannot admit, the contaminated sources of its own lust for power.

Under such circumstances, the subject cannot gain authoritative evidence – or interpret that evidence – of what is or is not common practice, and even at this petty level of convention is therefore lost in a world of half-seen and usually misinterpreted signs. The display here is, perhaps, of the neurosis of an age; but more significant is the notion that the expression of the feelings is sin and shame.

Shame and trauma

We can come to Blake via shame, which has to do with the vicissitudes of the exile of desire. In 'Then she bore pale desire' we find one of his many parodies of creation myth: an account of origins which, significantly, has no beginning. We must start from Blake's own principle, as encapsulated in narrative: that the world was the creation, not of a benevolent (male) almighty, but of a usurping (equally, or at least filially, male) power, Urizen, the god of this world. This structure discloses benevolence and love as the countenances of force and fear when 'adorned in dreams';[10] and it is probable that 'fear' is the 'she' of the first few words:

> then she bore Pale desire, father of Curiosity, a Virgin ever young. And after, Leaden Sloth, from whom came Ignorance, who brought forth Wonder. These are the Gods which came from fear, for Gods like these nor male nor female are, but single Pregnate, or, if they list, together mingling bring forth mighty pow'rs. She knew them not; yet they all war with Shame, and strengthen her weak arm.[11]

'They all war with Shame' means not, of course, that they fight her but that these other personified qualities, these other slow-moving and intertwined, Laocoon-like, giants are those who do Shame's work for her, who wear her insignia. The whole image is of distortion: 'Pale desire', which cannot fail to remind us of the pallor which invades Keats's systems from the underside, is the opposite of the sought-after restoration of the full sign which Blake, like Hegel, was to refer to as the essential motor force of human development.[12]

This, rather, is the quivering, enervate, emptied desire which is the product of repressive conflict. Curiosity, the 'Virgin ever young' – and here we must not discount Freud's myths of the origins of curiosity alongside the individual 'creation myth', alternatively described as a sexual theory[13] – is fount and product of sexual deceit, yet represented – in one of the more literal senses of that term – as female.

Behind all this skulks the equally female re-presentation labelled Shame, a reworking under the sign of contradiction of the unadmitted name-of-the-Father which forbids expression and forces men and women into the unreal realm where abstract qualities govern all, which is the region of narcissism; and here we loop back to the rhetorical issue of personification and its implications for the abdication of human social agency.

Here then we are on a terrain which directly develops from the eighteenth-century ethical code; and the issue Blake concentrates on is the replacement of people by monsters, whether through textual, rhetorical or developmental processes.

> Pride made a Goddess fair, or Image rather, till knowledge animated it; 'twas calld Self love. The Gods admiring loaded her with Gifts, as once Pandora. She 'mongst men was sent, and worser ills attended her by far. She was a Goddess Powerful & bore Conceit & Emulation. Conceit and Shame bore honour & made league with Pride, & Policy doth dwell with her, by whom she had Mistrust & Suspition; then bore a Daughter called Emulation, who married honour; these follow her around the World. Go see the city, friends Join'd Hand in Hand. Go see the Natural tie of flesh & blood. Go see more strong the ties of marriage love – thou Scarce Shall find, but Self love Stands Between.[14]

Here are the dominant signifiers in a code of relations between the genders: pride, honour, policy; and all hinges on self-love. A pride not to be translated in terms of self-respect, the integrated self, but as separation, aloofness, incomprehension, the ego bound, Urizen-like, in webs of his own devising, and constructing monstrous images of the females who put him there in a reworking of the inadmissible evidence of the womb. An honour akin to that of Antonia and Ambrosio, bound back to back, indissolubly, the offspring of conceit and shame. And a policy, the ethical calculation of Fielding, again housed in a female demonology; which reminds us of the gender specificities of the demonisations of the poetry of the Revolution.

Critics have differed about Blake's development of the 'Female Will', some claiming that it carried always a purely negative charge, others attempting an 'interpretation' of changes through elements in the biography.[15] Without deciding, we have only to turn to 'The Mental Traveller' or parts of the late Prophetic Books to see the grave reservations about the 'Female Will' being expressed; and we may find ourselves asking from a contemporary perspective, with others, how the very texts which achieve such a massive reworking of material about ethical pressure and rigidity nevertheless seem to capitulate at times in an apparently male supremacist space,[16] or, to put it another way, how the claims for gender even-handedness which emerge in 'Then she bore pale desire' can be so obviously undercut. The Garden of Eden does not seem at all a sufficient answer, considering how adept Blake was at adapting the Bible.

The lyric 'How sweet I roam'd' invokes the response of simplicity:

> How sweet I roam'd from field to field,
>   And tasted all the summer's pride,
> 'Till I the prince of love beheld,
>   Who in the sunny beams did glide!
>
> He shew'd me lilies for my hair,
>   And blushing roses for my brow;
> He led me through his gardens fair,
>   Where all his golden pleasures grow.
>
> With sweet May dews my wings were wet,
>   And Phoebus fir'd my vocal rage;
> He caught me in his silken net,
>   And shut me in his golden cage.
>
> He loves to sit and hear me sing,
>   Then, laughing, sports and plays with me;
> Then stretches out my golden wing,
>   And mocks my loss of liberty.[17]

The description is of a woman trapped by promises into bondage, within a recognisable, if sour, tradition of the depiction of marriage. The beauty and luxuriance of this proffered world lie in the realm of mere show: the 'golden pleasures' become the 'golden cage', and the natural liberty of innocence contrasts with the caged condition of the songbird.

Textual hiatus is evident in the specific absence: we learn nothing of the feelings of the 'trapped'. The last stanza is not narrated from her point of view; instead, it seeks out the protective and defensive markers of a quasi-objective discourse, and this sets the stage for the poem's curious inconclusiveness, in that the beginning lays an implicit plan for a more overt moral interpretation (*within* the text) than is eventually offered. An interpretation would be this: that the effects of entrapment, internal and external, serve to render the prisoner an object to such an extent that the phenomenon becomes re-presented attached to a desperate authorial abandonment.

This bird in a gilded cage has ceased to be human; thus the 'golden wing'. It is not a matter of being *like* a songbird, but of *becoming* a songbird, the stuff not of petty simile but of a certain kind of psychic identification founded on objectification and loss of agency. And this is also the becoming of the monster, a transformation from which the author stands back aghast, unable to produce a discourse of description because this 'objectified' self has passed beyond the limits of his comprehension. By the end of the poem, there is nothing recognisably human left to hold to, only the single baffling part-object, emblem of the desire for and impossibility of flight, but uninterpreted in the structure of the text itself.

The entrapping of women here, and the renaming which accompanies it, therefore do not proceed towards an argument about liberation but rather to one about the circular pressures of hegemony. The attempted representation ends at the gate of an encounter with fear, because whatever may emerge from the golden cage of the self may not be recognisably human, and this is the full depth of the violence done to the (female) psyche, a violence which may not be unravelled at the conscious level alone.

This is a violence which is made over ideologically, time and time again, into a pre-text for violation, whereby the psychic damage is relegated to an assumed pre-existing source and thus excuses are made for the obsessive repetition of that damage in the gender encounters of the everyday; it is also a violence before which, here, the poetic word flinches. And the alternative 'word' which most effectively describes this process, whereby also individuals are transformed into monsters, a psychic teratogenesis in which we can also sense the parallel inflections of Blake's Infernal Bible, is trauma.

We may therefore begin to describe this poem – and the prose fragment – as accounts of the genesis of a traumatised female consciousness, although in doing so we would not have probed the recesses and reticulations of the (male) ego's self-defences, a point to which we shall need to return. Jean Laplanche and J.-B. Pontalis define trauma thus:

> An event in the subject's life defined by its intensity, by the subject's incapacity to respond adequately to it, and by the upheaval and long-lasting effects that it brings about in the psychical organisation.
>
> In economic terms, the trauma is characterised by an influx of excitations that is excessive by the standard of the subject's tolerance and capacity to master such excitations and work them out psychically.[18]

In this clash of discourses, the concept of self-mastery, deeply lodged in Freud's own gender assumptions, enters at once into a curious relation with the violent mastery being exercised by the 'prince of love', perhaps himself a figure of some (illusory) psychological sophistication; the 'wound' which Laplanche and Pontalis go on to mention, and which we have now come across so many times before on the trajectories of the ego's dealings with the unconscious, an essential element also in the configuration of trauma, is here represented in the useless and encrusted wing.

The wing is, indeed, a symbol of the induced inability to escape repetitive cycling; and thus the female is figured as simultaneously disabled and angelic, in a familiar duplicity which reduces agency by a simultaneous upward and downward displacement which also replicates the contemporary dealing with feared materials from the public realm.

As monodrama, the poem may be said to display the introjection of a massive, deified social constraint; the repetition of event which is essential to trauma, whereby a (sexual) encounter triggers recollection of an earlier disruptive scene, is figured in the 'change' of tense into a continuous and changeless present. Thus, precisely, this poem enacts at an individual level the dealings with the hiatus, the gap, which we have seen displayed in the range of rhetoric applied to the French Revolution: it is the earlier disruptive scene which is crucial here, the past event which *must* be hypothesised to permit our fictional escape from the trailing and inconclusive mists of our personal history, but which also *cannot* be hypothesised because even to do that, let alone to imagine or to figure, would be to open a chink to the feared flood of repressed materials from the unconscious, and at the same time to engage precisely with the dialectic of change and changelessness in those ways which might open the precarious ego to invasion.

Thus a duplicity in the dealing with the past, which touches on a major motif of romanticism: the Janus-face which looks radically towards the new world, which seeks to do away with the stuffy order of classicism, and yet which looks with longing, nostalgia, and the gifts of a tender re-creation to the past, a past which can only exist 'over the shoulder', as it were, of that more recent eighteenth-century past which can thus itself figure only *as* the break, such that the moment of disruption is itself displaced into the least likely place, and what is saved for the vague and dreaming memory is another time, another place, before the sharp lines of rationalism, the sharp cut of the intrusion of the father; where medieval scenes offer only the undefined sense of a past forever lost and forever recapturable, not through an effort but through a complicity in forgetting.

But here again there is a mapping onto gender issues, a mapping of the father and the mother, of the cut and the healing, and a continuous displacement which marks, in part, the secondary revision of these imaginings; and to see further into this, we can turn to *Visions of the Daughters of Albion.*

Repetition and change: Daughters of Albion

In *Daughters of Albion*, Oothoon the virgin is betrothed to Theotormon, whom she goes to seek:

> Over the waves she went in wing'd exulting swift delight,
> And over Theotormon's reign took her impetuous course.
>
> Bromion rent her with his thunders; on his stormy bed
> Lay the faint maid, and soon her woes appall'd his thunders hoarse
>
> Bromion spoke. 'Behold this harlot here on Bromion's bed,
> And let the jealous dolphins sport around the lovely maid!
> Thy soft American plains are mine, and mine thy north & south:
> Stampt with my signet are the swarthy children of the sun;
> They are obedient, they resist not, they obey the scourge;
> Their daughters worship terrors and obey the violent.
>
> 'Now thou maist marry Bromion's harlot, and protect the child
> Of Bromion's rage, that Oothoon shall put forth in nine moons' time.'[19]

'Bromion rent her with his thunders' is a condensation of the two levels we have been discussing: the historical disruption and the personal violation. At one level, *Daughters of Albion*, as befits its title, is a poem about empire, and the events of this passage represent the destructive effects of a predatory mercantilism; but precisely by describing the ideological manoeuvring, at the level of the expenditures and balance sheets of psychic energy, which takes place at the site of simultaneous causation and effect within the constellation of colonial exploitation.

Bromion's violation of Oothoon takes place also, however, in a context where property, possession, ownership are played out across a wide variety of fields: Bromion sees Oothoon as his property – or, indeed, capital – which he is willing to 'hire out', after the fashion of hired labour, to Theotormon, but which will still remain 'stampt' with his 'signet': a violent image which, though, also returns us to one of the earliest of our images of the unconscious, as the seal whose pressings emerge all the more strongly as we strive to clamp down on the sources of life in which we cannot bring ourselves to believe.

With the entire field thus brought under the sway of the phallus as signifier,[20] Theotormon can be allowed to 'marry Bromion's harlot, and protect the child/Of Bromion's rage'; but this will be a superficial matter compared with the inalienable conquest (of land, of progeny, of the hated future) which Bromion has achieved in his lust for annexation, a lust which does not even need to be disguised by the 'pallid' signifiers of convention. Thus the 'recalling event' of trauma is fatally coloured (red on the map) by memory of the prior seduction, real or imagined, as is the case with the excuses for violation which provide the pretext for the guardian/monk.

There is a sense in which, of course, Blake is finding a suitable emblem, or rebus, for the contradictions of empire, and for those who perforce live on its poisoned fruits, who straddle the crucifixion tree; but what is more important in *Daughters of Albion* is the textual succession to the fatal event, the prefigured future to the failure of the 'visions'. Essentially, nothing 'happens' at all. Theotormon, confronted with the attack ('mounted', upon him, but only through a displacement of value from Oothoon), freezes:

> At entrance Theotormon sits, wearing the threshold hard
> With secret tears; beneath him sound like waves on a desart shore
> The voice of slaves beneath the sun, and children bought with money,
> That shiver in religious caves beneath the burning fires
> Of lust, that belch incessant from the summits of the earth.[21]

Theotormon is reduced to musing, to a parody of ineffectual contemplation (reflection), to the repetition and cycling which are the signifiers of disavowal, of the refusal of experience. He has been shown the trick of Satan on the 'summits', which is that action, tangling with the world of event and domination, can be evil; and has concluded from this, as the neurotic may, that *all* action is evil, that there is nothing to be undertaken once the true colours of action, of agency, have been revealed – or once, indeed, the prior model for action, the production of separation, difference, has been recalled. In this condition of fall (from the womb) there is nothing to be done.

Anything that Theotormon might *do* would run the risk of being tarred with the same brush (the brush which 'colours' slavery) as Bromion's violation. Specifically, presumably, any attempt at vengeance might be seen as playing Bromion's game; a patriarchal game which, of course, Theotormon is in any case enacting as he wears the 'threshold hard'. There is left only a hypothetical and inexperienced fantasy of self-castration as a removal of the pressure to signify in this contaminated discursive field.

Theotormon's disabling 'vision' is that things which he thought he had established as separate, along the path of abstraction – love and deceit – are found to be inseparable, bound to each other, back to back in the rebus, in a parodic non-copulation, and farther than this he cannot get (father to this he cannot be; father to what he cannot 'get' is his desire, which is now to be perpetually extruded from the system).

More significant, however, is what 'happens' (and this bracketing of event and passivity is symptomatic of the exile of desire) to Oothoon:

> Oothoon weeps not; she cannot weep! her tears are locked up;
> But she can howl incessant writhing her soft snowy limbs,
> And calling Theotormon's Eagles to prey upon her flesh.[22]

Why this distinction between weeping and howling? Apart from these three lines, we are told virtually nothing else about a female future. By far the larger part of the poem is taken up with lamentation, which is revealing in its way; yet in these lines the signifiers enter into a curious trajectory – confronted like Theotormon with a situation in which all alternatives are blocked, Oothoon does undergo a kind of change, becoming unable to produce a *human* response to her condition.[23]

Her tears are 'locked', just as Theotormon is locked, chained to the threshold of the cave (the cave of experience, the Platonic emblem reduced to a mechanical failure). Instead there is, as H.P. Lovecraft or any neoromantic horror movie might put it, only the howling and the writhing:[24] the loss of a distinctive humanity, and the becoming, again, of the monster, the soulless inhabitant of the cave who is also the prisoner for ever exempted from a world which she might 'contaminate' – with birth, with femininity, with the inaccessibility of primal crime. She is again the woman locked in a golden cage, the living and displaced proof of masculine monstrousness; for Oothoon is being represented as the victim of a trauma which occupies a space outside cultured time.

There is here, then, a critique of the ways in which women are forced away from the agential, into roles where the world, the external, can be referred to as something which *happens to*, in both senses. There is no available shaping by action or perception, only the lesson of eighteenth-century women's education, the learning to react within stereotype which is the paradigm for the feared (by the male) exile of desire. The representation is in trauma and consequent evasion of moments of crisis; which is itself the inadmissible *Trieb* of the male.

Laplanche and Pontalis delineate for us the double locks on the cage/cave:

> ... *theoretically*, the aetiology of neurosis is related to past traumatic

experience whose occurrence is assigned to a constantly receding date according as the analytic investigation penetrates more deeply, proceeding step by step from adulthood back to infancy; *technically*, effective cure is sought by means of an abreaction and a psychical working out of traumatic experiences.[25]

There is much to be said of these revealing metaphors of 'recession' and 'penetration', much that is relevant to the analytic process and to interpretation as a mode; here, however, perhaps it is necessary only to call attention to the ways in which the blocking off of avenues for 'solving' action (in a sense related to the acids of forging) relate to the claustrophobic tonal colouration of many of Blake's verbal and visual images; representatively, perhaps, in the plight of Nebuchadnezzar.[26]

The satirising of female role and of a presumptive male agency in Fielding is hegemonically bounded; Blake stretches this hegemony a little, with a detachment born, as it must always be, of unaccommodated fear. In this displaced form, displaced from the loss of agency related to the artisanate under the double pressure of changing employment patterns and association with Jacobinism, the fear becomes about what women in particular might become under the pressure of certain ethical codes; about dehumanisation and the 'manufacture' of monsters, as, of course, in *Frankenstein*.

There is a clear class component here, which differentiates Fielding from Blake, and it connects also with the chronological difference: behind the transition from 'wise' and soothing regret to a dialectic of panic and control, an emblematic dialectic for romanticism, we can detect the shadow of a massive shift in social structure. It is when we look into the shadow that we can see the attribution of trauma as itself an ideological device, a displacement of an awareness of rift and of a doubt about the safe continuity which 'ought to' pertain to mothering functions, to an absent nurture.

There is a statistical corollary in the eighteenth-century 'explosion' in figures for illegitimate births, a different 'teratology', and the claiming of female agency which lies behind those figures.[27] The historians of the family surmise a connection between the intrusion of the female body into a male-dominated space and the growth of the market economy, with its implications for the stated purposes of education.[28] Blake stands at the intersection of this development with a group of movements within the family, movements specific to the lower classes:

One might plausibly argue that in the course of the eighteenth century population growth decapitated the authority of the lower-class family by creating so many children that parents had nothing to pass on to their extra-numerous offspring, and hence no control over their behaviour. And cottage industry created alternative sources of employment to enable children to escape the authority of the family by physically removing themselves or otherwise acquiring economic independence.[29]

The statistics tell us about the extent to which this breach with the 'web of familial custom and control' was a phenomenon of the classes with which Blake was most familiar; but in any case, it is a feature of all industrialised – and, more to the point, industrialising – societies that a higher percentage of women in the lower social strata move into the labour force than of those in the higher groups.[30]

We need to add other facts: the rapid extension of the fertility zone in women's lives during the eighteenth century cannot be detached from the ground of feminist attack which, according to Sheila Rowbotham, was being laid at the same time.[31] The painful and systematic exclusion of women from trades, including, interestingly, mythically resonant ones like metal-working, the realm of Hephaestos, gives a representation of fear in the economic realm.[32] 'The traditional division of labour', according to Eli Zaretsky, 'was threatened as women and children joined men in the factories'; but of course, in many of the key areas of early industrialisation women *were* the labour force.[33]

What is happening between the 1740s and 1770s is that the whole hierarchical arrangement of sexual and economic space is shifting, and old strategies for negating female experience are becoming obsolete; it is thus necessary to 'forge' new ones. Blake, staring into the heart of a complex web of sexual threat and economic competition in the buzzing world of lower-class London, and encountering unexpected returns of a gender material previously thought safely repressed, did not find conventional strategies useful.

As a tide of acquiescence recedes, Blake's texts are beached against a discursive limit, whereon we may descry the form of the new 'Leviathan', which encompasses not only the coming of change but also and inextricably the dread associated with the rising of those very forms of oppressed and uncompromising consciousness which patriarchy has so effectively created; the forms of a newly rejuvenated narcissism.

Changes of the kind we are touching on mark an effective alteration in the social space in which people (here crucially displaced as women) can effectively survive on honour, policy and pride; and there is entailed a question concerning (re-)production.[34] How can a patriarchal society which has called upon women to reinforce hegemony through passivity now deal with the societal demand for female economic agency which, in turn, entails the suggestion, the counter-dream, that the cave was genuinely a thing of shadow, an adolescent error?

Oothoon appears to have no alternatives; she is conditioned to a certain 'in-look', frozen, without guides or guards. The question is of how liberation is to succeed repression; how *any* maturity might succeed the separations of the adolescent 'long hut'. To maintain the possibility of spontaneous individual freedom is to succumb to the pressure of cultural reproduction, to adopt a gentlemanly understatement of the repression which has always-already taken place. Yet to give that repression full weight, and admit the violence within the (male) ego, would be to admit to a reduction to passivity within the male role; and we may, as a concomitant problem, note that the narrative accounts offered by psychoanalysis – with the magic vanishing of the concept of repression which we may attribute to Foucault[35] – combined with the emphasis on the power of interpretation to 'penetrate' the unenlightened discourse of the 'patient' (the passive, with all its linguistic associations), contribute to this problem more symptomatically than heuristically. The struggles of vaunting totalisation and devalued rift link, indeed, across two centuries and two gender revolutions; and establish only but always the centrality of narrative form to the interrogation of the constitution of the gendered subject. Who does the 'showing' to whom in the 'de-*monstr*ations' of ideology?

The instituting of Blake

What, then, might all this mean to us now as we try to unravel the romantic skein? Blake, clearly, is the *auteur* who resists de-authorisation. Through all our awareness of the historical construction of subjectivity, of the controlling strength of discourses, of the diminution of the subject in the face of the limitless power of the signifier, the name of Blake is transmitted largely without 'difference', in either the heraldic or the Derridean sense. With other writers, increasingly we become coy, supply inverted commas, various kinds of parenthesis, the paraphernalia of erasure, so that 'Dickens' becomes shorthand for 'Dickens, if we were, in this interpretative community, still able to indulge ourselves for a moment in pretending that a text has an identifiable and unitary author'. But the name-of-Blake has already, it seems, absorbed these conceptual and positional niceties: the multivalent radicalism which is implicit in this name, for which the name is itself a sign, exempts critics of Blake from the alternations of doubt and anxiety which may afflict other, less privileged bands of apostles.[36]

Over here, under the sign of Blake, we take shelter behind the supposition that Blake himself, after all (and before all), knew the significant kinds of 'Other'-ness, bracketed his own texts away from the tug of the obvious, and thus we are not called upon genuinely to deconstruct, rather to discover the principle and procedures of auto-deconstruction in the texts themselves.

We might then be driven, as critics, to ask about the nature of this extraordinary authority, and thus about our investment in its maintenance: for power, as Foucault has taught us, is exercised not down the thin red line of repression but through a massive and webbed distribution of pleasures, whose shiverings and oscillations hold us transfixed.[37] Blake transfixes us, induces us to spin our own webs of discourse; in us, he produces selves, shapes we deem appropriate to the engagement – engagement as pre-marriage, as an appointment to be kept, as a battle. The wish, perhaps, is eventually to marry Blake in a perfected specular relationship which will absolve us of narcissism in our final committal; or, equally eventually, to 'engage' him in conversation (to peep behind the scenes); or to sally forth, armed and accoutred, to do battle with the giant.[38]

Blake's discourse about the fashioning of the self, as we have partly seen, is of a piece with his discourse about craftsmanlike fashioning: as we shape the object, so we shape an appropriate subjectivity. The crucial terms of this discourse of many levels are 'Gothic' and 'classical', and they are embedded in his own prior confrontation with authority, with Homer and Virgil: 'Grecian is Mathematic Form Gothic is Living Form, Mathematic Form is Eternal in the Reasoning Memory. Living Form is Eternal Existence'.[39]

But here, on this terrain of struggle and self-formation, there is an inversion, not entirely covered over by the grandiose claims of the Augustans. For the self mobilised in the face of the classical, perfected image (the statue) is not marked only by a sharing in this ineradicable beauty; it is produced also as, by comparison, dirty, inadequate, broken. It is sullied, as in Edward Young's obsessional lament, by a perpetual traversing between the earth and the stars;[40] that is to say, the overwhelming unity of the object refracts the gaze back into the interstices of our own body and splits us apart, offers us an image of formal cooperation before which we can only appear as shattered supplicants.[41]

Whereas the self mobilised in the confrontation with the Gothic, with the very images of shattering, of anger, of hurling apart, becomes enabled to congratulate itself on a relative wholeness, becomes capable, in fantasy, of gathering itself together as the focal point of the gaze; terror unites us, and concentrates the mind.[42] Thus in a reading of the Prophetic Books there is a submerged level of reassurance, for which the familiar discourse of 'difference' and of the un-dependence of the text serves only as a cover-story.

A myth among Blake critics is that Blake is infinitely recuperable, that the name-of-Blake cannot be erased;[43] suitably, there has already been a temporary, purging (nineteenth-century) absence. Thus Blake becomes Protean, able to take on any form. In our admiration for and propagation of this Protean shape, we perform simultaneously a celebration of our own ability to survive, to adapt our threatened interpretative craft flexibly to changing circumstances, to institutional pressures. We outlive censorship.

But if that kind of will to survive and understand has its origin in our accommodations with the supersession of the generations, the comprehension of 'generation', it must also have to do with gender, and there is thus a question to be addressed: what are the connections between this 'engagement' and the shaping of masculinity and femininity? Or: is it that in Blake, a figure anomalous along so many different axes (class, politics, reading) and yet so 'typical' of romanticism, we sense the wished-for presence of an overcoming of damaging differences in so many realms that we comfort ourselves, by empathising with this multiple transgression of boundaries, for our own incapacities?

> When weary Man enters his Cave
> He meets his Saviour in the Grave
> Some find a Female Garment there,
> And some a Male, woven with care,
> Lest the Sexual Garments sweet
> Should grow a devouring Winding sheet . . .[44]

But what is also at stake is this: 'Alas! the Female Martyr, Is She also the Divine Image?'[45]

An opposition relevant in this context might be articulated in terms of Northrop Frye and Derrida; of the will to global explanation and the desire for deconstruction; of system and process, in all their complexity of interrelation. But Frye and Derrida are themselves, of course, 'representations' through which we can glimpse the names of the older masters: Blake and Hegel.

And this opposition is also one in which we can trace the form of a collusion, as we seek for the inner meaning of these crucial dialectics.[46] Blake and Hegel are for us signs in a system, and the potential objects of a semiotic search which may uncover unconscious processes clustered around three nexi of romantic thought. Their texts need to be seen as structuring instances in an argument about the theological and the anthropological; an argument about the finite and the in-finite; and an argument about the nature and procedures associated with the 'wise man'.

All these arguments bear the ineradicable traces of a supreme articulation of a system based on male dominance, as indeed historically they must. As Hegel and Blake overthrow their fathers, and the reverberations of the struggle (against Kant, against Aristotle) continue to echo through the system, so too they set up the revolt of the eldest son as the model for our critical discourse, and become available for invocation as the guarantors of a radicalism which is nonetheless marked not by a rejection but by specific and sophisticated incorporations of the 'feminine'.[47]

In these tangential forms of romanticism, static dualism is transcended by dynamic dialectic: the locked noun becomes the energetic verb, and we are invited to participate in a flow of fictions which represent processes to which – so this fiction goes – no area of human life is foreign, in which we can both draw and leap the bounding line and penetrate all secrets, decipher the cunning of history, which is also the mystery of our birth.

Some dialectics

T.J.J. Altizer chooses Hegel 'as a guide to the dialectical ground and meaning of Blake's vision: for Hegel is the only thinker in the West who has created a comprehensive mode of dialectical thinking'.[48] That 'ground' is the recapture and reinterpretation of past systems of (theological) dominance.

> The ancient Poets animated all sensible objects with Gods or Geniuses, calling them by the names and adorning them with the properties of woods, rivers, mountains, lakes, cities, nations, and whatever their enlarged & numerous senses could perceive.[49]

> Every nation has its own imagery, its gods, angels, devils, or saints who live on in the nation's traditions, whose stories and deeds the nurse tells to her charges and so wins them over by impressing their imagination. In this way these tales are given permanence. In addition to these creatures of the imagination, there also live in the memory of most nations, especially free nations, the ancient heroes of their country's history . . .[50]

The nurse, as we know, gets short shrift for her role in the transmission of history, for she acts merely as the agent for a covert suppression:

> A system was formed, which some took advantage of, & enslav'd the vulgar by

attempting to realize or abstract the mental deities from their objects: thus began Priesthood ...[51]

The doctrines of the church have been armed with all imaginable terrors so that, just as certain magicians are supposed to be able to inhibit the use of physical capacities, these doctrines are able to paralyse all psychical capacities, or else to coerce them to function solely in accordance with this doctrinal imagery.[52]

This is a paralysing rememoration of a type we have encountered before, here deployed directly in the service of political conservatism and sanctioning class division: 'the result' was in the course of time 'profitable to the priesthood because the laity was encouraged to give freely to the priests, though the latter took good care not to squander their own acquisitions, and thus, in order to enrich themselves – the poor and needy! – they made the rest of mankind beggars'.[53]

> With what sense does the parson claim the labour of the farmer?
> What are his nets & gins & traps; & how does he surround him
> With cold floods of abstraction, and with forests of solitude,
> To build him castles and high spires, where kings & priests may dwell ...[54]

These are the monstrous phallic shapes, the forms of the bad father,[55] which dialectic purports to overturn, but without underestimating the resourcefulness of the enemy, who has, after all, been able to convince us 'that the Gods had order'd such things', and who has coalesced his procedures of power into a mountainous and unshakeable edifice, well-known also to Wordsworth, called positivity.

> It is clear ... that a positive religion is a contra-natural or a supernatural one, containing concepts and information transcending understanding and reason and requiring feelings and actions which would not come naturally to man: the feelings are forcibly and mechanically stimulated, the actions are done to order or from obedience without any spontaneous interest.[56]

The 'penetrating [sic] psychological account of the authoritarian personality'[57] becomes the root of a massive romantic rebellion, resonating down through Feuerbach, George Eliot, Swinburne; it is also the pretext for an un-naming, for a repulse of the dominating Name-of-the-Father.[58] 'It is better not to call an impersonal Absolute by the name of God': [59] better for many reasons, not least because the removal of sanction from the father signifies a possibility of redistribution of power among the brothers in the primal horde, the Zoas in Blake, for Hegel the 'shapes which the concept assumes' in the course of its dialectical history, and naming can begin afresh,[60] in a familiar twist of the narcissistic impulse to construct the new as a cover-story for preservation of the old.

The groupings of the Prophetic Books reflect this insistence on fraternal (political) equality, and at the same time the irritation caused in the machine by the ambiguous presence of the feminine, sign for a process of further subversive division which spreads out beyond easy schematic accommodation.[61] With the Name-of-the-Father erased, there is an endless spinning out of new sets of names, new attempts to trap an adequate power, to compensate for loss with the multiplicity of the polysyllabic Enitharmon/Jerusalem; in Hegel, *Geist* becomes the ambivalent signifier of namelessness, of a postponed shaping which cannot be known except in its avatars.

Thus what is happening in these texts is that the abolition of a mythical past unity represented as oppressive and stifling results in an endless yearning, a conjuring of names to fill the blank space and act as harbingers of a future reunification, within which, somehow, the harmony of the brothers will encourage the reincorporation, reabsorption of the female, and the 'emanation' will cease to threaten us with an irreducible 'Otherness'. But the home and site of this new anthropology for Blake remains Albion, remains the 'grand man', and succession remains within the male line; thus as readers we are allowed to retain our faith in phallomorphic hierarchy, while contentedly noting the presence of the feminine on the scene as a guarantee of our liberalism.

The signifier remains dominant, but absorbs into itself enough of the polymorphous plurality, enough of the unformed multivocality of the repressed, to reassure us that, *this* time, the revolution will not have been in vain, and that we are not involving ourselves in the re-establishment of a future patriarchy, of the 'once and future king';[62] Blake's very strictures on hermaphroditism are the evidence for an anxiety in the texts,[63] as we participate in a lengthy journey towards a salvation which will somehow also 'save' the female, but only in terms of a 'marriage' controlled by an unspecified and unspecifiable difference.

The dialectical systems of Blake and Hegel seek a reversal of the topography of common sense; there is no finite, stable bloc afloat in an uncomprehended sea, no totally interpretable sign surrounded by darkness. Instead, the finite opens like a flower, reveals infinity in a grain of sand; the outward search among the stars is known to lead only to an encounter with 'Og & Anak old',[64] shapeless sound and perceptual anarchy.

In the third chamber of the printing-house in *The Marriage of Heaven and Hell*, where meanings are inscribed, there is 'an Eagle with wings and feathers of air' who causes 'the inside of the cave to be infinite'.[65] The world is turned inside out, and art becomes a ceaseless incarnation of latent meanings, a ceaseless process of making into objects the previously unnameable energies at the earth's core. 'Artistic works are not abstract thought and notion, but are an evolution of the notion *out of* itself, an alienation from itself towards the sensuous':[66] metaphors of unfolding and metaphors of penetration, feminine and masculine, are sealed together into dialectical process and become the guarantees of reproductive motion.

'The apple tree never asks the beech how he shall grow'[67] because the apple tree is in itself a perfected life form: imaginative knowledge consists in entering the life, the heart, of the individual concrete forms of the world. Or, and here again we touch on the epistemological problem at the heart of psychoanalysis: 'scientific cognition . . . demands surrender to the life of the object, or, what amounts to the same thing, confronting and expressing its inner necessity.'[68]

The sexuality of the dialectic of finite and in-finite, which connects also with the psyche's enduring problems with the notion of 'control', is thus itself double: at one level, the flower-object unfurls and welcomes us, at another we penetrate and discover the secret sources of control and understanding, power and knowledge. 'Where man is not, nature is barren':[69] there is no need, here or elsewhere, to concentrate on the historically inevitable assumption of masculinity in the noun to underscore the structure of the assumed and actual verbs, to perceive the shadow of the male as the bringer of life, as the bearer of the seeds of meaning, as the cure for sterility.[70] Man as imaginer becomes the interpreter and therapist of the world, moving objects towards an undreamed-of consummation.

> What exists in nature is just a single thing, individualised indeed in all its parts and aspects. On the other hand, our imaginative mentality has in itself the character of universality, and what it produces acquires already thereby the stamp of universality in contrast to the individual things in nature. In this respect our imagination has the advantage that it is of wider range and therefore is capable of grasping the inner life, stressing it, and making it more visibly explicit.[71]

The power of the feminine is essential to the redemptions portrayed in the Prophetic Books, but only in so far as it complements the masculine, which alone has the power of naming: Vala has to become Jerusalem, has to take on a married name, before she is permitted her translation into the realm of the gods.

What Blake and Hegel thus mark is a transition in the self-representation of patriarchy, and it is one which conceals under a carapace of organicist metaphor an appropriateness to the new power-forms generated by the machine. Urizenic knowledge and control are grounded in territory and ownership: Urizen perpetually seeks his authority in the wide open spaces, posits an extension of his empire to the ends of the earth, searches for the (Kantian, or Aristotelian) categories which will serve as gridlines on the future map of the universe. The completion of his plan would be the culmination of enclosure, and of population control: the world would be subjugated to a total surveillance.[72]

But Urizen is inefficient about this, unsophisticated in his refusal to work with the feminine, in his rejection of his 'partner' Ahania, and as readers we know he is doomed, a dinosaur in a world where the swamps are drying up. His power can only become over-extended, and he gets repeatedly lost in prefigurations of Vietnam, mired in jungles where his dictates have only a muffled authority, unable to sustain the lines of communication which he has so meticulously established.

For Los, a degree of gender cooperation is possible, although he is always the senior partner:[73] instead of the massive attempt at assimilation of content which swells Urizen and topples him, Los seeks the perfect single form of power, a perfected single device (the phallus) which can be instituted in any field and yield results. Concentration on perfecting this device, whereby meaning can be inscribed at the heart of the object, will mean that in the end as one flower opens, so will all flowers open: where Urizen attempts to assert and save masculinity by a domination which entails reserve and withdrawal, by holding to himself an overview and refusing the contaminations of the bodily, Los gives form to the phallic act, penetrating the absences and converting them into adjuncts to his task. In so far as he works organically, with the affections and with relationships, he is seeking an ideal deployment of desire, knowing, unlike Urizen, that that deployment will be ideal only if it asserts a truly hegemonic ascendancy and can command acquiescence.

The wise man and the incorporation of the feminine

But this hegemonic attempt – and here the linkages between hegemony and narcissism become obvious – is riven with a contradiction, and we receive not one but two accounts of imaginative knowledge, itself under a double sign. While the phallus is asserted, it is also again withheld: although Los seeks a non-Urizenic type of unity, he also respects minute particulars, allows for plurality, portrays himself as a passive recipient of wisdom.[74] And while the Zoas scurry about trying to find a form of organisation for themselves, father Albion sleeps, passively awaiting an inevitable resurrection.

There is thus the possibility, prefigured in Jesus rising without assistance from the grave, of a second stage of immaculacy, of an Albion purified of conflict and of dominance, a father who will be purely the sum of his sons, no longer encompassed in mystery and taboo. In the aesthetic realm, this temporary witholding of the phallus as principle of unity until a new form of organisation can be found is paralleled by the replacement of Urizenic force by the less overt force of the gaze, before which the flower is induced 'spontaneously' to open and yield its secret. Power is no longer to be exercised merely through weaponry and instrumentation, but by means of a patient staring into the vacuum, a conjuring, in the fullest sense, of meaning.

Thus a tainted masculinity is purged and finds for itself a new, less offensive and more effective shape appropriate to the ethos of 'fraternity'; this connects with arguments about political democracy, and also, in a more complexly inverted way, with the problems of *Daughters of Albion*, and also serves as a figure for the cooperation required by specialisation of labour. The father-as-lord becomes the father-as-friend-and-mate, tamed yet replete with socially useful wisdom.

> The Wise Man ... is fully and definitively reconciled with everything that *is*: he entrusts himself without reserve to Being and opens himself entirely to the Real without resisting it. His role is that of a perfectly flat and indefinitely extended mirror: he does not reflect on the Real; it is the Real which reflects itself on him, is reflected in his consciousness, and is revealed in its own dialectical structure by the discourse of the Wise Man who describes it without deforming it.[75]

Intertwined with the radicalism in Blake's texts we thus find the traces of a specific type of positive authority, which is essentially unquestionable: understanding, in a time of epistemological and intrapsychic crisis, the limitations of the expanding and imperial intelligence, these traces set up a different location for the discourse of wisdom, and simultaneously assert the absolute co-extensiveness of the imaginative (male) envisioner and the 'infinite' field of vision, with obvious consequences for the concept of interpretation.

Perhaps, then, it is in these traces that we can detect the sign of Blake, and come to see the textual hiatuses around the issue of the Female Will not as aberrations in a radical discourse or as difficulties in our own self-assimilation to the sign,[76] but as the evidence of a specific and unacknowledged *plaisir du texte*. The father dies, but we know that in us (males) he will be reborn; meanwhile his penetrative power is developed afresh, and he relocates the operations of power within each tiny locus of vision, at the controls, as it were, of the microscope, as Foucault would have him do.

And at the same time, a cover-story is developed, which is that really the male does not have to assert his power through binding and deformation, but can derive the necessary authority from his natural equivalence to the perceived world, a world which he does not need to interpret because it will reveal itself direct through his transparent skin, without resort to the recourses of the unconscious, which are also the effects of historical seepage. Perhaps, then, Urizen is after all a paper tyger, as Kant was to Hegel: a travestied form of domination, under the cover of which a narcissistic myth can be reshaped.[77]

The pleasures to be derived are clear, as is the historical pretext: the texts prefigure anxieties about the role of the 'paterfamilias' in an economy demanding unaccustomed mobility and threatening the male with a home-lesssness which would strike at the root of power, and they suggest a series of strategies for coping with this crisis in masculinity. More significantly, the complex sign of Blake represents the harnessing of this redeployment to a battery of revolutionary ideas, so that this reshaping of the primary family can claim a radical reputation.

The feminine is not cast into the outer darkness under the new regime of power which Blake and Hegel figure: instead, she is incorporated as the negative moment of dialectic, as the moment which represents plurality and perpetual change, reproduction and movement.[78] Yet what is reinforced is the feminine as absence, the passivity of the Female Will, to be fructified by male insight, to be brought to life by masculine agency, as in a now familiar pattern of evasion to be referred back to the rage of womb envy.

And thus of course also, the revolt of the son can be seen as a willed transcendence of the mother: old Vala, Mother Nature can be pronounced barren, a tissue of delusions (a delusion of tissue), desexualised, so that our future mating with Jerusalem can be freed from the trammels of condition-ing, so that we can begin again in a brave new world where relationships are no longer bound up with the transference and where we can, with Paine and the other revolutionaries, inscribe totally fresh patterns in the un-foldings of destiny.

Blake and Hegel resound through history as the progenitors of male neologism, counters, still to be mobilised, to be possibilities of real neolalia which pertain to the feminine. The coining of new terms is not only a major mark of the texts themselves; it also continues to generate novelty in the critical writings which are superimposed on the original texts, in the massive systematisations of Frye, in the endlessly slipping and sliding discourse of Derrida.

For Blake and Hegel are the signs for the possibility of an 'unnameable' discourse; the dialectic is not restricted by boundaries of epistemology or by the rigid structures of a coherent science of knowledge. Here poetry, philosophy, narrative, drama are mixed into new forms, 'phenomenology' or new epic, monodrama or the travails of the spirit,[79] forms which offer the coherence of narrative, the ego's essential disguise, but twist it into new and experimental forms as the older versions fail before the disruptions of history and the self.

Thus the overcoming of the Name-of-the-Father, at a formal level, becomes also the overcoming of the names of the genres, with all the multiple ambiguities of genre/gender/generation available for spinning out and weaving. Hegel's dialectic, writes Marx, is 'a scandal and an abomination to the bourgeoisie',[80] but that is only so in so far as we continue to accept a version of bourgeois society as essentially bound to an anal-repressive constellation: what is also produced by the bourgeois order is surplus, a surplus which can be readily translated into 'play', and Blake and Hegel become the authorities through which we can justify a romantic removal of the text into the realm of the self-moving and self-generating, where fictions of omnipotence are constructed.

By taking history up and sublating it in these discourses, Blake and Hegel produce a paradox whereby history itself is flattened out: according to the dialectic, the 'two classes of men' are always with us,[81] there is 'a perpetual war and contention',[82] a perpetual play of difference. What we invest in this structure is a wish for there to be no real 'Other'-ness, a wish to go behind the mirror and see the world from a double perspective, stereoscopically, so that neither parent shall be alien to us.

Thus comes the fascination with birth and reproduction in the Prophetic Books, which can be seen as a twisting series of accounts of origins, which do not reach a conclusion. Was Urizen the first-born, or was it Tharmas? By what process do the Emanations arise? Onto birth is superimposed almost immediately – as Melanie Klein would indeed have it – a structure of splitting: the female characters in the Prophetic Books are perhaps not born by 'natural' means, but are simply the result of reduplication in the unstable personalities of the Zoas.

Thus the Emanations are a temporary accident, the outcome of and evidence for problems within the supposedly unitary consciousness. Thus at this level too the feminine is to be superseded, reincorporated, *aufgehoben*. But if the origin of the female is to be seen in the splitting of consciousness, we can trace here a familiar neurosis.[83] The problematic material, painted large on the historical canvas, has to do with the relations between agency and feeling, with how to be an active participant in the world while at the same time experiencing the world's pain: with, again, the exile of desire.

Just as the troubled consciousness divides, produces on the one hand a purified and effective agent, while reserving the feelings for a different, invisible self – the subject-of-activity splits off from the subject-of-perception – and in doing so traces a trajectory with an access closer to the truth than the embattled ego could ever guess, so the Zoas can only be free to carry out their work of regeneration if they split off their femininity, that reservoir of agony which would otherwise act as a brake.

This structure is, of course, familiar from Western legend, and represents a sophisticated view of the dispensability of women, which reverberates in the sign of Blake at many levels. It is present in Catherine-as-absence, or Catherine-as-disciple, or as the Catherine who failed to understand her husband's concern with 'higher matters'; but symbolically it is more powerfully there in the un-tutored quality of Blake, in the supposition that his texts emerge 'un-educated', betrayed only in the limp of Hephaestos.

Thus, being un-tutored, Blake was un-mothered: in him a process of creation has occurred which required no female participation. When Mary Shelley recounts the same fiction, we detect in it the neurosis of an age, the deeply-laid womb-envy at the root of the narcissistic 'lust' for knowledge;[84] but unless we can detect it also in male writers – in Coleridge's exiled dejection, in Shelley's hermaphroditism – then the use to which we put Mary Shelley becomes duplicitous, and we may grant the validity of her account while at the same time reserving our suspicions of a freakish female perception.

The womb in Blake is dark, and sleeps: it awaits awakening, and yet we may doubt that this transformation will ever arrive, for the babe, the child, springs time after time fully-armed from the mother's body, and thus it becomes again the absent space between the father's agency and the child's maturation: the hiatus, the rip of history, the going into the dark. Thus the frightening space within the body is collapsed in on itself, folded neatly away like the grave-clothes to await the life-giving ministrations of the male.

Alternatively, the female becomes the walled and impenetrable, a figure whose (maternal) rejection excuses the rejections of the male:

> And she is all of solid fire
> And gems & gold, that none his hand
> Dares stretch to touch her Baby form,
> Or wrap her in his swaddling-band

But She comes to the Man she loves,
If young or old, or rich or poor;
They soon drive out the aged Host,
A Beggar at another's door.[85]

The old man is driven 'far away', 'sore distrest/Untill he can a Maiden win',[86] until he can find a figure of female purity, a woman who is not yet possessed of the dreaded (carnal) knowledge and who is thus available for awakening, like the 'girls of mild silver, or of furious gold':[87] the lineaments of a Rousseauistic absorption with the young woman as territory to be explored, awakened, colonised returns in a cloud of masculine self-pity, the 'unknowing' of the all-knowledgeable and totally reflective ego.

Haunting

We can make some generalisations about what is marginalised in Blake's texts, what function the many spectres, ghosts, phantoms perform. Partly, what comes back to haunt the writing is the spectre of the failure of the revolution, the revolution which did not occur in England and has thus remained as a state of unfulfilled desire, classified as an unnecessary residue. Partly also, this connects with the thwarting of epistemological shift, summarised in Schelling's well-known accusation of Kant for leaving us, as his successors, wandering in a field of spectres, disabled by dualism yet unable to impart life through the dialectic of perception.

More significant, though, is another impression about agency, about the sparking events of the Fall. The Prophetic Books turn back and inward on themselves, each account of the descent from the stars bracketed as a piece of motivated and partisan dialogue, so that no true account is sanctioned. However justifiable the historical fear, a fear of censorship or compromise, which produces this set of partial texts, the sign remains and is associated with a refusal of effective political action.

To turn back to the critical and political *uses* of Blake: if even Blake had to speak in codes, perhaps this can be taken as a justification for the development of a creative and critical practice which is itself increasingly divorced from the public discourse of power; and so, in the here and now, we resign ourselves to an activity of apparent decoding in which nevertheless the language in which we produce our evidence and results is itself as effectively encoded as the Ur-texts which we concern ourselves with translating. Myth becomes its own justification, and as critics we join in a discourse over the heads of the participants in historical action.

Albion is haunted by the possibility of the failure of unity, the ineffectiveness of the phallus:

> Why roll thy clouds in sick'ning mists? I can no longer hide
> The dismal vision of mine eyes. O love & life & light!
> Prophetic dreads urge me to speak: futurity is before me
> Like a dark lamp. Eternal death haunts all my expectation
> Rent from Eternal Brotherhood we die & are no more.[88]

There is a loop here: it is the fear of death or disappearance which urges Albion to make his presence known in language, yet it is also precisely that fear which at every moment converts his discourse into code, which entails a recognition that every sign involves a negation. Discourse may point towards plenitude, but this is a useless knowledge in a state of fragmentation: over Albion's shoulder lies the dark realm of that which cannot be uttered, the unutterable womb which 'shadows' his discourse and produces the ghostly as a constant accompaniment to the search for light. The 'ghostly' is also the form of Vala:

> O be thou blotted out, thou Sun! that raisedst me to trouble,
> That gavest me a heart to crave, & raisedst me, thy phantom,
> To feel thy heat & see thy light & wander here alone,
> Hopeless, if I am like the grass & so shall pass away.[89]

The shining of the sun of enlightenment brings no hope to the female; on the contrary it reveals her unreality, produces woman as absence, as the not-yet-incarnated because unfulfilled by the birth of the son: for the woman is not the agent of discourse, but the passive recipient of 'impressions', a sensing object which is simultaneously 'stamped' with the male-determined sign of 'the feminine'.

Resurrection requires the death of this definition of womanhood. At the culmination of *Vala, or, The Four Zoas*, this supersession of the ghostly is coupled with the reabsorption of Enitharmon into the male Urthona: 'earth-owner', possessor of Mother Nature, incarnation of the denial of the infinitely unfolding tendencies of the womb, and representative simultaneously of enclosure in its historical senses:

> Urthona is arisen in his strength, no longer now
> Divided from Enitharmon, no longer the Spectre Los
> Where is the Spectre of Prophecy? where the delusive Phantom?[90]

Los is released from thrall because Enitharmon no longer remains to limit his claims to power and insight: now he can achieve the 'full speech' of the future, the discourse beyond hiatus, because the feminine, the negative, has acquiesced before the illimitable power of interpretation. It is the discourse of power itself, of course, which generates ghosts:

> What may Man be? who can tell! But what may Woman be?
> To have power over Man from Cradle to corruptible Grave.
> He who is an Infant and whose Cradle is a Manger
> Knoweth the Infant sorrow, whence it came and where it goeth
> And who weave it a Cradle of the grass that withereth away.
> This World is all a Cradle for the erred wandering Phantom,
> Rock'd by Year, Month, Day & Hour . . . [91]

If Vala is correct in identifying herself here with the grass, then the power of woman may indeed be classified as a ghostly supplement, for it is her own substance she weaves into a cradle for the boy-child: thus the survival of the male is predicated on the continual self-destruction of the female, and on the ideology of sacrifice which legitimates this process. The dialectic of harmony is also a bitter battle for space and time, or between rival conceptions of space and time, which are also rival processes for reproducing the coordinates of the psyche.

Bromion in *Daughters of Albion* is beset by the mutual ghosting which follows from gender division: 'is there not eternal fire, and eternal chains?/To bind the phantoms of existence from eternal life?'[92] But in Blake's texts, it is not the souls of the dead which come back to haunt us but the severed elements of the living body, the globes of blood, the hurtling bones, the senses floating on their unrooted filaments. Urizen tries to form a shape out of the shattered body, to put together these unaccommodated part-objects through investing a semblance of organic desire:[93]

> Horrible hooks & nets he form'd, twisting the cords of iron
> And brass, & molten metals cast in hollow globes, & bor'd
> Tubes in petrific steel, & ramm'd combustibles, & wheels
> And chains & pullies fabricated all round the Heavens of Los[94]

This exercise of phallic violence, filling the hollow globes (the breasts, the womb) with the fluids of masculine industry, is designed to sever and expel the feminine, to 'tear bright Enitharmon/To the four winds': under the guise of making, which loops back to definitions of romantic poetry itself, what occurs is an unmaking, but to Urizen's horror this very unmaking, this ravaging of the body, produces its own shape:

> Terrified & astonish'd, Urizen beheld the battle take a form
> Which he intended not a Shadowy hermaphrodite, black & opake;
> The Soldiers nam'd it Satan, but he was yet unform'd & vast.
> Hermaphroditic it at length became, hiding the Male
> Within as in a Tabernacle, Abominable, Deadly.[95]

So the attempted expulsion of the feminine encounters the forms of resistance, and is twisted into a 'hiding' and implanting of the masculine, as the male is hidden literally in the text: Blake deleted 'male' in the second of these lines and wrote 'hermaphrodite' over it. But what Urizen cannot achieve in the way of narcissistic perfection occurs under a more diffuse agency later in *The Four Zoas*, when the terrifying 'globes', which also carry the signification of Vala, of the planet earth, of ecological integration, of maternal nourishment, are banished:

> The Expanding Eyes of Man behold the depths of wondrous worlds!
> One Earth, one sea beneath; nor Erring Globes wander, but Stars
> Of fire rise up nightly from the Ocean; & one Sun
> Each morning, like a New born Man, issues with songs & joy[96]

All is oneness and timely order: the stars are indubitably themselves, single points of power and light, models for a version of individualism in which the masculine has always already seen itself falsely born, and which at the same time stands in for the unassimilable but unforgettable unitary origins of narrative, before the 'Fall' of which Urizen's weaving of webs is the attempted unravelling. The globes, however, threaten with the thought of what they might contain: through a familiar metaphorical shift, as eyes they may observe us; but worse, they refract Blake's obsession with blood, and may thus threaten with the unbearable rememoration of the mother's blood coursing unstoppably through us, with those memories of dependence in which we are, after all – and before all – 'unmanned'; not simply 'New born' each morning either, as we would like to believe, but bearing the knowledge of our own origin within the womb, a knowledge itself womb-like in its enveloping presence, its power behind our squared shoulders. And it is thus that we spend our time merely seeking to replicate in the dialectical imagination a process of reproduction which we cannot emulate.

Reflexivity

The basic terms of Blake's myths are expulsion and reincorporation; these are the activities, under the sign of complex kinds of compulsive repetition, around which the Prophetic Books are structured, and they come to bear the signification of the available ways of dealing with the troublesomeness of the feminine 'Other'. Habitually, critics treat this as one level among many others: centrally, it may be said, the myth of the Fall and resurrection is epistemological, or 'psychological', or societal, but it is a mark of Blake's 'genius' that he has lighted upon a 'structure', an archetype in its strictly Jungian sense, of such manifest power and fertility that we can trace it across all these realms, can sense in the texts the glimmerings, admittedly without total reasonance – yet – in the echo chamber, of an absolute symmetry, albeit 'fearful'.

Thus we are carried by Blake, as by Hegel, to a vantage-point from which the multifarious patterns of the world are fully visible, even if, when there, we speak in coded whispers, victims of an awed hush. If, we say,we wish to derive enlightenment about the unconscious structurings of patriarchy, then we might turn to other writers: surely Blake offers us enough sustenance without this added frill.

Thus in our readings of Blake, in our engagements with the sign, we are permitted to re-enact a customary displacement, and to sublimate our dread of primal division. As in Freud, indeed, the most that can be uttered about the feminine is that it is at root very like the masculine, another exemplar to be held to the strict accounting of neuter adjectives; alike in the processes of development, in the ambitions for harmony;[97] and over and above this, the feminine has of course a special quality to bring to that postponed resurrection, that overcoming of doubt and dissent, although that quality, that power is displaced.

It is displaced from a feared psychic area around the issue of secrecy, what is held in the body, in the memory; the recollection of priority, a recollection about which men do not wish to hear, whether it emerges in the form of claims for an always already prior matriarchy, or in demystification of the female body. The 'Tree of Mystery', we are encouraged to believe, really grows in the 'Human Brain';[98] what prevents us from absolute knowledge is a resolute deflection of perception rather than the endlessly reticulating structures of patriarchy.

But of course, if we tie patriarchy to a feudal parody like Urizen, really a figure of fun and constantly afflicted by the strange and ironic properties of farce, constantly also amazed by his own failure to dominate, we have a handy caricature of masculine power onto which we may load our own anxieties as we adopt the belief that revolution will, by some 'necessary' process, lead to a supersession of this patriarchy, that the liberation of the sons will save the 'Daughers of Albion' by some symmetrical process of mechanical linkage.

But Blake is the poet of the shattered body, as Hegel is the historiographer of the shattered psyche: in Blake's 'corpus', in his textual body, the signifier undergoes a progressive expansion as it tries to catch and hold the perpetually escaping substance which resists naming. The

Prophetic Books re-present the babble of voices, trying to be heard, each outdoing the other with a 'new' account of history, whose newness is only the product of a process of forgetting which has also forgotten the imperatives which dictated the original urge to forget. Here also we hear a new attempt to implant a hope for a future, a future which will be in continuity with the past and thus whose 'differance' serves only as the essential guarantor of stasis and incorporation, a resistance to fantasy.

Each of the voices, each inflection of discourse, tries to 'seed' the future so that a new beginning can be made, avoiding the contaminations of the primal knot. It is here that Blake's extraordinary authority may be located: in his provision of a multiplicity and complexity of codes which, in themselves, in their very brilliance and metaphorical applicability, guarantee the fertility and historical adaptability of the masculine intellect.

Despite Urizen, the Ur-myth here is an inversion: it is Enion who numbers Tharmas's nerves, who challenges a dumb and ox-like power to give an account of itself, and who is thus held to reduce ideal, instinctual man to misery.[99] Reincarnated as Vala, she then suffers under a lengthy vengeance disguised as transformation, so that she may herself become the 'golden city', the objectified good mother for whom we yearn and with whom, in the absence of the father, we are at length permitted a plenitude of relation; in whose reincarnated and expanded womb we are at length permitted to reside, and whose many 'gates' will at length be opened to us.[100]

But in fact we do not need to turn to the complicated narratives of the Prophetic Books for a model of the pedagogic practice sanctioned by the sign of Blake, a practice which colours our own engagement. The symbolic incorporation of the feminine is already significantly present in the *Songs of Innocence and of Experience* (1789–94). In the lyrics we have already, and conveniently available, a sign for gender relations in which, despite our critical animadversions on the complexity of connections between and among them, pedagogically it is often only the songs of Experience, the discourse which predicates agential involvement with the world, which can be *taught*, with the world of innocence as pretext.

Yet again, there is a revealing contradiction, for in some ways Blake is held back from pedagogy: the assumption is that here is the ground for an imaginative involvement which transcends mere edification. 'The tygers of wrath are wiser than the horses of instruction';[101] or, at greater length:

> Whoever seeks mere edification, and whoever wants to shroud in a mist the manifold variety of his earthly existence and of thought, in order to pursue the indeterminate enjoyment of this indeterminate divinity, may look where he

likes to find all this. He will find ample opportunity to dream up something for himself. But philosophy must beware of the wish to be edifying.[102]

The appointment we have to keep with Blake will not be of a commonplace character: as our perceptions of the writings alter, so we will ourselves alter and grow. Thus we are persuaded that our reading of Blake enables us to transcend the discredited habits of over-analytic masculinity, that a 'feminine' power of instinctual recognition is drawn out and born in us: in our reading, we ourselves perform an incorporation, develop an encompassing imagination which is apparently distanced from masculine pride.

The pedagogic practice surrounding Blake corresponds to a rite of initiation; after the easy slopes of the lyrics, and the complex maze of the annotations, comes the great encounter with the Prophetic Books, in a carefully graded ascent in which only the few manage to reach the summit, shrouded as it is in the mists, precisely, of interpretation.

Thus we proceed, like the dialectic, through the stages of maturation, to the point where instruction is left behind and we commune together in whispers, before the hieroglyphs of knowledge left behind by the *pater absconditus*. And as we deconstruct the standing stones, so simultaneously we breathe life into them and they begin to dance, welcoming us into their midst and inviting us to a communion of delicious conflict. Thus maturity demonstrates a circularity and we are permitted solemn play, games from which we will never be called in.

But to read Blake's texts as subversive without recognising the extent to which they are themselves politically subverted by the shapes imposed on and by sexuality and by historical dislocation is to refuse to press towards a realisation of historical entrapment, to refuse at the most difficult point – the point at which we all wish to refuse – to recognise the exclusions which are nonetheless present, and which challenge the process of signification itself; to refuse to probe the re-lapses of the sign and to settle for Blake's texts as applicable commodities rather than as themselves participants in the vicissitudes of history, politics, patriarchy.

Blake and mysticism

It is possible to consider much Blake criticism as *appropriative*. That is to say, loosely but in what I take to be an essential context, that critics of a mystical persuasion have found Blake mystical; critics opposed to mysticism have found him down-to-earth, historically grounded. This contrasts strongly with, say, the criticism of Jane Austen, where socially conscious critics have usually enshrined a wish to demonstrate the narrowness of her views and *mise-en-scène*. Blake is a writer around whom criticism clusters, rather than against whom criticism takes up antagonistic stances.

This begs a large number of questions; one I believe we need to think about as we interrogate the boundaries of the historical and the psychological concerns the meaning of mysticism. Generally, in the theological literature as well as in the literary–critical, it figures as a sign in a system, the opposite pole of which is immersion within and responsiveness to immediate historical circumstances. While wage-slaves labour, or while classes and fractions arrange themselves in intricate patterns of hegemony, the mystic's face is turned away, upward or inward. And yet, of course, this opposition cannot bear much scrutiny. Indeed, the critic professing materialism while making such an assumption has only fallen into a trap; has given away, in the very act of vindicating a materialistic world-view, his or her unexamined faith that such a worldless position is indeed possible, and that the motion of turning away has a chance of successfully evading the real.

For what, after all, is the nature of the transcendence or, alternatively, the interiority which is thus posited and safeguarded? If our subjectivities and fantasies are indeed structured by historical circumstance, there can be no reason why the contents of mystical experience should be less amenable to interpretation than any other experiential plenum, although their relation to the moment of interpretation itself may be complex.

On the contrary: if we talk about interiority, then we are surely permitted to examine the moment accounted as 'mystical' precisely in the terms some mystics themselves have used, Blake among them, as a moment not of escape *from* but of specific embedding *within* the time-continuum.[103] There would then be no reason why this moment of fascinated concentration should yield less to interpretation than more extended and diffuse types of apprehension; the unfolding of the particular flower, petal by petal, is of no less intrinsic interest than the taxonomy of flora.

Yet what might these contents be? Here again there is a contradiction. The materialist might well claim that any moment which eludes expression would indeed be one which can perform no service in the systemic investigation of forms; yet it is never actually with such moments that we are called upon to deal, since they can by definition have nothing to do with writing. We cannot be interested in some mysterious and always deferred moment of unexpressed vision in Blake, but only, and precisely, in the linguistic expression of that moment; and mystics have indeed frequently waxed prolix in their descriptions.

Whatever 'mysticism' may be, the mysticism with which we have to do in the study of writing is not a jot less expressible, or indeed expressed, than any other type of claimed insight, no matter how many negations linguistically surround it, no matter what the writer's own apologies may be for the paucity and inadequacy of his or her discourse. Mysticism therefore is a mapping of language among other such mappings, distinguished not by excision from time but, certainly, by a sense of difference in time-apprehension, a difference the evidence of and substance for which can only, for us, be discursive. In Derridean terms again, we cannot get beyond the supplementarity; and it is significant that the classical tradition of interpretation of mysticism, not wishing to own to this inevitable embedding, turns repeatedly to Kant's purist categories as a source of heuristic method.[104]

How, then, can we move beyond this false structure, which is also the central structure of idealism? Blake, we should note, although he uses the term 'visions' and its cognates as a central sign, refers to the 'mystic' only twice, and one of those occasions is in a deleted plate from *America* (1793), where he is obviously describing the dragon force of mystery:

> the vale was dark
> With clouds of smoke from the Atlantic, that in volumes roll'd
> Between the mountains, dismal visions mope around the house
> On chairs of iron, canopied with mystic ornaments
> Of life by magic power condens'd; infernal forms art-bound ...[105]

This 'magical condensation' is defined as a distortion; we can relate it to a false version of the naming activity of the gods, a naming which does not serve to assert particularity but which takes its place instead in the armoury of mechanisms of control.

If in Blake we see a further reticulation of patriarchy, one more appropriate to new social complexities, such that the overtly dominant figure of Urizen is superseded, by Los, certainly, but thus by a force whose 'penetrative' power is in fact much greater than Urizen's, then we may see in Blake's work a moment at which Urizenic rationalism is indeed overcome by a power of imagination; but that power has just as much difficulty with the feminine as did its predecessors, placed as it now is under the tortuous sign of incorporation.

In the process, then, of attending to the margins, the shapes and pressures which, unaccommodated, return to haunt the text, the spectres, ghosts, phantoms; in what is, indeed, a parallel movement, we thus need to sophisticate the notion of mysticism. The mystical moment can be known only in the expressed; but that 'expressed' itself takes a specific form, whereby it is forever haunted by the inexpressible. The sign, in its very presence, points us inexorably and constantly towards absence, towards a movement from and above the world; in one sense, this is true of all language, but mysticism is distinguished by a tonality which we can refer to as 'gratitude', an imprint of pleasure which asserts that expression is saved, only but always, by the notion of a supernal audience, 'present' in some sense even in the darkest moments of spiritual convolution.

In Blake, then, I would suggest that we do not need to engage with an argument about the 'reality' of his visions; but rather to attempt to discern within his texts the structure of presence and absence, the flutterings at the edges of discourse and the modes in which they are in- or discorporated in the plenum of language. The crucial mystical moment can be, and has been, defined as a 'yes' and a 'no';[106] the question, however, must be about the relatedness of these terms, about the fullness and emptying of the sign, about substance and shadow, and we can come at these issues best, I suggest, not by trying to assess the 'content' of Blake's vision, not by a mechanical listing of features of the world to be taken or left behind on the posited journeying beyond, but by trying to construct an intertextuality in the light of which Blake's specific textual stance can be inserted into the gallery of vision whereby the whirling stance of the mystic 'caught' between naming and the unnameable can be held for a momentary regard without being frozen by the critical gaze. And I hope that by constructing this intertextuality we can explore further the issues of narcissism and gender which are central to romantic discourse.

Kenosis and the vortex, interpretation and fantasy

The central concepts which Altizer uses in connection with Blake revolve around a particular meaning for the phrase 'death of God' and originate in a revival and reticulation of the old theological dispute about 'kenosis'.[107] 'Kenosis' is definable as 'the self-renunciation of the divine nature, at least in part, by Christ in the incarnation';[108] and it is that 'at least in part' which is traditionally at stake in the theological controversies. We need also to have in mind the key biblical passage, which, in a modern translation, runs:

His nature is, from the first, divine, and yet he did not see, in the rank of

Godhead, a prize to be coveted; he dispossessed himself, and took the nature of a slave, fashioned in the likeness of men, and presenting himself to us in human form . . .[109]

Without following through Altizer's detailed arguments, I would want to say that this problematic touches very closely on some of the basic structures in Blake's work, and raises some of the most important questions. How may we accurately describe the relation between fallen and unfallen form, between, say, Jerusalem and Vala? What are the limitations of Albion's sleeping condition, and, concomitantly, what is the status of his dreams? What is the strict relation of terms in the phrase 'human form divine'?

In the context of the mystical, these questions can be generalised into, precisely, a revision of conventional assumptions about fullness, emptying and time. It cannot be, for example, the case that Vala's apparently temporary supersession of Jerusalem during the whole course of human history can be characterised simply in terms of replacement, of presence and absence; but nor, on the other hand, can we hold that this 'replacement' operates purely in the world of appearance and perception.

What is at stake is what we might term time's essential duplicity: a recognition that continuity and extension are themselves ordered fictions, and fictions with, at that, overt social and psychological purposes – the ego-protecting promotion of a time-bounded logicality which defines inclusion and exclusion. The mystical opposes this logicality, not by supplying an alternative order but by suspending us, the readers, in the dizzying moment of the unlimitedly spontaneous; by constantly reminding us that the mental operation by which we perceive relatedness assumes, all the time and everywhere, a massive simultaneous perception which in turn defines the innate fictive structure of discourse.

The act of 'dispossession' of which the author of Philippians speaks is not an act of sudden freedom. It is instead depicted as a taking on of an alternative slavery, since of course it is a liberation into the 'human condition'; yet in it we see the possibility that there is a slavery in mysticism too, enjoined by a responsibility to recording an always-remembered disruption. The mystic is in thrall to the Fall.

And this connects very closely to Blake's thinking on the 'Vortex':

> That every thing has its
> Own Vortex, and when once a traveller thro' Eternity
> Has pass'd that Vortex, he percieves it roll backward behind
> His path, into a globe itself infolding like a sun,
> Or like a moon, or like a universe of starry majesty,

> While he keeps onwards in his wondrous journey on the earth,
> Or like a human form, a friend with whom he liv'd benevolent.[110]

How can we 'live benevolent' in the company of the vortex, the whirlwind? Or: how can we live with the knowledge of that extraordinary constitutive power glimpsed in the individual consciousness, *and yet* carry that power with us, in hiding, on our ordinary journeys?

Blake's argument, like that of Meister Eckhart and others, was that we do; and to the extent that we do, we live over a void and we spin webs of interpretation to protect ourselves from falling. The mystical appears as the quiver in the web, the reminder of breezes blowing, for the vortex remains cogent only by external force. Our 'incarnation' brings us this side of the mirror; but we are left with an option about which way we then choose to face; or rather, on what we choose to concentrate as we too are whirled, experiencing the world we have left as a series of images, passing too fast for conventional apprehension, but visible too frequently not to leave a stain on the retina.

This provides a key for thinking about the relations between mystical apprehension and the need for interpretation: the types of interpretation which I tried to enumerate above, in literary and cultural criticism and in psychoanalytic discourses, often take the form of a continuous raising of the question, 'What are we incarnating?' And the function of a notion of the 'unconscious' in any of these discourses is the same: it is to remind us that, in so far as we are incarnating, for ourselves, an apparently inaccessible interiority, we are simultaneously incarnating the social and group pressures by which that interiority has been formed, and in the context of which it is inevitably and unknowingly shared.

Albion dreams his own societal position, incarnating himself through his series of representations of other 'characters', experiencing their life as a squeezing, as a painful forming of himself which appears to have nothing to do with his 'self' as a self-cogent and separate entity. It is in the mystical moment that this 'crowding' forces itself upon our attention, when we come to see that, in whatever position or role we like to see ourselves, we are necessarily, in our very individuality, 'representing' or playing out the fantasies of others, standing in for something larger than we wish.

One of the best accounts of this process, which tries to utter the discourse of group analysis in the same breath as the 'literary mythic', is John Broadbent's essay 'Darkness'.[111] Its primary concern is with Conrad's *Heart of Darkness* (1902):

> We penetrated deeper and deeper into the heart of darkness. It was very quiet there. . . . We were wanderers on a prehistoric earth . . . We could have fancied

ourselves the first of men taking possession of an accursed inheritance, to be subdued at the cost of profound anguish and of excessive toil. ... We could not understand because we were too far and could not remember ...[112]

'We may see these as stations of the cross', Broadbent writes of the stages of this journey, 'on a journey past "falls" back to the beginning of the world; or back to the primordial in oneself under analysis perhaps; or as stages in the membership of an institution, a marriage, the life of a group'. However we see them, they indicate that we live as individuals by incarnating wider forces; and the question is raised as to whether, by reflexivity and the assimilation of projection, we can move beyond the slavery implied by the myth of kenosis. Or: if indeed we could see these levels as one, as Blake tried to do in the structure of the Prophetic Books, how would we be able to recount this perception without being bound to the time-norms of the interpretative, the spinning out of the web of deepening discourse, which is itself a known misrepresentation of the simultaneity of apprehension?

Broadbent mentions Conrad's comment on Marlow, as a narrator:

to him the meaning of an episode was not inside like a kernel but outside, enveloping the tale which brought it out only as a glow brings out a haze, in the likeness of one of these misty halos that sometimes are made visible by the spectral illumination of moonshine.[113]

And he comments:

Those statements do not excuse his [Conrad's] mistiness as a writer but they do sum up a difficulty that members have in a here-and-now group ... They also suggest something of the nature of interpretative remarks: that meaning is already latent among people, and may merely be brought out, made manifest, by the flow of the telling, the interpreting; yet all the interpreter's glow can do is reveal the meaning as hazy: and what he says may be moonshine.

I would want to connect this with Blake through an argument about authority. Blake's authority as a narrator hinges on his mysticism because it is only there that he can locate the draining away of the self which accompanies an increasing reflexivity about the interlocking projections and introjections of which the world is constructed; only there that he can find a way of bringing out a set of perceptions which offer a simultaneous *plenitude*, to do with the wealth of the social world, the effects we have on others, the dominance of structure, and *absence*, as individuality whirling in the vortex, gaining purchase only through acts of interpretation which are always already surpassed. Kenosis must include reminder, and they must be supplementary to each other; shapes swim in the heart of darkness, yet they are all shapes of the 'Other', holding us in a binding rigidity.

'Good' interpretation thus makes things fall apart, as Los strives to break the cement-like function of Urizenic perception with a sudden act of penetrative dislocation, also figured ambivalently as transcendence and aspiration.[114]

Some contexts: Blackwood, Lindsay, Swinburne, Beckett

A second useful analogue here can be found in Algernon Blackwood's mystical novel, *The Human Chord* (1910). The text supposes the possibility of massive change, a sudden romantic transcendence of the material universe; but, like Conrad, Blackwood is reluctant to specify the nature of the change. He does, however, describe the means. A chord is to be uttered; for its perfect utterance, four voices must perform a perfect harmony. These voices, in fact, range across genders and classes; and we are reminded of the many 'fours' in Blake's texts, and also of the quaternaries in terms of which I have tried to characterise the interpretative process.[115]

The plot, such as it is, hinges on one of the characters, Spinrobin, progressively realising the choice which confronts him as he decides whether or not to take his place in this fatal choir. There is no doubt that success for the group would mean the end of time; possibly new time structures would evolve, but more probably time itself would be superseded and the universe held for ever within a single moment of mystical apprehension, in which this little group would finally stand, eternally, as the representation of the very notion of combination and interaction. All else would flow into them; and here again we touch upon group fantasies of omnipotence and their narcissistic root.

Spinrobin is thus faced with a paradox: the moment of full apprehension will simultaneously be a moment of individual disappearance, because the very terms in which he might consider his individuality will be transcended. He opts against; his alternative is human love, marriage, the preservation of self under the guise of a simple dialectic. He realises that the wielding of power, the donning of authority, the premature return to godhead will also involve the arrival of an unchangeable absence in which he will drown.

The difficulty here is that the image of a harmony to end all harmonies is strongly connected with metaphors of phallomorphic aspiration. Broadbent makes the point about *Heart of Darkness* that both of the women in it, Kurtz's tender and sensual selves, are nameless; indeed, at the end his 'Intended' asks Marlow to tell her what Kurtz's last words were, and Marlow says that he spoke her name, even though we know that Kurtz's last words were 'The horror! the horror!'.[116] This, then, *is* her name, as far as the text is concerned; and similarly Blackwood connects under the same sign femininity/weakness/inability to realise the vision, the very 'muddy hole' of materialist trammels in which Kurtz's body is thrown, and which here in a different guise prevents Spinrobin's flight to the stars.[117]

If we assimilate mysticism to notions of a unitary, climactic naming of God the Father, then the problem becomes focused, as it was indeed for Blake in his spinning out of the complexities of 'emanation'.[118] Thinking back to the model of group dynamics and its significance for the construction of subjectivity, it is tempting to see this structure of aspiration as a displacement: under the guise of further revelation, what we in fact enact is a further removal into a place of absolute comfort, and this again is where the tonality of gratitude appears. Mystical experience, though, since it is mapped in discourse, is not an invariable, and in exploring its contents it is hardly surprising if we find at the heart of Western recountings the installation of a phallomorphic deity.

David Lindsay, in *A Voyage to Arcturus*, a book of visions thinly overlaid with narrative, attempts a questioning of this content. Maskull sees a figure walking towards him, and experiences a

> surprise, for this person, although clearly a human being, was neither man nor woman, nor anything between the two, but was unmistakably of a third positive sex, which was remarkable to behold and difficult to understand.
> ... Just as one can distinguish a man from a woman at the first glance by some indefinable difference of expression and atmosphere, altogether apart from the contour of the figure, so the stranger was separated in appearance from both. As with men and women, the whole person expressed a latent sensuality, which gave body and face alike their peculiar character. ... Maskull decided that it was *love* – but what love – love for whom?[119]

This attempted supersession of 'differance' is accompanied, however, by a difficulty of vision; the figure shimmers, escapes from its own 'contour'.

Maskull needs to coin a new pronoun for it, something to hold on to to combat namelessness; and here we find echoes of Blake. In Blake's works, the word 'nameless' occurs eight times, and we can structure these references. There is the 'nameless female' of *America*; and the 'nameless shadow' who occurs twice in *The Four Zoas*. There is the composite form, the 'nameless shadowy female' who is mentioned in *Europe* (1794) and twice again in *The Four Zoas*; and there are the further mutations of the 'nameless shadowy Vortex' of *The Four Zoas* and the 'nameless Shadowy Mother' of *Milton*.[120]

Female/shadow/mother/vortex: in the passage from *Milton* which we quoted earlier, the vortex is that which we continually leave behind us, and yet it is that with which we learn to live as a 'benevolent' friend. The problem, metaphorically, is how to probe the shadow: to do so, as both Los and Urizen find, is to convert this restless unconscious substance of femininity into a phallic icon. The possibilities of harmony slide under the sign of aspiration. In the mystical moment, we are not required to perform the masculine act of interpretation; yet if we do not, we can bring nothing of our revelation back with us.

Swinburne clearly reflects on this problem as well, and his answer here enters into a now familiar doubleness. There is a possible version, or a possible fiction, which posits a female origination which sets up flimsy masculine deities as a comfort; partriarchy is thus a kindly device invented by mother to protect us from the terror of the womb. The alternative fiction is that this very fictional structure is designed to keep us in the 'shadow', to prevent the emergence of the aspiring purity of the phallus. Albion serves Jerusalem; or Jerusalem makes us forget to put on our sacerdotal robes, in a priesthood where raiment is sexually ambivalent yet women are exiled from the cloth, or the tapestry.

> I that saw where ye trod
>   The dim paths of the night
> Set the shadow called God
>   In your skies to give light;
> But the morning of manhood is risen, and the shadowless soul is in sight.[121]

These lines of Swinburne's occur in his poem 'Hertha' (1871). Hertha is an alternate and, to modern consciousness, apparently feminised version of the name of an ancient German goddess of the earth, more usually known as Nerthus. She was, perhaps, a fertility goddess, although the relevant passage in Tacitus is not clear.[122] At all events, she was connected with a specific ritual, in which she and her chariot had to be washed in a sacred lake by slaves who were subsequently drowned: the moment of incarnation was 'shadowed' by slavery and by a drowning in the well of unrecountable experience. But the name-of-Nerthus does not seem etymologically clear either: it may come from the Greek word for the dead, although she is referred to as *terra mater*.

Swinburne's purported algolagnia makes him a significant commentator on these processes of sexual ambivalence; but of course his contorted naming of the 'nameless shadowy female' recounts a long cultural history, which again we would expect to find occurring within the theology of mysticism itself. Which it does, mainly in the guise of a debate about the relation between mysticism and theism. Steven Payne, for instance, tries to distinguish theistic from non-theistic mysticism, claiming that Christian mysticism cannot be sensibly seen against a culturally undifferentiated context.[123] He takes W.T. Stace to task for citing Sanjuanist passages to show that John

> describes with great subtlety and wealth of detail how, in order to reach union, the mind has to suppress within itself all sensations, images, thoughts, and acts of will. It is the same process of emptying the mind of empirical contents as we find with Eckhart, with the Upanishadic mystics, and indeed with all mystics who have been sufficiently intellectual to analyse their own mental processes. ... And the only result of getting rid of all mental contents (if it does not produce unconsciousness) can only be an undifferentiated unity.[124]

There are many ways of relating this to our general issues: for example, the passage suggests a further twist to the concept of emptying. But what is more important is the way in which it takes up the various comments on differentiation and undifferentiation which comprise this romantic and post-romantic intertextuality.

It is the case that when groups of people arrive at the mutual fiction of omnipotence which we are now finding ourselves frequently mentioning, they come at it in one of two ways. Either they believe that they have submerged their differences, gender, race, class, skills, and their power thus derives from a version of telepathy based in cloning. Or they believe that they have arrived at a distribution of skills, talents, tasks, so exact that they can function as a tiny State. Blake suggests from his experience of harmony and narrative that these may be parts of a twofold evolution: that the 'State-like' relations between the various Zoas and their Emanations, where all is clear function and ascribable purpose, may be a prelude to a situation of undifferentiation and loss of individuality, as in the vineyards and winepresses.[125]

At one level, of course, this seems a sensible way of saying that life precedes death; but the question that remains is one of consciousness. What is the shape of the group which is to come, and how much of our present version of consciousness shall we be able to bring to it? When the feast is announced, are we expected to bring our own dishes? If we do not, will we find that we are being entertained by Timon with stones and water; where will the *wealth* – a term used in similar context by Payne and Altizer – be, where will the rich multiplicity of content – which *depends* on narrative and interspersion – find its place?

And in the Blakean context, we can see two possible answers textually evidenced through the crucial process of naming. With a name like 'Urizen', we are invited to speculate precisely on the relation between inherited wealth of association and newness. Of course we can talk about 'your reason' and 'horizon'; but we conduct such an interpretative discourse against a background of felt inadequacy, in the ambiguous light of the haze, the 'misty halo' as Conrad has it, of breaking into components that which has its force only in relation to a different version of time. The dreams of Albion, or indeed the dreams of Coleridge, do not 'transcend', in any literal sense; but they are equally discontented with the immanent, because the immanent disregards the real epistemological problems of incarnation, at the quite practical level of relating the sense of consciousness to the knowledge of artificial constraint, those pressures from the 'Other' which we know to be constructed yet constitutive.

The state that Blake is reaching out for, we know, is the state of 'organised innocence', and we are now in a position to describe that condition. It would be achieved by the individual, presumably, at the point where he or she had, firstly, made the leap into realisation of the constructed nature of subjectivity, the move, that is, from Innocence to Experience; and secondly, achieved a degree of relativity about this process which *nevertheless* enabled him or her to continue to act in the realm of freedom. But the problem is obvious. What we have here may be some kind of non-supernatural transcendence, but it may equally well be a regression, and a regression achieved precisely through the complexities of narrative, the endless treading on the escalator which brought us down from the imaginary heavens.

This doubt about regression is simultaneously a doubt about the authority we might have over the narratives the ego constructs: in the moment of mysticism, or during the patient undoing of the dreamwork, whose is the voice which speaks through us? And will the entity to which it belongs always resist our naming, always remain the 'nameless shadowy female' despite our apparent efforts to 'repatriate' her? These are fears which recur in systematic form in Beckett, and particularly in *The Unnamable* (1953):

> And sometimes I say to myself I am in a head, it's terror makes me say it, and the longing to be in safety, surrounded on all sides by massive bone. And I add that I am foolish to let myself be frightened by another's thoughts, lacerating my sky with harmless fires and assailing me with noises signifying nothing. But one thing at a time. And often all sleeps, as when I was really Worm, except this voice which has denatured me, which never stops, but often grows confused and falters, as if it were going to abandon me.[126]

And sometimes, indeed, Blake's figures say to themselves that they are in a head, Albion's head; and sometimes again they attempt to build themselves a body out of shattered fragments to protect themselves from the cold winds, from the terror of being vulnerable to these unassignable voices which are the voices of language itself and also the sounds which come to us when, in the mystical moment, we attend deeply to silence.[127]

Blake's characters, Los and Enitharmon particularly, are frequently frightened by others' thoughts; they live in a universe where the saving boundaries are down, and there is simultaneous transmission. They do, of course, try to cheer themselves up, as does Beckett's narrator;[128] the thought that you are being formed by the Imaginary of others is indeed uncomfortable, and it cannot be wished away by a simple repetition of the long cultural history of 'signifying nothing'. This universe is 'intentional', in Franz Brentano's sense;[129] but that does not mean it is transparent or lucid. How, then, can we show the necessary gratitude, if the world proves to be an unnatural or 'denaturing' mother, and if, as well, we are terrified that even this false mother might abandon us?

It is then in the context of this ambivalence towards the female that Blake, Swinburne, Blackwood turn towards the skies, looking for the clear word, the word which we may utter in harmony with the universe without sensing it bouncing back at us mockingly in another's voice. But the project does turn back on itself, at least for Beckett:

> ... those are words, open on the silence, looking out on the silence, straight out, why not, all this time on the brink of silence, I knew it, on a rock, lashed to a rock, in the midst of silence, its great swell rears towards me, I'm streaming with it, it's an image, those are words, it's a body, it's not I, I knew it wouldn't be, I'm not outside, I'm inside, I'm in something, I'm shut up, the silence is outside, outside, inside, there is nothing but here, and the silence outside, nothing but this voice and the silence all round, no need of walls, yes, we must have walls, I need walls, good and thick, I need a prison ... [130]

Mysticism is not the inexpressible; but it is bound up with language which attempts reflexivity about its own ambiguous power. From the fearsome materiality of language, its constraint and history, we plan to flee to a realm of new sounds; but the plan is always botched, always betrays itself in the traces of fear, boundness, confinement which prevent the flight to the stars. Between the name of the father and the nameless female we are stuck, unable to use or not to use language, unable to experience limitlessness or limit, constructing prisons but not even able to trust that their walls and stones will remain real against the underminings of the Imaginary. The aspiration is broken to pieces on the 'infusile' rocks of language:

> You, you take form,
> I, I am reborn endlessly:
> both to the pursuit of the union.

My joy, your body,
Your delights, my presence

I give you appearance,
You make me infinite.

We two, a single body,
A new being is born,
The You-I, the I-You.

Between us no difference any longer,
I-You, You-Touka.[131]

Mysticism and psychosis: the dark dialogue

The words of Toukaram, as above, fall apart on the 'you' and the 'I', on
the irreducibility of naming. Ben-Ami Scharfstein, in his astute book on
mystical experience, gives us a list of mystical traits which can be linked
with psychosis: 'the psychotic experience of time, mode of speech,
hallucination, certainty, bliss, depersonalisation and loss of identity, and
sense of unreality'.[132] The 'mode of speech' category turns out to be another
failure of incarnation, another kenosis bound to slavery:

> Speech may cease to have any public meaning, for the differences between
> speaker, person spoken to, words spoken with, and subject spoken of may
> vanish and only a subjective thing-like word or word-like thing be left. ...
> Thus, in one case, the letters of the French alphabet were felt to be each a
> different part of the speaker's body, and he guarded the parts against infection
> by pronouncing the letters in the right way and order. The emptiness of speech
> ... is really its transformation into an idiosyncratic magical being, which is
> created by utterance to guard, to avenge, and to grant and be fulfilment.[133]

Emotive, conative, metalingual and referential functions are collapsed:
according to, for instance, Roman Jakobson's theory what we would be
left with, what the psychotic may be left with, is a conflation of the phatic
and the poetic, contact and message fused into a frozen form of incor-
porative desire with no beginning or end, no source and no 'emanation'.[134]
There is a paradox here, and it is one which we can find in Jacob Boehme
and other mystics: that when all the distractions of human communication
are wished away, if only for a moment, what is left is not as light as a
feather, but instead an object of extreme materiality, the word thoroughly
incarnated and unleavened by the human, the unthinkable resistance which
we have been keeping at bay.[135]

Thus, in psychosis, the intimation of transcendence is inevitably accompanied by an awareness of 'interference':

The point seems to be, so far as I can grasp it, that during an exhilaration the mind penetrates infinitely more deeply into all things, and receives flashes of almost divine light and wisdom, which open to it, momentarily, regions of thought hitherto difficult or impossible of penetration. But, except in the milder forms of the exhilaration, the mind's own restlessness, and impatient activity, interfere, for the time being at least, with the just application and the rational and appropriate, not to say the sane, use of what is has thus acquired.[136]

'Someone', says Berryman's demented priest, 'interferes/Everywhere with me'.[137] It is important to underline that I am not in any sense suggesting that we 'diagnose' Blake's type of mysticism as psychotic; what is at stake is the way in which mysticism maps itself in language, and the construction of a general frame within which Blake's texts might be viewed. This frame must inevitably include that realm of experience in which the word becomes itself fully materialised in the very act of transcendence, a phenomenon which Blackwood's fable, in retrospect, appears to be about. The interference, the disharmony in the chord, afflicts Blake's figures, Albion himself and his warring members; the tremors in Urizen's webs, Los's sense of loss. For Tharmas, even the most inward visions are betrayed into fragmentation and the pained stretching of nerves, in language very similar to that of Judge Schreber:

With my mind's eye I *see* the rays which are both the carriers of the voices and of the poison of corpses to be unloaded on my body, as long drawn out filaments approaching my head from some vast distant spot on the horizon. I can see them *only* with my mind's eye when my eyes are closed by miracles or when I close them voluntarily, that is to say when they are then reflected on my inner nervous system as long filaments stretching towards my head, sometimes withdrawing from it.[138]

Thus Tharmas:

>   he sunk down into the sea, a pale white corse
> In torment he sunk down & flow'd among her filmy Woof,
> His spectre issuing from his feet in flames of fire.
> In gnawing pain drawn out by her lov'd fingers, every nerve
> She counted, every vein & lacteal, threading them among
> Her woof of terror.[139]

Tharmas's lament is also, of course, an account of narrative: narrative as the dismembering of experience, as the capitulation in a version of time which leaves us extended on the rack and deprived of any authority to own to simultaneity. It is also an account of the work of the Blakean dark female, but again here there is a crucial doubt about agency. Certainly Enion is the victim of at least as much pain and disorientation as Tharmas;

and this is a particular instance of Blake's general narrative difficulty about where to start. A myth of origins seems again essential; but every such myth contributes to the artificial severance of continuity, spreads the mystical moment out to dry on the beach.

Just so in Blake, every act of naming is held in a peculiar provisionality; it is not so much that many figures flow into each other, finding new names as they do so, but that the activity and interplay of the names themselves is primary. We need to see Blake's texts as playing on the reflexivity of words, his emphasis on movement and stasis as itself a problem of language, of describability and the conditions for comunication. In 'The Dark Dialogues', W.S. Graham charts some of this trajectory:

> I speak across the vast
> Dialogues in which we go
> To clench my words against
> Time or the lack of time
> Hoping that for a moment
> They will become for me
> A place I can think in,
> And think anything in,
> An aside from the monstrous.[140]

But the hope is perpetually defeated, deferred; the sense that one can make a 'home' in language, and thus a specular and 'tamed' Other, a domesticated tyger, something for which to be grateful, is always deferred, as the experience recedes. But that deferral, of course, will not make the hope drift away, will not enable the mystical search to be abandoned: always over the frame of the constructed universe, over the clenched body of the constructed and narcissistic subject elbowing for room, there are fictions to be drawn, as covering, as painted backcloth, as the sign of an absence which haunts and hovers:

> This is no other place
> Than where I am, between
> This word and the next
> Maybe I should expect
> To find myself only
> Saying that again
> Here now at the end.
> Yet over the great
> Gantries and cantilevers
> Of love, a sky, real and
> Particular is slowly
> Startled into light.[141]

Here, then, is the difficult work of obliterating the disruption, of making a space within which threat can be comprehended; a version of creativity which is at the always occluded apogee of the romantic trajectory.

PART 4

ROMANTICISM AND THE UNCONSCIOUS

Psychoanalysis and the text

I have tried so far to look at some of the shapings of romanticism from two vantage points: that of the 'outer world', by which I mean to refer to those features of introjection discernible in the texts which appear to be responses to fears engendered by changeful circumstance; and that of the self, the patrolling ego which, in its circuits of its perceived universe – a universe always perceived, naturally, as whole – encounters various vicissitudes which shake it in its narcissistic preconceptions and render its movement visible as it scurries to bury the traces of the unendurable sharer of power.

I propose now to follow up these interpretations by taking the third available vantage-point and examining some of the shapings we can find in the depths. In saying this, I am not directly indicating a move of vantage point *to* the 'unconscious', since it is matters occurring in the unconscious which I have been trying to discuss so far; rather, I am thinking of the actual model of the psyche which we now take as current, and the currency of which shows its roots precisely during the romantic period, and of taking that model as a template for interpretation. Some of the main evidence I shall use here comes from Gothic fiction; and I see no reason to part very far from the conventional interpretations of Gothic as representing a 'darker side', a world of pain and destruction which shadows the daylight love and ethereality of the presented romantic emotions.

I shall also be arguing at this point for a shift of terrain within the available interpretative methods, and shall be in particular using concepts drawn from the British School of Psychoanalysis, and particularly from the work of Melanie Klein. In bringing Gothic fiction together with object-relations psychology, I believe I am not simply practising an arbitrary yoking together of the heterogeneous. Kleinian psychology, as I read it, is a set of mechanisms at the service of the production of accounts of what it might mean to be human. It does not shirk the complexity of the connections between thought and feeling; it does not shrink from owning to the destructiveness which proves so frequently disastrous to the best-intended schemes of political and social progress; it attempts to describe the growth of the individual in ways which assume that from the outset he/she moves and has his/her being in a recognisably constituted social world.

In these respects we need then to adduce Gothic fiction as a set of analysable displacements of the meaning of being human; a series of strainings at the limits of mortality, reason, order. It is as though a concept of humanity under threat generates a terrain in which this threat can be explored and the centres of humanness tested in, as it were, a cultural laboratory. Thus there is an ambivalence in Gothic fiction as it both tests and saves a notion of the human which is inevitably bent into the prior service of a societal status quo.

The narrative and interpretative attempts of Kleinian psychology stand, I would say, in strong contrast to the field of the Lacanians. There are many things one could say about this contrast, and what it itself symbolises as a contemporary cultural divide. There is a question about the nature of the purchase on experience of Lacanian psychoanalysis, and I believe it possible to unearth within Lacanian texts a cerebrality, an abstractness which, even while we see the intelligence of the dealings with structure and form and the value of the insight into levels at which, indeed, the unconscious may operate like a language, appears nonetheless inextricably linked in with an evasion of the real, 'irregular' complexity we find in the best psycho-analytical writing.[1]

This hiatus in Lacanian thought would not, perhaps, matter very much were it not for the fact that, after all, Lacanianism purports to be a variant of psychoanalysis, and if there is one thing of which psychoanalysts should beware it is of the deep psychoses which frequently underlie the excessively high valuation of mind. Sándor Ferenczi, to name but one analyst who writes about this, referred most individual and cultural madnesses to the intense desire for rationality, itself a mask for disgust for the body and for the material world, a disgust which would need much patient historical unravelling.[2]

Lacan, as I see it, is caught in this trap. It is also worth underlining that this syndrome, the syndrome, we might call it, of the disembodied brain, is undoubtedly connected with masculinity; that is not to say that it is exclusively an illness of men, but masculinity, the rejection of the body, and the primacy of impulses of self-destruction and the physical destruction of others are very closely tied together, in this culture at least, and the directly phallic stance of Lacanian thought and writing stands as a further vitiation of its value.

Behind this lies a principal question: what are we doing when we psychoanalyse a text? It needs to be said that we are engaged in a very different enterprise from anything we might practise within a real relationship with other people. According to Freud there are only three ways of recovering and exploring unconscious material. One is through dream; the second is through parapraxes, slips of the tongue, behavioural eccentricities and so forth; and the third, which of course bases itself largely on work with the first two, is in the practice of analysis itself, through the use of the principal tools of free association.

None of these methods for the recovery and exploration of unconscious material is available in the written text.[3] The text may recount dreams, but it does not dream of itself. The nearest equivalents it may have to parapraxes are printing errors; these might indeed be interesting, but are hardly likely to yield a rich crop of meaning. And although we may put questions to the text, we can expect no answers. Indeed, in our interrogations of the text, as we have seen in our quaternary diagrams, the psychoanalytic situation is reversed; it is the text which remains mute, while we, the critics, conduct our more or less impassioned monologues and dialogues across its inert form.

The text itself cannot be analysed, and even if the author can be this will have little relation to the central tasks of criticism. The best we can say is this: that we are making use of psychoanalytical concepts, and maybe also of a psychoanalytical *stance*, as tools with which to elucidate our experience of the text. That may sound imprecise; but the hinge has to be the category of our own experience, because whatever our approach to literature is, it will always be our own experience of the text which is at stake. And, of course, there is no reason to suppose that this experience need be pristine or uninformed; clearly, whenever we approach a text we bring with us all the baggage we have acquired through previous cultural contacts, our knowledge of the language, our various historical senses, our aesthetic formation and so forth.

I say 'to elucidate our experience of the text'; but I would want to add a further point. Psychoanalysis, essentially, is in the business of making interpretations,[4] and it is for this reason that in an attempt at interpretation we may find analytic categories useful. But the status of those interpretations, whether offered or withheld by the analyst, is highly provisional; and, indeed, this may also be the case with literary interpretation. It may be interpretation which is the endpoint of our endeavours; but it is inevitable that in putting forward an interpretation of a text we are simultaneously putting forward an interpretation of ourselves, and also, in most cases, an interpretation of a particular moment of contact between the culture we inhabit and a different one, a moment of contact across the parabola within which whole realms of human experience may be contained.

Psychoanalysis and Gothic

Gothic fiction has been a godsend to psychoanalytically minded critics; and it is not hard to see why this should be so. Gothic fiction deals intensively and to the point of naïvety in symbolism; it does not take much analytic skill to probe the skeletons of *Mysteries of Udolpho* (1794) or the inner significance of the portrait in *The Monk*. One variant or another of described mental abnormality occurs in all the relevant texts; it would take considerable blindness to avoid noticing the diagnoses of insanity which are offered on every page, although that is not at all the same, of course, as taking those diagnoses at their face value.

For all that, there has not been a satisfactory general study of the Gothic from a psychoanalytic viewpoint; these kinds of analysis tend to emerge piecemeal in the general run of Gothic criticism.[5] There are, however, one or two points on which we need to concentrate. First, we need to note the considerable historical continuity between the forms of Gothic fiction and the forms of psychoanalytical writing. Put at its simplest, quite a number of Gothic novels are really structured as case histories. Sheridan LeFanu's *Uncle Silas* (1864) is an astonishing case in point. We might also think particularly of James Hogg's *Confessions of a Justified Sinner* (1824), with its doubled account of what we could crudely refer to as a phenomenon of massive defensive splitting of the psyche; but the structure is also visible in many lesser-known works. In Sophia Lee's *The Recess* (1785), for example, a very early Gothic novel, we are invited to adjudicate as readers between two different diagnostic accounts which in several crucial respects flatly contradict one another.[6]

And this, of course, complicates the business of critical interpretation by appearing to offer us a further strategic alternative. If it is impossible on technical grounds to analyse either the text or the presumed author, either the irrefragable presence or the dominant absence, perhaps after all it may be possible to conjure a patient for our process by analysing the character or characters whose reality we are offered for inspection – and not only from the outside.

We have to be clear that if we do this we are in fact engaging in a further participation in the potentially unlimited flow of fictions which we have earlier designated; which, in itself, may be a perfectly worthwhile activity, but is not to be confused with the analysis of real people. It is significant that even critics alert to this problem, to the fictions of character and the ways in which the very notion of character needs to be deconstructed so that one can see the bundle of codes, categories and markers out of which fictional persons are built, nonetheless seem able to believe that, for the specific purpose of discerning an 'unconscious', we can, in a peculiar double suspension of disbelief, take a 'character' as in some sense real.[7]

There are, of course, other connections. Freud was himself a devotee of just that period and type of German writing, epitomised in Goethe's *Sorrows of Young Werther* (1774), which proved inspirational, if parodically so, to the English Gothic novelists. This is important because, after all, the great German romantics were themselves trying, for the most part, to diagnose a cultural condition, a condition in which, of course, they themselves knowingly participated. It could be said that this kind of writing reached its finest if most opaque flowering in Hegel's *Phenomenology of Spirit* (1807), where the passing sicknesses of civilisation and of the individual psyche are welded together in a single narrative account of a historical condition. The basis of that condition, according to Hegel, can be summarised as 'alienation'; and it is worth noting that among the many meanings of that tortured and tortuous word is its application to conditions of mental dislocation.[8]

In drawing psychoanalytical writing and Gothic fiction together in this way, the principal question which arises concerns the pleasure of the text. Why do we read Gothic novels? Why do we read Freud's case histories? There are some obvious symmetries of reading structure. Of course, in the latter case we may have a genuine professional interest; but in the absence of that, I suggest that the pleasures to be derived are not dissimilar. What we have in the texts are two sets of depictions of psychotic states of mind; the 'dreadful pleasure' evoked by Gothic fiction, whether it be *Mysteries of Udolpho* or *Frankenstein*, is not merely the terror of falling from high precipices or of encountering the fearsome sight of the monster playing Boris Karloff and hurling small children around; it is also the terror that we may be in danger of losing our wits, that the madness exemplified in the text may end up by removing some of our own usual life coordinates and leaving us adrift.

Certainly Coleridge felt that danger as he read through and reviewed some of the early Gothic texts;[9] and yet he was aware, as we need to be, that with this terror there is also a considerable admixture of pleasure, of several kinds: the rather unpleasant pleasure which comes from viewing a character in worse psychological shape than oneself, but also the deeper, and only tangentially regressive, pleasure of being able to peer backwards through our own personal history, because all psychotic states are simply perpetuations of landscapes which we have all inhabited at some stage in our early infancy. Madness is not something peculiar which grows on people; it can more usefully be seen as the radically inappropriate persistence of visions of the world which are perfectly 'natural' in their rightful place and time but which should, by some standard of integrated functioning, have faded long ago from the inner eye.

And obviously, in Freud's texts too we can observe these states and their operations in the world, and measure our experience against these extreme accounts of cultural dislocation. It may be helpful at this point to recall Barthes's term, the 'enigmatic code': the way in which we identify those parts of the text whose primary function is to keep us persisting in our reading by focusing our minds on unanswered questions,[10] upon a certain pattern of hiatus and expectancy, upon a continually postponed hope for a resolution of the uninterpretability of change. The detective story and the thriller are the principal forms in which the preponderance of the enigmatic code as an organising textual principle is high; but it is high too in Gothic, although of a different order.

We may take *Frankenstein* as an example. In the classic detective story, the forms of the organising enigma may be neatly classified. There is the central question of who committed the crime. Often, of course, there is greater secondary elaboration than this: was a crime committed at all? or, will X, who, we know, did not commit the crime, manage to demonstrate his/her innocence? and so on. The enigmatic code in *Frankenstein* is a great deal more open-ended than that, and this may be significant for its curious survival under the unlikely guise of mythic enstellation.

The extraordinary longevity and power of adaptation of this particular text are connected to the double level at which the central enigmatic question operates: the level of character interaction and the level of world-historical consequence. We wonder, of course, and increasingly as the novel continues, what the outcome will be of the burgeoning conflict between Frankenstein and his creation, but we are also brought to wonder what the effects will be on the world in general of a belief in the existence, revelation and public performance of this non-human creature.

And this, I suspect, could be traced through the entire enigma-system of the Gothic. Because it deals in material which exists through its challenge to the boundaries of the 'natural', therefore it is always difficult to see what the implications might be of the outcome of specific action for the world at large. Whether or not Philip Marlow identifies the murderer, the world as a whole will go on in very much the same way as before, a point Raymond Chandler indeed continually sardonically underlines; but if indeed it should prove that the ghosts Emily sees at Udolpho are real, then the impact of that tiny example of the supernatural, of that minute seepage from the uncontrollable world, would radically undermine a great number of metaphysical and political presuppositions, or ways of interpreting under the multiple sign of possessive habitation.

And this version of an enigma-system, with its looped lines implicating our psychic survival in a vindication of a specific view of internal textual events, can be connected with the codes at work in Freud's case histories. If indeed it is the case that people – and, of course, in the emblematic case of Schreber, very important and public, very 'adult' people – are themselves the open recipients and bearers of a version of being human which is not in general accord with our conventional perceptual or linguistic criteria, what does this do for the ordinary consensus on which social life and organisation are based?

Despite claims to the contrary, psychoanalysis has actually been quite shy of moving into the realm of cultural diagnosis. Freud's only significant attempt, *Civilisation and its Discontents* (1930), was a late work and lacks very much detail. The question needs to be put, however, at this level as well as at the others: is psychoanalysis capable of proffering an interpretation which transcends the individual? Of course, in one vital sense analytic interpretation does just and only this, in that the unconscious necessarily overflows the boundaries of the individual; or rather, it is precisely the sum of the signs of that which has always defied perfect containment. It is the unconscious which has a strength of relatedness to the world of flow by which the individual psyche is structured, through the processes of quasi-biological accretion. The more specific point here, though, is whether interpretation can find any purchase on the societal world which constitutes the node of the individual and the universe, the mediation of all relatedness – and which in fact itself structures the relations within which the individual, otherwise lost in Heideggerian 'thrown-ness', literally 'finds' him/herself.

The question of the diagnosis of an age is coterminous with the possibility of diagnosing a literary (or other) genre, considered as a historically bounded set of attempts to structure and explicate feeling. We think naturally of Marcuse, Reich, Brown, the sequence of attempts to characterise capitalism through the use of psychoanalytic experience and conceptual categories.[11] It is, of course, historically obvious that the Gothic coincides with a specific stage of the reorganisation of British society and economy, and that in this respect the demonstrations of historical linkage which we have attempted in connection with romanticism in general should also be applicable here. Yet here we are not talking about anything as simple as that which might pass under the label 'industrialisation'; but rather attempting to capture an experience of changes, the alchemical joyful paradox of a quintessence of transformative process, and particularly a series of glimpses of how the beleaguered narcissistic ego might experience expectancy and change, an experience which would necessarily take the form of a defensive 'dealing with' and managing.[12]

I am assuming, with Freud, that the experience of change is fearful, whatever our position on the time scale. We might then well expect to find a fiction of fear arising at a time when conventional social norms (and I speak here only of the dominant form of awareness in the period itself) were evaporating; but clearly in order to avoid a myth of relative historical stability we need to go farther than this. After all, the emergence of the Gothic is, even by the standards of romanticism, an extraordinary phenomenon; a new, and very large, audience for fiction which had been contentedly reading Fielding and Smollett, with their emphasis on London taverns and country retreats, suddenly chooses to start to read stories set in medieval Italian abbeys and mysterious Spanish courtyards. Why?

Part of the answer presumably lies in the concept of sublimation, in its historical connectedness with the category of the sublime. We may put it like this: that when the prospect of uninvited change, of approaching hiatus or of the approaching need to relive 'at home' a gap already feared as it opened up in the distance, becomes pressing, there arises a need to safeguard the objects in one's internal world; and to contemplate whether they are capable of survival in this soon-to-be-changed scenario. Clearly there is a danger of grandiosity in this more or less desperate attempt; and as with the more recent disaster movie, there may be an associated steady interrogation of those qualities to be sorted as essential or supernumary to the prevailing fantasy of the coming tasks.

In Gothic fiction we see a prolonged contemplation of the objects in the individual's internal world; and at the same time a repeated vindication of the individual's ability to survive (despite) threat. Emily survives; many of the crucial figures in Gothic mythology – the Wandering Jew, the Ancient Mariner – are archetypal survivors, and indeed often their narrative function seems simply to be to evidence the possibility of survival, albeit in a mode displaced from the historical to the transcendental. And, of course, it is not by accident that the notion of narrative suspense goes through such an increase of intensity with the Gothic authors; clearly the conditions of fear, threat and dependency are precisely in the area where suspense becomes a key datum of everyday experience.

Narrative and symbolism: Melanie Klein

The mention of 'internal worlds' suggests a brief excursus into Kleinian theory. The cruxes here are the way in which individuals form internal worlds, and the characterisation of life problems as series of attempts to square the contents of the internal world with the outer world and the ways in which one might from time to time experience it. Klein, it is worth re-emphasising, was a Freudian; her own analysis was carried out by Ferenczi, briefly, and then by Karl Abraham. The crucial questions I want to address now are; what were the differences between her theory and practice and those of the psychoanalytical orthodoxy? and what use might these ideas be when we come to consider literary phenomena – in general, that is, before going on to think about the Gothic?[13]

We can summarise the distinctiveness of Klein's position very briefly. Firstly, her work is distinguished by its attention to infancy and very early mental states. Although it is a simplification, I nonetheless think it fair to say that she rejected Freud's theory of the instincts; she was much more interested in how very early experiences shape the internal world of the child, and in particular in how those experiences may have bearing on patterns of emotion – hate, envy, guilt, reparation – which may continue to reverberate through adult life.

In her attention to the infant, Klein's emphasis was always on the central relation with the mother; in reality and in fantasy, as actual nurturer and also as the fictive precursor of the expected and hoped-for principle of nurturing which conditions much adult response. This reliance on the recollection of experiences of being nurtured tended largely, for Klein, to reveal infantile predispositions which were not gender-based; and thus the gender-differentiated symptomatology of the Freudians disappears, or is diffused, to be replaced by a seeking which is based more on the problems of the (relative) absence of the parent.

She was absorbed, even more than Freud, by the phenomena of the transference and the counter-transference in analysis, and it is not hard to see why. Her belief in the supreme importance of early stages of infancy and her reference of psychological problems to damage caused in these early stages entailed a strong interest in the patterns of early relationship which might be re-enacted in the analytic situation; and clearly the fact that she was a woman underlined the importance of working through feelings about motherhood and nurturing which Freud had to a large extent ignored, or at least relegated by his attention to penis-envy and other gender-specific formative hypotheses.

Klein's interest in early infancy and the transference points to her main clinical work, which was in the sphere of psychotic states of mind; an unusual slant for a psychoanalyst of her time, since the principal criterion for identifying psychosis had been precisely as that order of mental disturbance which analysis could not reach. Finally, Klein did a great deal of work on the inescapability of envy and destructiveness as components of the infant experience which cannot be expunged by later developments and which thus continue to operate within the conventional interchange of relationships and social existence. It is, it seems to me, in terms of this destructiveness and, precisely, its links with envy, a 'dog-in-the-manger' quality, that we can sense the importance of Gothic fiction in its guise as a reservoir of conservative scorn while the world around burns; precisely, again, a refraction through a narcissistic fantasy of omnipotence to the crumbling of the island.

Klein's work is referred to as 'object-relations psychology' because, in her analysis of infant states, she supposes that our earliest experiences are in relation to specific part-objects, and principally the breast; and that, later, children embark on a process of putting these part-objects together as whole objects and thus of conceiving of the totality of the mother and then the father. It is the series of relations between the infant and the part-objects, which is also the relatedness, the specular dialectic between the gazer and the shattered body, and then the whole objects, which is crucial to healthy development. If any of these objects becomes damaged (through introjection of bad feelings, through frustration, or whatever) in the child's internal world, then that will be the basis for disturbance in later life.[14]

It is in the relation between external and internal objects that Klein believes the origin of symbolism to lie. Freud considered that all interest in the 'world' was a displacement from an interest in, or rather, curiosity about, one's own and one's parents' bodies. Klein agrees with that; but she considers that the wish to possess or attack the mother's body is the fundamental epistemophilic relation to the world, and is thus imbued with all the primary processes of guilt and reparation. All external objects are, according to Klein, symbols of the child's and the parents' bodies or parts of them; and the construction of a work of art is in part a symbolic externalisation of the inner world within which these objects exist, and in part an attempt at reparation for the past sins of which the still existing child in the artist frequently considers him/herself to be guilty. Thus works of art frequently contain representations, revisions, reconstructions of damaged internal objects; and symbolism as such is based in a wish to effect some connection between the damage which exists within the inner world and the objects in the world outside which may in some powerful way relate to our not-absent experience of that damage.[15]

Art is the recovery and restoration of damaged and lost internal objects. And this damage occurs at a very early age; for Klein claims that the origin of symbolism, being a displacement, is coterminous with the prevalence of sadism at a particular point of the child's development.

> The child expects to find within the mother (a) the father's penis, (b) excrement, and (c) children, and these things it equates with edible substances. According to the child's earliest phantasies (or 'sexual theories') of parental coitus, the father's penis (or his whole body) becomes incorporated in the mother during the act. Thus the child's sadistic attacks have for their object both father and mother, who are in phantasy bitten, torn, cut or stamped to bits. The attacks give rise to anxiety lest the subject should be punished by the united parents, and this anxiety also becomes internalised in consequence of the oral-sadistic introjection of the objects and is thus already directed towards the early super-ego.
>
> ... it is the anxiety arising in the phase that I have described which sets going the mechanism of identification. Since the child desires to destroy the organs (penis, vagina, breasts) which stand for the objects, he conceives a dread of the latter. This anxiety contributes to make him equate the organs in question with other things; owing to this equation these in their turn become objects of anxiety, and so he is impelled constantly to make other and new equations, which form the basis of his interest in the new objects and of symbolism.
>
> Thus, not only does symbolism come to be the foundation of all phantasy and sublimation but, more than that, it is the basis of the subject's relation to the outside world and to reality in general.[16]

Klein and Gothic

We can move directly from these concepts to Gothic fiction; for instance, to *Castle of Otranto*, and with a certain justice as we approach a work which has so frequently been taken as the 'originator' of the genre, and which so clearly bears the marks of an immersion in and rehabilitation of childhood. It is a text which, very obviously, abounds in part-objects, in separated fragments of the disunited body, which figure in, among other scenarios, the massive and baroque evasion of incest which twists its way through the evolving narrative.

For the second edition of the novel, Walpole added an epigraph: *vanae / fingentur species, tamen ut pes, et caput uni / reddantur formae.*[17] This is a corruption of a text from Horace; the original meaning was: 'Idle fancies shall be shaped [like a sick man's dream] so that neither head nor foot can be assigned to a single shape'. Walpole's version, significantly and, I believe, unconsciously – and playing around the resonances of 'species' – reverses the impact of the text to read that 'nevertheless head and foot are assigned to a single shape'. The reversal is vital, and tells us that, in this new genre of supernatural or improbable fiction, the bits and pieces of the body which we are offered have some grounding in dream and sickness; and also that they need to be taken precisely as symptomatic of damage experienced in the relationships between real people.

Thus in *Castle of Otranto* we are brought, for instance, to an encounter with the enormous casque, or helmet, which is offered to us as a part of the body of a deceased giant who is, of course, the absent ancestor. When our hero, Manfred, first encounters this object, we have this description:

> The first thing, that struck Manfred's eyes, was a group of his servants, endeavouring to raise something, that appeared to him a mountain of sable plumes. He gazed, without believing his sight. 'What are ye doing?' cried Manfred, wrathfully; 'where is my son?' A volley of voices replied, 'Oh! my lord! the prince! the helmet! the helmet!' Shocked with these lamentable sounds, and dreading he knew not what, he advanced hastily; but, what a sight for a father's eyes! he beheld his child dashed to pieces, and almost buried under an enormous helmet, a hundred times more large than any casque ever made for human being, and shaded with a proportionable quantity of black feathers.[18]

Such a passage as this, from one vantage-point, exemplifies the melodramatic quality of the text; and has also been seen as evidencing Walpole's incompetence in the sustained evocation of fear.[19] But there are other things to be said about it. We might well suggest, according to Kleinian theory, that this incidence of an accommodable part-object, and especially in an incident which also recounts the death of the child, relates particularly closely to that problematic stage in which the child has to learn to make the transition from observing his parents as bundles of objects whose relevance to him/herself is defined merely in terms of gratification, and to begin to take note of the ways in which these bundles of more or less gratifying physical objects appear, in disconcerting ways, to possess a level of independence which threatens the child's own apprehension of the purposes of the universe – which, until this stage, have largely consisted of the gratification of the child.

We can thus see that we are back with the major psychic themes of romanticism; with narcissism, and with what theatens narcissism, breaks up its artificial syntheses, and operates to disturb the gratifyingly united picture of the universe which it seeks to create; the ambivalence, in short, of the specular, of the staring down into the pool.

And we can go further. This scene is expressionistically emblematic of the process which Lacan describes as the passing under the name of the father:[20] the dead prince is that child who has been called upon to take on the role of the father – and in this case, with certain associated feudal responsibilities – but has been, rather directly, crushed by them. We could alternatively see here a *jouissance* around the issues of prohibition and transgression. And in Kleinian terms, we can add something further to this interpretation: what we clearly have here is an unhappy, or disastrous, accommodation with the head, or penis – a failure of patriarchal descent which is, in the end, what undermines Manfred himself: and it is this which effects the major connection with the incest theme.

Turning from *Otranto* to *Frankenstein*, we can follow through some of this thinking about part-objects. After all, what is the monster if not an attempt to bring together the parts of the inner world to form a whole which can somehow achieve cogency and validation in the outer realm? We need to remind ourselves of several crucial features of *Frankenstein*. First, Frankenstein's own education, or worldly initiation, is a peculiar one. He says:

> My temper was sometimes violent, and my passions vehement; but by some law in my temperature they were turned, not towards childish pursuits, but to an eager desire to learn, and not to learn all things indiscriminately. I confess that neither the structure of languages, nor the code of governments, nor the politics of various states, possessed attractions for me. It was the secrets of heaven and earth that I desired to learn; and whether it was the outward substance of things, or the inner spirit of nature and the mysterious soul of man that occupied me, still my inquiries were directed to the metaphysical, or, in its highest sense, the physical secrets of the world.[21]

Clearly, those 'physical secrets' are precisely the goal of the 'curiosity' which Freud speaks of as the root of the epistemophilic urge, and thus as the heart of the knot which generates the ambivalence of narcissism's doomed search, wherein the fear of knowledge provides the block on advance, while at the same time acting as the limit of consciousness and thus providing the unsought boundary with the hidden world.

The category in Frankenstein's education which is missing is thus that category which embraces all reality-testing; the category which embraces encounters with the real world in its societal organisation. It is this category which seems to Frankenstein to hold no interest; to supplant it he turns to the two extremes in a symbolic self-crucifixion, to the so-called 'metaphysical' (one of the thieves shall be saved) and to chronic introspection (and one shall be damned), as if thus he could solve some riddle of the construction of his own personality, could purify the base metal and precipitate gold.

The young Frankenstein is thus given to us, the readers, as a name for a syndrome which abandons reality-testing, for one reason or another, and which prefers to work on a direct link between the inner world and untested fantasies of the universe. But this is, of course, a mask for destructiveness: such willed ignorance of the real world reflects also a need to wish it away, a drive towards obliteration, a wish to deal only in the inner world and in the gigantic shadows which that inner world throws on the screen of experience if we choose to ignore the checks and balances of external constraint.

It is thus not surprising that we find Frankenstein describing his creation of the monster in these terms:

> I wished, as it were, to procrastinate all that related to my feelings of affection until the great object, which swallowed up every habit of my nature, should be completed.[22]

This is in the context of a passage where Frankenstein is saying that he wished to suspend every tie of affection with real people, and principally with his family, while he was engaged in his version of creativity. I have no wish to pun on Mary Shelley's use here of the term 'object'; nevertheless what is happening is that we are being offered an account of what might occur when creativity is practised and developed in an arena where the internal world has been fatally damaged. Clearly there is a sense in which Frankenstein's work is reparative, in the sense in which Klein uses the word; a sense in which his effort to construct an object for himself is itself connected with his apprehension of the failure of loved objects in his own life.

It is here that Klein's description of the transition from a world based on part-objects to a world where real relationships can be established, and where one's experiences of the unconditional love of the mother can be continuously transformed into further experiences of loving and being loved that can at least appear to have independent and volitional validity, is useful. Because Frankenstein is stuck with the bits and pieces. It is clear –

Mary Shelley tells us so – that the inner world of the story has become a charnel-house, a place where all that exists are the fragments of the body which cannot be connected together to comprise a meaningful and functioning whole. This is not only so if we fall into the fiction of considering the enterprise from Frankenstein's point of view; the very structure of the novel itself, beginning as it does with the series of letters, reinforces our sense of being in a world where the fragments cannot be made to coalesce.

And thus it is that Frankenstein embarks on his great surrogate activity, a displaced Noah. If the outer world is not experienced as real, if it is perceived as a shadow form in which consequences cannot be produced or expected, then the monstrous truly appears in that one might try to set the internal fragments themselves in some kind of order and expect real life to result. The actual physical fragments from which Frankenstein has assembled his monster are themselves beautiful; and human. Yet what is the outcome:

> How can I describe my emotions at this catastrophe, or how delineate the wretch whom with such infinite pains and care I had endeavoured to form? His limbs were in proportion, and I had selected his features as beautiful. Beautiful! – Great God! His yellow skin scarcely covered the work of muscles and arteries beneath; his hair was of a lustrous black, and flowing; his teeth of a pearly whiteness; but these luxuriances only formed a more horrid contrast with his watery eyes, that seemed almost of the same colour as the dun white sockets in which they were set, his shrivelled complexion and straight black lips.[23]

It has never been easy to get a picture of this monster; certainly little in it suggests the various cinematic representations of the twentieth century. Some parts, certainly, are good, others bad, as one might expect, but it is the disunity of the whole, the inability of these various parts to cohere which is the main source of Frankenstein's dismay, and thus of the endless persecution to which the monster is subjected throughout the rest of the novel.

What we then need to say about *Frankenstein* is that it confronts us with a scenario in which the damaged inner world of which Klein speaks is incarnated; and the result of that incarnation is the imposition of an endless destructiveness, based in mutual envy.[24] Crucially, the monster envies Frankenstein his freedom of action, which is intimately associated with his command of language; what Frankenstein envies in his creation is his apparent ability to give free vent precisely to his destructive and envious impulses. The landscape here is one in which inner and outer worlds have become fatally fragmented, and we can connect the nature of this fragmentation with the phenomena of Gothic in general, with, for instance, the extraordinary paintings of John Martin, where the dislocation between the puniness of the human figures and the grandeur of the destructive landscape is the very incarnation of the landscape scenes we encounter all the time in Radcliffe.

Both *Otranto* and *Frankenstein* confront us with psychotic states. These are the landscapes of childhood, where enormous monsters rush around after us threatening to tear at our vitals, while all the time we suspect that they are of our own making. It is not enough to speak of instinct, rather we are referred back in both cases to the hiatus: to difficulties of parenting, of succession, of the handing down of behavioural patterns within the pseudo-family. For it is the collapse and ineffectiveness of the family which is at stake in these texts, and in almost all the other Gothic novels, with their insistent harping on the state of being an orphan.

It is at this point that the socio-psychological questions begin to re-appear, for we need again to recall that one of the principal experiences of the industrial revolution was of a massive and irremediable dislocation of family life.[25] But there are other related points about Gothic fiction which we can also explore in Kleinian terms. What happens, for instance, in *The Monk*, as in many other Gothic texts, is that there is a total absorption of an object; and this is a phenomenon which Klein describes. In fact, Freud describes it first, defining introjection as the sole condition on which an object may be given up.[26] In other words, it is only by tangling with and absorbing an object that one may be allowed to develop to a further stage in which the external occurrences of that object may appear unnecessary.

Klein adds to this point: 'If the object is introjected in a situation of emotional conflict it is more likely to be introjected into the superego'.[27] In other words, the phenomenon of introjection happens all the time, but if it happens at a time when the psyche is peculiarly vulnerable then one of the possible consequences is that the introjected object may take over one's life, and effectively prevent the possibility of reality-testing. It is these conditions which, according to Klein, produce the main defensive strategies. In other words, when the introjection of the object becomes too intense, phenomena occur within the psyche which may prove unamenable to the usual processes of social restraint. Klein describes these processes under two main headings: projective identification and splitting.[28]

Splitting is only too obvious as the major motor principle of the narrative of *Frankenstein*; projective identification may well be the main process described by the other main Gothic fictions, the intense identification with the hero and heroine despite a lack of any obvious reason for their assumed supremacy. And it would be at that point that one might begin to consider what the fundamental principles are behind the ways in which narrative itself functions: through a process of identifying and destroying centres of consciousness, in other words, through a process of making and destroying projective identifications.

The process of maturation as Klein describes it is the evolution from the paranoid/schizoid position to the manic-depressive position.[29] In other words one moves in infancy, or so it is hoped, from a stance in which every phenomenon of the outer world appears as persecutory and thus threatens one with the splitting or disintegration of the self, to a stance in which one might achieve a reasonable oscillation between feelings of hope and despair. This is, one should add, the best that can be hoped for. I would suggest that Gothic fictions, like so many other romantic phenomena, for the most part deal in interruptions, hiatuses in this maturing process; and that part of the evidence for this has been the succession of critical attempts to explore the categories of the 'explained' and the 'unexplained' supernatural. Presumably the 'explained' supernatural is that experience which proves amenable to the categories one might use in so-called adult life; while that which remains unexplained adheres to the paranoid position.[30] *Northanger Abbey* (1818) and similar tales of recuperation would thus serve as attempts to regain for adulthood what might be essentially the property of childhood, as Austen more or less overtly says.

To add two further points: it is apparent that the hero, so aptly named Wringhim, of *Confessions of a Justified Sinner* is precisely a representation of the mechanism of splitting which takes place, according to Klein, when there have been problems with the figuring in the internal landscape of the mother or the father. Equally, Klein talks about the damage which may ensue from the child's unestablished fantasies about the presence of the father inside the mother; much of the material about Schedoni in Radcliffe's *The Italian* (1797) fits in with this analysis. Why, however, and the question still remains with us, the Gothic? Why then, and why like that? And how can we match this with our wider analyses of romanticism?

The infant, it is plain from Klein's accounts of her own analysis of children, is at all times evolving symbolic systems in order to prevent him/herself from having to experience loss. That resistance to loss may in some extreme cases become a resistance to development or change of any kind, and some psychotic manifestations like autism arise from this syndrome. The issue is the prevention of whole objects, and the fear is that those whole objects, if they were allowed to appear, would reproduce the persecutory valency which the infant has experienced in relation to the breast.[31]

I would suggest that this resistance is at stake in Gothic fiction, and that this may condition the narrative forms with which we find ourselves dealing in the Gothic. The enigmatic codes permit of only two alternatives, explanation or non-explanation; in both cases there is a problem about how to do justice to the unresolved complexities of adult existence. And this has to do precisely with the fears of change which we have been exploring throughout; here is a genre which is peculiarly a set of narratives which emerge in a world where either the questions which narrative might pose are unanswerable, or the answers might be too fearful for the individual mind to hold in the face of social change.

It seems to me that the Kleinian concepts are indeed capable of generating accounts of history, although clearly historical process cannnot be mapped in a one-to-one way onto the development of the psyche. But more importantly, Gothic fiction, because of its overt dealing in symbols, becomes a special case, in two ways. On the one hand, we might say that its expressionism renders its meanings peculiarly available to analytic interpretation. But on the other, one also needs to say that psychoanalysis itself, and especially of the Kleinian kind, can provide us with some clues about why this type of fiction arose when it did: about, in other words, the ways in which external fears are linked in particular ways with attempts to constitute and handle the internal world onto which fiction so often gives access, and about what those linkages might be for Gothic fiction, arising as it does at a time when processes of maturation and shapings for family and nation which had become imbued with an aura of tradition were being visibly threatened by a set of changes the endpoint of which could be seen but dimly if at all.

Emma, Wuthering Heights *and the family romance*

The grand narrative, we might say – the narrative so many of the romantics sought – is the narrative of the family. The metaphorical and the metonymic, condensation and displacement, take their places as steps in the dance, devices through which we seek to render tolerable what would otherwise be an intolerable boundedness, a claustrophobic scenario in which, endlessly, mother says that she told us so, that she had always prefigured this invariably present end. It is against this overweening prefiguration that the urgency arises, the necessity of preventing the formation of an object whose wholeness, far from stopping at the guarantee of nurture, would in the end reduce our attempts at independence to nothing. It is only because of a conventional transmutation of genders under the sign of the fear of the womb that we witness this anxiety about dependence figuring for the romantics rather in a sequence of arguments against God, a sequence which harps upon the obliteration of human-ness endemic to theological systematisations.

The Castle of Otranto, The Cenci (1820), the myriad displaced forms of imprisonment, the narrative of Byron's maniac: here are the limits on a conceptualisation of family which reduces the individual to the status of an outcast. In romanticism the solitary may stand over against familial bonding; yet he/she can also be found *within* the family, the isolated heroine who cannot share the common perceptions of dinner-table or nursery yet who has nowhere to go other than into an internal exile which, by a wonderfully liberating paradox already prefigured in the Richardsonian letter, turns out, like the door to Alice's garden, to open upon a realm of delights which may be summed up in terms of access to a new and non-familial public.

Thus the dialectic of overhearing alluded to by critics: that which is confided is simultaneously broadcast, and the extremes of introspection and public transmission become a dual sign of power which is reckoned capable of eclipsing the too-present sun of the parents. We may thus see romanticism as a squeezing through the keyhole; beyond the confinement lie the broad open spaces, the new unseen readership among whom our words might echo without the inevitability of ricochet. Here seeds can be sown, yet we may not need to encounter the reaping of dragons; still less need we live with the pallid and barbarous reflections of old jealousies which constitute the fouled marriage bed of family. Each Hamlet is free now to speculate upon procrastination without being called to ready account.

Thus romanticism is able to cast itself upon the winds, or upon the waters, without searching deep into the attendant risks. The paradox is everywhere evident, particularly in the shapes of autobiography: the young sage confiding to his diary, or to his college friends, his fears of failure and of, more dreadfully, lack of fame, while below this there surges a confident certainty that this narrative of doubt carries with it an absolute certainty of later celebration. In the diaries of the English and German romantics, we can collect together an unparalleled series of prefigurings of global fame, such that each life appears to be lived under the unmediated sign of the future, a future in which genius will have its day because, in the new market, recognition can be manipulated.

Thus the combined hope and fear of an aristocracy of the emotions: we think of the destructive but energising group relations sessions in London or on the shores of Italian lakes, where the payoff for honesty will come in an arena where the rewards are freed from the mother-string. We throw the image of narcissism on the waters, become lost in the tides of speculation, knowing that the narrative of this loss will be a *lisible* product, will complete, through text, the transmutation of base metal into gold, fluid currency into capital accumulation, fluxile self into immutable record. None of this, of course, is to talk about accreted intention; but it is to point to a rock amid the floods of uncertainty, and also to a recourse against the masses, an assertion of individual value which simultaneously and surreptitiously reintroduces the mass as the quantitatively essential auditorium within which the text will live and move and have its being.

I do not want to write in detail about *Emma* (1816) or *Wuthering Heights* (1847), but to propose them as signs in an imagistic system. On the one hand, the drawing-room, immune from the elements, a place for weather reports; on the other, the windswept reception hall, the site onto which figures are always blown in attitudes redolent of the moor, the crag. Figures dissociated from a landscape, or a landscape encroaching upon the interior; a threatened dissolution, one way or the other, always saved by the re-establishment of boundaries, the dismissal, by various means, of the upwelling which would break down the walls. The house may survive full or empty; contents may differ, even to vanishing point, but the archetype of the *oikos* remains, a guarantee against the encroachment of changing spaces.

Or we may oppose them another way: clarity of family line, accompanied by an extended hierarchical awareness which successfully fits even far-flung attachments into the familial model, or an unintelligibly complex family tree which, however far it is unwound, will always prove to contain more baroque corners, more places behind the arras wherein unimaginable couplings have taken place and are now being recorded in all their plangent and noisy secrecy.

Or we may point up both of these narratives – and well-guardianed settings – as recourses against incest; and still wonder why. Incest figures here as the short-circuiting of narcissism.[32] Narrative, in the interpretation we have been advancing, is essential to narcissism; the pride in system, in speculation, in posing problems which are always-already solved and which therefore successively vindicate the supremacist battles of the ego, works itself out only at length, only through entering and tracing the crevices of the signifier, by proving at every stage the possibility of establishing a new patterning of the universe, through spaces and times.

This entails necessarily a deferred act. Were there no such act, there could not be time, at all; because time here appears only as deferral, as prevention, and thus inextricably as lust. And so family itself is a deferral, a postponement, and one in which fantasies proliferate: if only we were to .... But *if* we were to, then at a stroke we would lose mastery; for such (textual) mastery can be demonstrated only in the spinning out, in the weaving of voices and codes, in the withholding of that knowledge which, if shared, would render narrative a series of silly jokes, silly because they are old and because their punchlines have already been available to us, time and time again.

Emma and Catherine know their doom, their promise; that which is unknown is the category of vicissitude, the identity of adjuvants, the endless paraphernalia of postponement. There is nothing new in this, except that everything is new: the precise shapes of house and land which now appear as containers for desire, the intrusion of passion into the drawing-room, the invasion of the peaceful (if windy) moor by human and familial hierarchies and jealousies. A double invasion, which is self-cancelling: even as passion is to be known, it is subordinated to the tie of the supremely ordered past, for otherwise we should – as usual – risk revolution.

For the narcissistic ego, everything is a challenge, a territory to be mastered and to be added to the empire. There can be no stasis, no absence of the westerly wind, for stasis figures as a lockedness into a pattern of relationships which exists only as a pretext to be transcended. Thanatos cannot be faced because it resists incorporation; easier to turn that desire for incorporation inward and, at a level lower than that of overt gender, to construct fables of the suppression of the feminine, because impotence is the doom to be feared and to be re-presented as the consequence of incest, of abandoning the familial convention.

Everywhere, of course, the pace of the closing down of nature is accelerating; and the high revaluation of the open spaces accompanies enclosure in all its historical and psychic ramifications.[33] Berryman's 'violent and formal dancers' are habilitated in Highbury, but are no less present in the rushing to and fro on the blasted heath. The whipping on of action is compulsory, compulsive, the stirrings of dead leaves the witches' portents which will bring us to life and potency once more, will remove or allay our fear of being the passive outcroppings of a deeper life which can be known only in a more than specular recognition.

Shelley

The 'Ode to the West Wind' (1819) is a poem about power and impotence, and finds the poet inspecting a set of fantasied relationships with an imaginary source. That source, the invisible 'breath of Autumn's being', is the wind, and is at the start and end of all things, 'destroyer and preserver'; it bespeaks the romantic dilemma of transience, the paradox whereby only change is permanently known. Abstract continuance pertains only to precisely those qualities of flow which ask the poet a ceaseless question about his own ownership of his self.

> If I were a dead leaf thou mightest bear;
> If I were a swift cloud to fly with thee;
> A wave to pant beneath thy power, and share
>
> The impulse of thy strength, only less free
> Than thou, O uncontrollable! If even
> I were as in my boyhood, and could be
>
> The comrade of thy wanderings over Heaven,
> As then, when to outstrip thy skiey speed
> Scarce seemed a vision . . .[34]

Here we have a sequencing of hypothetical relationships, which we may enumerate. The first is that of the leaf to the wind, and is imbued with a characteristic doubleness centred on the term 'bear': the leaf is 'borne' by the wind, in a relaxation into complete passivity, but is at the same time the offspring of that wind (and, of course, this set of stanzas is fixed within a rememoration of childhood).

In the relationship of cloud to wind, we have a movement forward, perhaps into adolescence; at any rate into a sharing of power, such that the cloud may at least appear to have volition, may appear to possess some freedom in the confrontation between that which moves and that which is moved. But the oscillation between power and impotence rapidly becomes more complex than this, when we come to the image of the wave: the powerlessness of the 'panting beneath' veering into the sharing of 'the impulse of thy strength', as though this is a power which can be somehow donned; or gained by a process of osmosis or infection.

And here again, it seems, we touch upon the father, and the difficulty of taking up a power which one may regard as a false inheritance, a structure of surmounting a felt gap in the immediate past which, as we are coming to see, is crucial to romanticism. It is as though the effort is to shoulder a space in a world which is already filled by the massive forms of patriarchal power; and indeed, the series of strong mythic images centred around the 'pumice isle in Baiae's bay' may in their very rebarbativeness stand in for this whole weight of past tradition which excites, obviously, a mixture of fear and reverence, but, more than that, carries a weight of envy.

This becomes apparent in the next image, the 'comrade of thy wanderings', which moves from this attempt at equality and fraternity into the competitive imagery of 'outstripping' the wind's speed. This change of imagistic stream is underlined in its uncertainties by the curious structure of 'scarce seemed a vision', which leaves the reader unclear about the reality being talked about, just as, in fact, the adolescent here is sharing an experience of uncertainty about his relative power.

The dialectic is one of freedom and constraint; and there is a difficulty in severing this dialectic, with its essential emphases on maturation, from the fantasies of omnipotence which we here encounter again. And, as we have seen before, such fantasies inevitably slide into a depression centred upon the loss of an ego which has placed its hopes in a purely imaginary transcendence:

> I would ne'er have striven

> As thus with thee in prayer in my sore need.
> Oh, lift me as a wave, a leaf, a cloud!
> I fall upon the thorns of life! I bleed!

> A heavy weight of hours has chained and bowed
> One too like thee: tameless, and swift, and proud.[35]

One of the things happening here is a taking on of age, an assumption of past years which in the context can seem merely presumptuous. But then, there is really no alternative: if the self can survive only by constructing fictions of absolute freedom, then it cannot pass through the mazes which truly lead to maturity, but must instead seize wisdom, as it were, all at once, in a movement which attains to age without labour and naturally tends towards a febrile exhaustion.

The 'striving' is offered to us, but is not substantiated; indeed, one could say that the real striving which is at stake in Shelley's work is, as it were, a 'striving to strive', a strenuous wish to be engaged strenously, whereas there is always a pressure away from this engagement and up, indeed in Blackwood's terms, to the skies, into an orbit related to that orbit we have come across before in terms of the human chord, wherefrom few distinctions can be sustained.

It is not difficult to see this as poetry of the untrammelled narcissistic ego, a poetry in which, while worldly power has to be seen as evil and restrictive, nonetheless the psychic root of that societal 'striving' cannot be excised; nor indeed can any desire for its excision be conjured. Instead, what we have is a movement towards the pure specular relationship, within which there are no boundaries between self and world and consequently no limitations on the ego's claims to self-motivation:

> Make me thy lyre, even as the forest is:
> What if my leaves are falling like its own!
> The tumult of thy mighty harmonies
>
> Will take from both a deep, autumnal tone,
> Sweet though in sadness. Be thou, Spirit fierce,
> My spirit! Be thou me, impetuous one![36]

The movement through the ambiguities of 'both' to 'be thou me' effectively obliterates the painful divide between desire and achievement, as Narcissus stares down into the pool and perceives an alternate self which is not merely identical in every physical respect, but which has also the added gift of being freed from the experience of pain. If one can make the journey between the two selves, then one can prove the inauthenticity of the unconscious (all one finds is a further reticulation of ego); but one can also partake of the condition of the gods, while watching the agony of the world being showered liberally on the self which has been left behind.

What this is is a masculine self-birthing fantasy, which reverses the orders of pain and fulfilment and reminds us once more of *Frankenstein*. So by the time we come to Shelley's wishes for the future, it is not clear whether any distinction remains between the apparent persons of his discourse:

> Drive my dead thoughts over the universe
> Like withered leaves to quicken a new birth!
> And, by the incantation of this verse,
>
> Scatter, as from an unextinguished hearth
> Ashes and sparks, my words among mankind!
> Be through my lips to unawakened earth
>
> The trumpet of a prophecy! O, Wind,
> If Winter comes, can Spring be far behind?[27]

The 'new-ness' of this birth relates back to the fantasies surrounding revolution, the desire for a total obliteration of origins, and thus the hope for the removal of that fear which cannot be eradicated simply by fantasising the womb away. That hearth may indeed remain 'unextinguished', but it nonetheless figures as a place from which to escape, a reminder of claustrophobia which has to be left behind even on pain of death.

Yet the process of wakening also goes through a curious reversal; for this 'unawakened earth' is surely also Blake's sleeping womb, which awaits the ministrations of the male in the guise of both prophet and fulfilment. Shelley is here his own John the Baptist, as the instrument becomes the message, the prefiguration becomes the achievement. Thus the seasons do not merely anticipate each other; rather, they collapse in on themselves, since time itself has to be negated in order to complete the forgetting of priority which is essential to masculine fantasies of birthlessness.

We are thus confronted, throughout the poem, with a chthonic vision, from 'the wingèd seeds, where they lie cold and low' to the 'blue Mediterranean' being 'wakened' from 'where he lay,/Lulled by the coil of his crystàlline streams'. But the attitude towards this earth-birth is double. The power which may seep into the nervous system through this proximity of attachment may also stand as a sign for the impossibility of escape from bonding; and this double-bind returns us precisely to the condition of the adolescent, a coming to terms with the many forms of dependency and the ever-present threat of a retreat into a narcissism of style as a vindication of the hypothesised impossibility of coming into one's very own and golden kingdom, the 'old palaces and towers/Quivering within the wave's intenser day'.

Repetition compulsion and the search for wisdom: the wanderer

I want to suggest now a romantic scene, which is a room, quite probably a bedroom, or at least bearing some alternative taint of mortal sickness. The furnishings have a customary heaviness: this is Wells's red room again, or the room where an unnamed Frenchman, pregnant with unannounced discovery, is to disclose a doubt about the necessity of breath.[38] There are plush wall-hangings; and on small and ornate tables, themselves the products of some long-past crusade, stand one or two of the effigies of alchemy.

There is, then, despair in the room. There is also stasis, feasibly the stasis of procrastination: a room, this is, out of which the inhabitant has started many and many a time, without achieving his ends. Here he remains immured, and ponders upon guilts: guilts past and familial, guilts present and to do with a failure of nerve, possibly artificially induced, and guilts future, a feared erosion of the possibility of action.

In terms of the protagonist, we have a small repertoire to choose from within the tradition, although no two of them can coexist in this room. There is the high-domed philanthropist, worn down by ennui and anxious about the vanishing of his martyred feelings. He is haunted by hopes: hopes vested in himself by long-dead relatives and mentors, and hopes that he has himself vested in the rest of mankind. Their refusal to live up to the necessities of his expectation, which are the necessities of a transcendental myth, plunges him into a particular hell.

There is the character of mastery, for whom these small tables hold no secrets (though they secrete no gold), who has been dabbling in these codes of life and death to a point of jadedness, and who now expects to see nothing further along the arc of manifestation. He may even have familiars who inhabit the blackened spaces of the room, the untranslateable and burned corners of the palimpsest, from whose yellowing pages issues a whiff of brimstone. Or there is the (comparatively) innocent hero of alternative romantic dreams, the youth of dashing good looks, a quiff of unruly hair falling over his blazing eyes and over-scarlet cheeks, dissatisfied with human lives and loves, inventing forms for a different future, a difference which will produce transcendence itself as the response to ennui and for whom all these alchemical games are played in the awaiting of a more carnal consummation (which is thereby not a whit less symbolic), the site of an irrefragable ambivalence.

Probably there are one or two more; but now the scene comes to life. Our protagonist throws himself back in his chair, in an agony of remorse or despair; or remorse about despair. There is nothing left, nothing to be done. The drapes are thus conjoined in a doubled refusal: this is a place which cannot be invaded, but similarly these closed and incense-ridden curtains permit no alarums and excursions, there is no point of impingement which could relativise this moment of loss, of indulgence, of sweating forehead and mind fragmented on the very cusp of totalisation.

The curtains blow aside, and there he stands – we have many pictures of this moment from the penny dreadfuls, from illustrators of Ann Radcliffe and others, from later illustrators of the *1000 Best Ghost Stories*. He is tall and pale, and robed, and he quivers in the throes of some unimaginable tempest. His physical presence is filled with signs; it is, indeed, coterminous with the notion of the sign, this new and archaic creature brings with him the category 'sign' to impose on loss (to impose a rereading of loss).

This imposition of sign is re-echoed in his physical stance, the arrangement of, for instance, his arms and fingers. He points, yet he clutches his seething breast; he indicates an unanticipated future, and he recollects the unremembered past. His position is the very acme of frozen movement. He is passing through, but motionless; he incarnates the *gestus*, the forgotten realisation of 'being towards'.[39] Our hero he reminds of – everything.

Partly because he is, indeed, an extension of our hero; he may, for instance, resemble him, as Christopher Lee can come to resemble Peter Cushing. Or he may even replace him in our readerly appetites – when we thought we had the place of the tall, dark stranger adequately filled, here comes the sign of excess, a stranger even taller, even darker, even more available to symbolic interpretation.

Let us return to his signs, for they are the stigmata. This may be literally so: he may display his scarred hands. But it may be more that he brings with him a whiff of the flame, the possibility of a narrative of previous scarring which will parallel and offset the newly and suddenly febrile narratives of our hero. His experience is – already – obviously greater; he is ageless, yet he carries with him something of the gusto – to use Hazlitt's term – of our hero's vanished (or denied) youth.[40]

As yet, he does not speak. The place from which he has come does not deal (primarily) in words, and there is the chance that his voice has grown rusty from disuse. In this supposition – bound, as it were, in the resounding Miltonic depths of it – he immediately renders the endless and futile ratiocination of our hero a thing of the 'superficies': the possibility immediately becomes available to us that all this soul-searching, all these student years, all this patient training of the indissoluble mind and heart, may have simply been reticulations of a 'verbal way' which, decisively, does not lead to God.

For indeed, this may *be* God; or it may be the devil. Speech would probably confirm us in one of our directednesses; but before speaking, he sighs, and thus we are introduced to a new dimension. This homeless spirit is not a harbinger of certainty, either for good or for evil; he comes rather to remind us of the grandeur of doubt. Similarly, he does not bring with him a simple mastery, but a supplementary mastery which resides only in the interstices of victimisation, his credentials for which he proceeds to recount to us.

In part, of course, he comes, this wanderer, to bring us fresh and convincing evidence. God is indeed unjust, he claims: he has condemned me to a lifetime of wandering, for some venal sin, and there is no appeal against his rigid justice.[41] Thus our hero may come to understand in a different dimension the pains he believes himself to be going through, may come to see them as steps to an understanding of the diverse purposes of God.

But the speech of the wanderer is always double. For behind this apparent assertion of a type of justice lies an intensification of a primal cry, the cry which is simultaneously for and against vengeance; he thus equally brings us closer to an understanding of God, and repels us from the substance which that understanding discloses. And the site of this ambivalence is marked by a question: why have I been subjected to this fate? But for the expected answer, the evidence is always inadequate.

This summary makes it sound as though it is the wanderer who is the supplicant, moving through time and space searching for answers, unguents, balm. And of course this is right: the wanderer cannot *answer* our hero's questions, however long a lifetime may have lain behind their asking, but what he can do is supplant them by greater ones of his own devising. The question then for us as readers becomes: what is the relatedness between these new supernal questions and the mundane problems of despair and ennui; in what area of ourselves resides the wanderer? Thus for the hero, the wanderer comes as a supersession: but always and only as a *temporary* supersession, for what has appeared here tonight, drawing aside these red plush curtains, may appear in any number of similar rooms. Thus, again, is there wisdom here? And if so, what relation has it to internal wisdom, what external, historicised 'differance' may we apprehend here – does the lesson preached at us by the wanderer demonstrate any sign of an enviable burgeoning of experience?

Our answer to that will depend on our apprehension of the nature of repetition, and here we are plunged from one romantic motif to another, ably summarised in Hegel's adaptations of Vico's notion of *ricorso*.[42] 'Could we have our time again', is the ambiguous phrase which swims into view, both plea and prelude. What kind of experience is available on the spiral?

The essential feature of the spiral, and the reason why it is used as a seating form in the context of the experiential analysis of group dynamics, is that it encapsulates within itself a set of questions about origin and destination. It may be seen, by individuals in their places, as folding inwards or outwards; as in movement or in stasis; and, even more significantly, as arranged in concentric circles (which it is not).[43] The spiral can thus be used experientially to demonstrate a lust for circular order, the seven circles of hell, as it may be, or circles of knowledge where access and denial are easily assimilated to notions of hierarchy, thus providing evidence for the basic correlations of knowledge and power. And, if we transpose this spatial figure back into the temporal (whence, of course, in the guise of the wanderer, it came), we begin to see the meaning of the various historicist dialectics of romanticism – not as 'accounts of history' but, precisely, as sites for, arrangements towards, interpretation. The event thus gains its meaning from structure, as we know; but here from the peculiar structure of apparent structurelessness, the trajectory, the orbit, the originless unfolding of the cometary path with its false regularities and millenial connotations. And the comet – the meteor, as the romantics knew it – is the exile, the wanderer par excellence, the visitor in the face of which we shall have to make up our minds, live, if for but a little while, with the predication of our deaths.

But now we can see the relation between hero and wanderer under a different guise: for here we have the ambivalent forms of dependence, a dependence between the static and the temporary, but with this relationship itself crossed. Which is the static: the form of the heroic but stuck consciousness, or the endless unconscious *ricorso* of the wanderer who cannot escape his destiny? Which is the temporary: the unrepeatable (to the individual) manifestation of this same wanderer, or the tiny life of the hero, destined to be swamped as soon as the candle is blown out in this red, red room; which now, of course, stands revealed as the womb, which is the only site in which these questions about origin and destination, temporality and permanence, can be asked?

Dealings with the uncomprehended: the ancient mariner

The question posited by the wanderer is nothing less than: what is the true account of the universe? And this can be rendered as a point of judgement about metaphor and metonymy – whether it is the depths or the linear chains which have any kind of predominance. Where does the learning come: through the embellishment of chains or through submission to fate and the still, small voices which may, if we are lucky, result from such submission?

And thus we might ask, for instance, what is the true account of 'The Rime of the Ancient Mariner' (1797) (in the senses both of the true account it gives of the universe, and also of the true account we might accede to of the poem itself; but these two questions are one). The 'Argument' of the poem reads thus:

> How a Ship having passed the Line was driven by storms to the cold Country towards the South Pole; and how from thence she made her course to the tropical Latitude of the Great Pacific Ocean; and of the strange things that befell; and in what manner the Ancyent Marinere came back to his own Country.[44]

This is not, it seems fair to say, the précis that most of us would offer of the poem; so it seems reasonable to ask what kind of an *account of an account* this is. It is, of course, a 'naturalising' account in several different senses. It produces a certain kind of harmony with contiguous forms of writing – with the travel book principally – and at the same time it relegates the 'strange things', the marvels, to the last sentence – and thus, perhaps, to the status of an optional extra, if we cannot find that within our reason which will render this content innocuous.

And yet we stick on certain features of this 'argument'. The importance, for instance, of precise geography: the 'Line', the 'South Pole', the 'tropical Latitude'. The globe on which these marvels will occur is precisely demarcated, it is already the site of Urizenic webs and grids. And thus, of course, the passing of the line, as celebrated in naval ritual, attains to another symbolic potential.

For the line which is crossed is obviously – the argument says so – a line between passivity and agency; yet, of course, this signification is crossed, since it is absence of agency which drives the ship to this irremediable action, and the gift which is conferred in this underworld is not the gift of forgetting, the offering of Lethe, but the reverse: the renewal of agency – or, we might say, a new getting in touch with potency. This repotentiation, we may note, has very little if anything to do with the mariner himself, who up to this point has not been sensed as a protagonist in the narrative; which raises questions about the function of the 'of' in the title of the poem, and in particular about the importance of the reading as 'sung by' (the ancient mariner), which fundamentally affects the relations between individualism and community in the poem.[45]

We have thus here a myth of resurrection, of being reborn from the dark encounter, and, probably even more importantly, a homecoming, although, as we reach the end of the poem itself, we become aware of how flimsy that homecoming is. But then, we already have here two 'countries' counterposed, the 'cold Country' and 'his own Country'. If this is a journey of initiation, then the first encounter which originates the action is held to be with the cold and distant, the unresponsive. And perhaps this in part accounts for the mariner's plight later on; that his awakening (into maturation), his coming to awareness, has indeed been on a version of the 'cold hill side', and thus it is that this awakening is to a world without true reciprocity, a world burdened by human incomprehension and by divine malfeasance. For it cannot be doubted that this 'lesson of the master' is, in the end, sterile:[46] the world of the ancient mariner is one in which the link between development and interpretation has been severed, or rather, it is that world in which such a link has never intrinsically existed, such that when it does occur, as in the blessing of the water snakes, there is no choice but to take it as a sign of grace.

Sterility and grace thus become the 'poles' between which the mariner – as, among other things, a figure of patriarchal consciousness – is said to move. Here the sterility would be the recognition of abandonment (apparently by God, but more probably, through the gender cross, by women), and the grace would thus be required as a re-acceptance into the human community of that part of the species which has no irreplaceable part to play in the reproductive cycle.

That cycle, we are here told, has four parts: coldness and warmth, strangeness and return. In some sense, of course, they recapitulate each other in the Hegelian sense, the coldness being caught up in the strangeness (figured jointly as a point of stasis), the warmth looking towards the return (and thus encompassing the possibility of movement). Yet here again we come across the problems of linear and circular accounts.

The potential for linearity is clearly demolished in the very first stanza of the poem, wherein we become aware of a multiplicity of fictions which subvert the clarity of ballad narrative. There are several examples in this stanza, but, to take only one, the business of 'one of three', in its very underlining of the trinitarian assumptions of the poem, thus also sets up a small variety of narrative versions for us. We are ostensibly given only one, but this clearly does not in itself disprove the existence of other versions, unrecorded and even non-verbal as they might be.

Thus in the background, through the keening of the wind in the sheets, we hear other voices, even as we hear other imagined responses; and as readers we are inserted into an endless proportionate series, which is at the same time an outcropping of randomness: 'Now wherefore stopp'st thou me?' This cycle, then, may be stopped at any point: the quaternary becomes the trinity, which can only happen through the obliteration of one of its parts. According to Jung, this abolished 'fourth part' would necessarily numerologically be a female part; and here we begin to glimpse what is under erasure in the 'Rime'.[47]

For there is, of course, a wedding in the offing, and thus a bride, but the consummation of this wedding will be endlessly postponed while this repeating account is given. As in *Dracula* (1897), an eve-of-wedding fantasy, with all its regalia of ambivalence and fear, becomes cited as the 'origin' of narrative.[48] It is on, indeed, such a night as this, a night whose business is with the affections and the flesh, that the voice of narrative as deferred gratification, as the will of Scheherezade, will be raised, to the drowning of other voices, as the other representatives of 'mere' humanity are drowned on the flood of the symbolic, the luminous ocean.

Thus recapitulation, *ricorso*, enters into its proper place as the great alternate to reproduction: the making of the same and the making of difference become the structural subplot which underpins the detail of the narrative. And what we are told is that the effect of narrative is not a raising to consciousness, but a submersion; first in story itself, and then in the sense we are given at the end of the poem: 'He went like one that hath been stunned,/And is of sense forlorn'.

The overarching fiction, of course, is of the otherness of the mariner and the guest, with all its connotations of locked stasis and passing: which ship, indeed, passes which in the night, what wandering star produces, by a process of 'differance', its pole star, and by what fixed geography are we to reckon the randomness of the attack of story. This represents the attack on children by story (the coming of reading skills); and thus the displaced attacks on the parents which, Klein tells us, provide the motor force for the elaboration of symbolism,[49] and the attack which is of the heart, which is representative of the chronic intrusion of the inexplicable and uncontrollable into the orderly form re-presented itself by the archaism and fixed enstellation of the ballad.

It is at the point at which the ship crosses the line that the wedding guest, the unwilling auditor, hears a quite different sound, the 'loud bassoon' which reminds him unavailingly of the realm of the real: but already by this time the power of the symbolic code has mastery. There is a battle being fought; but it is being fought by somnambulists, the mariner aware only by a process of continuous recall of the originating events of his catastrophe, the guest 'spellbound' and in thrall to the narrative – of himself – which he finds spilling from the lips of the stranger.

It is a battle which has resonances for us: for it centres again on the question of the ego's maintenance of its defences, but now with an added twist. How far does the ego have to dip into the reserves of the unconscious in order to provide itself with the stock of tales which will protect it from dissolution? And here we begin to sense an unnerving paradox: that the chest of available riches in which the ego habitually deals, the fruits of the mind, may indeed be a *trompe l'oeil* trunk, with a false base which opens onto who knows where. Perhaps all this finery of speculation, all this pride of intellect, is itself merely the almost ejected coinage of the id, with which it wishes – or needs – to have no further dealings.

If this were so, then indeed the notion of justice would finally be revealed as a mere efflorescence of decay; and, by the same token, the historical notion of a new dispensation would stand revealed as a mere effect of unaccommodated desire, which at the interpretative level might well occasion a descent into the abyss, a resignation to the restrictive interpretation of *ricorso* which, in itself, may be bound to avoid the trajectory and the stars and lead back into a conservatism, that conservatism characteristic of Coleridge's later years.

Amontillado

We may attempt to pursue this trajectory further in the works of Poe, the master and self-conscious narcissist whose speculations on the quasi-scientific also place him on the edge of precisely the dual realms of knowing that we are discussing. Reading through his tales remains a peculiar experience. In some ways, of course, they can readily be seen to be by the same hand. There are the continuing and, indeed, at times irritatingly repetitive preoccupations, ranging from premature burial at the 'Gothic' end of the spectrum to the fascination with specific technological developments – the balloon, mesmerism, various types of medical progress. These are most clearly linked through the primary motif which asserts that technological development is that which forces us to forget, to consign to oblivion those inconvenient parts of life which are not reducible to reason or habit.

There are also similarities of form caused largely by the actual production circumstances: it is not entirely a joke, for instance, when Poe asserts in 'How to Write a Blackwood Article' (1838) that no story can be published in *Blackwood's* unless it contains at least one erudite quotation from the classics, even if on occasion it is not entirely to the point.[50] Indeed, in Poe an awareness of interlocking discourses which carry their own signification prior to the inscription of specific and local meaning reaches an extreme point.

And yet it is the significant differences which attract our attention. Across the whole corpus, there are only a few tales which appear to muster the writer's entire concentration. They are often the shortest; they are often marked out by not beginning with the 'naturalising' preambles which figure in so many of the texts. They are, by and large, the tales which are well-known: pre-eminently, perhaps, *The Cask of Amontillado* (1846), *The Fall of the House of Usher* (1839), *The Masque of the Red Death* (1842), *The Pit and Pendulum* (1842), *Ligeia* (1838), *The Tell-Tale Heart* (1843) and a few others – *MS. Found in a Bottle* (1833), certainly, with its extraordinary image of the great ship of death, and *The Man of the Crowd* (1840), which still remains an originating image of urban alienation.

The oddest thing about this group of stories and, in a way, the guarantee of their quality and their access to the cultural unconscious, is the remarkable sense of *déjà vu* which attends them. They are stories, of course, which have sunk deep into the unconscious of the West; but it would be a one-sided judgement which left it at that without adding that, therefore, they must be reworkings of psychological materials which were already foci of interest and disturbance, materials, I would say, at the heart of the romantic project.

And this cannot be divorced from a question of style: it is often in these stories that Poe moves directly into an incantatory mode which dissolves historical location and immediately encourages the reader to see them as parables of a continuous present rather than simply as accounts of events which can be designated as past – and here, of course, we come upon the peculiar mode of temporal life of the unconscious. The stories are themselves – or appear to be – acts of rememoration, usually without a salving grace; these are events on which the mind cannot cease to play, and their only solution or resolution is death.

What needs, then, to be described is a difference of intensity: it is only on rare occasions that this full intensity can be brought to bear. It is brought to bear in a different way in the 'detective' stories, such as *The Murders in the Rue Morge* (1841) and *The Mystery of Marie Rogêt* (1842–3), but here in the service of a quite different structuring, which is dialectically related to the first. That is to say, there is an obvious connection between the emphasis on problem-solving rational power, personated in Auguste Dupin – a power which itself, by a paradoxical process, takes on the contours of the supernatural – and the fears of the dark, of entombment, of collapse and decay with which the name of Poe has come to be exclusively associated.

The detective stories are predicated on an 'if only': if only the human reasoning capacity could indeed be made as strong as this, be freed from its damaging obsessions and addictions, then our fears and terrors would disappear and we would be fully at home in a world which, alas, persists in presenting itself to us under the guise of mystery, the incomprehensible, the shiver of doubt. If we could exile the unconscious, erase memory, then we could come into our own and golden city.

The Cask of Amontillado is a particularly fascinating tale in this respect, because it unites, or attempts to unite, the universe of terror and the universe of order. Montresor's revenge, *outré* as it is, is nonetheless predicated on the basis of close and attentive planning. He has a distinct and amused eye for detail, on which he prides himself; there is an inseparability of madness and method, alluded to again in a more whimsical vein in *The System of Doctor Tarr and Professor Fether* (1845), in which the lunatics actually do take over the asylum, although their winning attempts to build a substitute order are fraught with difficulty since at any moment one of them is likely to remember that, at heart, he is a frog or a tee-totum.

The most pleasing twist to *Tarr and Fether* is that, when all is revealed and the lunatics show themselves in their true colours, there remains a puzzle about Maillard, the apparent director. He, clearly, is a lunatic, and the one who has managed to impose his version of tainted order on his fellow-inmates: but he is also, it transpires, the real Maillard, who was indeed the director of the asylum until he 'lost his wits' and was himself incarcerated. The result of his incarceration was that he formed the opinion that he was, really, the best man to run the show; and at first glance it is not easy to say whether his conviction, classified as insane or not, has been proved wrong.

Returning to *The Cask of Amontillado*, we again find Poe overturning a world, but less in terms of the ever-ambiguous structures of madness than in terms of discourse. We need firstly to note that the whole story is an elaborate structure of puns. There are, obviously, the names : 'Montresor' and 'Fortunato'. There is the moment when, already within the damp cellars, Fortunato coughs and Montresor feigns solicitude for his health. 'I shall not', observes Fortunato, 'die of a cough'. 'True – true', responds Montresor.[51]

There is the visual pun of the arms of the Montresor family (arms into which we hope we shall not fall): 'a huge human foot d'or, in a field azure; the foot crushes a serpent rampant whose fangs are imbedded in the heel'. 'And the motto?' inquires Fortunato: '*Nemo me impune lacessit*', comes the reply. To classify this as a pun, of course, is to call upon the Freudian theory of the joke, as a socio-linguistic interplay involving three positions: the teller, the hearer who understands and the hearer who does not.[52]

Not all of these positions need to be occupied at the level of the Real: but unless there is, at least implicitly, a duality of reception postures there is no psychic release, no laughter – and, of course, no reinforcement of the bond thus formed between teller and understanding hearer, a bond which may well be the principal social effect of jokes. Here, of course, Montresor and the reader (and, at a different level of narrative structure, the narrator and the reader) are ranged against Fortunato, although this does not preclude the psychic countermove whereby we rebel against the position of conspirator in which we thus find ourselves.

Behind the puns – and the most elaborate is the play on 'masonry' which continues throughout, as brotherhood but simultaneously as the culmination of a murderous vengeance – lies something else. Fortunato's death is offered to us in the guise of a progressive relocation of meaning. At the beginning of the tale, he is drunk, and thus not well equipped to follow the intricacies of Montresor's word-play. He is duped, certainly, into a belief in a false version of power; it is intrinsic to Montresor's plan that Fortunato must be the one eager to visit the vaults, and thus that, at the level of discourse, the desire is clothed in the victim's words and not in Montresor's. Fortunato's cough prefigures his descent into speechlessness, as does his apparent inability to derive meaning from the Latin motto.

In this context, the moment when Fortunato makes a masonic ritual gesture figures as an attempt to fight back, to impose a meaning on Montresor; but Montresor counters by producing the trowel, thus simultaneously regaining semiotic power and relegating Fortunato's universe of discourse to the ineffectually symbolic. Behind all this, there is also the shifting meaning of the world 'Amontillado', which Fortunato can only interpret literally, whereas Montresor progressively translates it into the indeterminate source-word, the primal sound, converts it into an artificial imitation 'shifter'.

When Fortunato is first chained within the recess which will become his tomb, for instance: '"The Amontillado!' ejaculated my friend, not yet recovered from his astonishment'. 'True', replies Montresor, 'the Amontillado': but by this time it has become clear that the Amontillado stands, for Montresor, for the consummation of his desire, his vengeance decked out in a quite different sign of which he and he alone is the custodian. It is after this point that Fortunato is reduced to non-linguistic communication – a 'low moaning cry', followed by 'furious vibrations of the chain', the chain of meanings, and then 'a succession of loud and shrill screams'.

When these prove of no avail, Fortunato's final resort is to attempt to unravel the discursive trickery which has been the means of his downfall: it is, he asserts, all a joke, and in this he is absolutely right. But the joke is indeed a structure of power, and it is this precisely because it patrols the open gateway to the unconscious. This is finally reinforced in the last exchange between the two men, when Fortunato screams, 'For the love of God, Montresor', to which Montresor replies by merely repeating his words, while we, the readers, know that the meaning he is ascribing to them is quite different and, by this point, incontrovertible, since Fortunato's version of events, his alternative narrative which might break open this quasi-aristocratic sealing of history, is about to be silenced for ever. '*In pace requiescat!*' as Montresor concludes his account, an account which has now attained to the status of the true since his joke has taken on the full material regalia of power.

Berenice and the pit

We can pursue this individualistic conquest of narrative through *Berenice* (1835), which is a less well-known tale but equally significant in terms of psychic structure, and represents a different version of the obsessional intensity which is worked through in *The Cask of Amontillado*. In an almost hallucinatory way it reminds the reader of *Ligeia*, as though the tale itself has not really come loose from its creative surroundings, and is but one frame in a continuing tapestry. There are also, of course, *Morella* (1835) and other tales of the death and return of the female, but with a different denouement. Egaeus is, as is again customary in these tales of Poe's, betrothed to his cousin, Berenice, and we are immediately told that Berenice is a victim of the also familiar wasting disease which appears to afflict most of Poe's heroines as the inadequately evaded wedding night comes closer.

But Egaeus himself is also sick, and in a way that Poe is at great pains to delineate carefully. It is a psychological morbidity; a 'morbid irritability of those properties of the mind in metaphysical science termed the *attentive*'. Here we see the familiar marks of a 'neurasthenia of the ego', which Egaeus clarifies as follows:

> Yet let me not be misapprehended. – The undue, earnest, and morbid attention thus excited by objects in their own nature frivolous, must not be confounded in character with that ruminating propensity common to all mankind, and more especially indulged in by persons of ardent imagination. . . . In the one instance, the dreamer, or enthusiast, being interested by an object usually *not* frivolous, imperceptibly loses sight of this object in a wilderness of deductions and suggestions issuing therefrom, until, at the conclusion of a day dream *often replete with luxury*, he finds the *incitamentum* or first cause of his musings entirely vanished and forgotten. In my case the primary object was *invariably frivolous*, although assuming, through the medium of my distempered vision, a refracted and unreal importance. Few deductions, if any, were made; and those few pertinaciously returning in upon the original object as a centre. The meditations were *never* pleasurable; and, at the termination of the reverie, the first cause, so far from being out of sight, had attained that supernaturally exaggerated interest which was the prevailing feature of the disease.[53]

There is an attempt here to distinguish between the productive intensity of the poet and the unproductive intensity of the neurotic; as a psychological description, though, interest focuses more on the determination with which

Poe classifies objects in the outer world in terms of their 'intrinsic' importance, thereby performing a massive act of projection while remaining apparently oblivious of this transfer of the mind's contents.

The passage is also important as a description of a desire on the part of the writer, and thus serves as a key to Poe's tales. The problem, clearly, is exorcism: once in the mind – and they may be said to be 'always already' in the mind – the kinds of fear which Poe writes about do not go away. Meditation and contemplation make them all the more intense; the shadow side of narcissistic involvement. Narrative structure is useless as a palliative, because there is *no way out* of these stories. Medically, we might refer to the condition as satyriatic: a permanent morbid excitement with no moment of relief. Epistemologically, it becomes a question of non-differentiation of the object, a problem of arbitrary fixation through fear of change and historical succession; or rather, of a fixation which chooses helplessly to remain with the confines of its own assignations of arbitrariness.

Yet there is another view. As the brief story unfolds, Berenice comes to Egaeus, near the point of her death:

> The forehead was high, and very pale, and singularly placid; and the once jetty hair fell partially over it, and overshadowed the hollow temples with innumerable ringlets now of a vivid yellow, and jarring discordantly, in their fantastic character, with the reigning melancholy of the countenance. The eyes were lifeless, and lustreless, and seemingly pupil-less, and I shrank involuntarily from their glassy stare to the contemplation of the thin and shrunken lips. They parted; and in a smile of peculiar meaning, *the teeth* of the changed Berenice disclosed themselves slowly to my view. Would to God that I had never beheld them, or that, having done so, I had died!

The rest of the story is predictable. Berenice dies and is buried. Egaeus goes into a trance, and when he is woken from it by a servant his attention is called to various objects in his room: his clothes, 'muddy and clotted with gore'; a spade against the wall; a box on the table which 'slipped from my hands, and fell heavily, and burst into pieces; and from it, with a rattling sound, there rolled out some instruments of dental surgery, intermingled with thirty-two small, white and ivory-looking substances that were scattered to and fro about the floor'.

But this apparently arbitrary obsession is, of course, open to interpretation, of various kinds. The delusive smile which discloses terror is frequent in Poe; there is a variant on it in *The Facts in the Case of M. Valdemar* (1845), when the dead man speaks but only with his (blackened) tongue, and thus the words come from him but are not of him. There is also lurking here some further echo of the 'body in fragments': Egaeus clearly finds it impossible to compose for himself an entire and integrated picture of his beloved, and that itself has a clear root in the kinship problems which, like the incest of *Otranto*, underlie the text.[54]

Egaeus cannot, indeed, compose and hold a whole sign, so has to perform a practical synecdoche, taking a part to stand for the whole and to represent sureness against the inevitability of decay. It need not, of course, have been the teeth; but then if we return to the problem of the satyriatic, of unslakeable desire, then presumably the only solution would be the removal of the offending organ. Egaeus has taken steps, either to avoid castration by a displaced *vagina dentata* or alternatively to reincorporate that parody of femininity within himself; yet it is significant that, at the end, he is unable to open the box, and it is only through the 'accident' of dropping it that the teeth are conjured to appear.

I want to point to a connection between Poe's intensity and his use of the apparently arbitrary: it is as though, in most of the stories, it is necessary for him to set up a structure of probability, but this, oddly enough, has the effect of reducing narrative conviction. It is only in those stories in which he dispenses entirely with the mathematics of probability that we sense the urgency, the desperate sureness which attends on indispensable unconscious functions, and on the need to display the romantic qualities of narcissistic transcendence.

And thus the double-bind: all the writer can be sure of is that which he cannot 'know', according to any model of consciousness. Either we follow Poe, rather tediously, through the mazes of an intelligent but contorted and sometimes ill-informed mind; or we accompany him with a savage simplicity to regions where the only evidence is the pressure of the narrative itself, and its replicatory undying quality.

The Pit and the Pendulum, the best-known of the stories, should therefore be a test case; and it is. We can, of course, analyse it in conventional psychoanalytic terms. Briefly, this is another fable of the 'red room', like Wells's, in which the identity of the fear which inhabits the haunted chamber is finally clarified as fear itself. And from the red room and its increasing constriction we are immediately in the territory of birth, of the womb, of primal fear. Nothing, our hero concludes at last, can prevent the increasing heat and decreasing size of his environment from forcing him down the pit; nothing can prevent his entry into the world of cold mortality, figured as an invisible death. There is no alternative to being born; but neither is there anything more terrifying, because by being born one enters into the cycle of life and death, forced out onto the dangerous road of mortality.

And yet, of course, this does not occur. There is a final paragraph:

> There was a discordant hum of human voices! There was a loud blast as of many trumpets! There was a harsh grating as of a thousand thunders! The fiery walls rushed back! An outstretched arm caught my own as I fell, fainting, into the abyss. It was that of General Lasalle. The French army had entered Toledo. The Inquisition was in the hands of its enemies.[55]

This is an extraordinary denouement, largely in that it pretends to no connections whatever with the body of the text. It is an absolute subversion of the idea of narrative development, the perfection of the *deux ex machina*.

We can speculate a little more on its form. The central figure is saved by a character who is military, who represents secure strength, and who, uniquely in the story, is named. If we put these features together, we can produce a psychic peculiarity: that Poe, terrified in this case at the prospect of ejection into the world of death, experiences the 'name-of-the-Father' not as domination or oppression but as salvation. Lasalle is linguistically the 'room' under a different guise, the presumably more capacious room offered by masculinity, a masculinity which is armed and therefore sure of its power.

Silence, enclosure, dark heat

The hero of *The Pit and the Pendulum* is thus rescued by an act of differentiation; his recognition of a named individual, unlikely under the circumstances as it might appear, is presumably a harbinger of the return of his own name, which has been held in suspension. What is terrifying is *silence*: the silence which might be associated with premature burial, or, as in *The Cask of Amontillado*, with having one's wished-for version of events silenced; or, more importantly, that silence which betokens namelessness.

Thus Poe's continual insistence on the names – Berenice, Ligeia, Morella, Eleanora, and more so again in his poetry. Yet these names provide no escape, for they are, typically, the names of the female, the names of the Other. In *Silence: A Fable* (1838), the Demon describes the site of terror in terms which originate in, but significantly differ from, those of Coleridge:

> The waters of the river have a saffron and sickly hue; and they flow not onwards to the sea, but palpitate forever and forever beneath the red eye of the sun with a tumultuous and convulsive motion. For many miles on either

side of the river's oozy bed is a pale desert of gigantic water-lilies. They sigh one unto the other in that solitude, and stretch towards the heaven their long and ghastly necks, and nod to and fro their everlasting heads. And there is an indistinct murmur which cometh out from among them like the rushing of subterrene water.[56]

Here there is silence, or at best a sound which bears no differentiation. There is also no possibility of escape, because the motion of these waters is in no direction, they are stuck forever in position no matter how they might heave and boil with frustration.

But, more than that, there are two rivers here: the pinioned river of the surface, the imagined possibility of subterranean 'rushing' below. Poe makes this related claim, in *MS. Found in a Bottle*: 'I have been all my life a dealer in antiquities, and have imbibed the shadows of fallen columns at Balbec, and Tadmor, and Persepolis, until my very soul has become a ruin'.[57] But this paradoxical wealth of experience does not help him at the confluence of the two rivers. How can it be that a dual suffering is experienced: that on the one hand there is the fear of being becalmed, the fear of motionlessness, while at the same time there is the equal terror that, at some other level, everything is passing by, passing away? At neither point, within neither scenario, is there scope for human action; yet it is, I would say, in his descriptions of the static, the ever-repetitive, the inescapable, that Poe comes closest to a realisation of the romantic problem of intensity and narrative.

It is at this peculiar still point, for instance, that the denouement of *Berenice* begins. It is 'an afternoon in the winter of the year, – one of those unseasonably warm, calm, and misty days which are nurse of the beautiful Halcyon'. There is something about these surroundings of motionless warmth, the arrested river, which endlessly replays the comfort which preceded exile, and something about the quality of the air in these conditions which renders the memory peculiarly susceptible to an indelible engraving, one which is desperately unwanted but which cannot be avoided.

The same thing happens in *The Assignation* (1834), when the hero gets his first glimpse of the Marchesa Aphrodite. 'A snowy-white and gauze-like drapery seemed to be nearly the sole covering to her delicate form; but the mid-summer and midnight air was hot, sullen, and still, and no motion in the statue-like form itself, stirred even the folds of that raiment of very vapor which hung around it as the heavy marble hangs around the Niobe'.[58]

The plot of *The Assignation* consists of the hero stumbling into knowledge of a relationship between the Marchesa and a young man *who remains nameless throughout*. This relationship, although the narrator does not at first know it, is about to issue in a death-pact, and the narrator is called upon to be an unwitting witness of the suicide of the nameless acquaintance. But the plot is singularly ambiguous, even for Poe; the acquaintance certainly dies, of poison, but not before the narrator himself has drunk of the same wine, partaken of the same fate of historical and familial refusal.

I do not mean to suggest that Poe intended this ambiguity; that would be very unlikely. But it still exists, and serves to call into question the relation between these two nameless characters. But then, the narrator's senses have already been confused by a specific romantic environment, one which mediates in a significant way between the dark heat of *The Pit and the Pendulum* and the lost and silent warmth of the river:

> Rich draperies in every part of the room trembled to the vibration of low, melancholy music, whose origin was not to be discovered. The senses were oppressed by mingled and conflicting perfumes, reeking up from strange convoluted censers, together with multitudinous flaring and flickering tongues of emerald and violet fire. The rays of the newly risen sun poured in upon the whole, through windows formed each of a single pane of crimson-tinted glass.

Here again is the fear of enclosure, of an environment so total and so undifferentiated that the individual disappears, becomes merely an effect of the rich patterns. In this world, breath itself ceases, as it does for the unfortunate M. Valdemar, and as it does again in the quizzical tale called *Loss of Breath* (1832).

Loss of Breath is written in Poe's lighter mode, and concerns a man who unaccountably ceases to breathe and is therefore consigned to the underworld, although he has no doubts that he is still alive. There he encounters a prodigiously fat man – or rather, the corpse of such a man – and proceeds to meditate upon him:

> He has never ascended the summit of a hill. He has never viewed from any steeple the glories of a metropolis. Heat has been his mortal enemy. In the dog-days his days have been the days of a dog. Therein, he has dreamed of flames and suffocation – of mountains upon mountains – of Pelion upon Ossa. He was short of breath – to say all in a word, he was short of breath.[59]

The story of the *House of Usher* also begins on a 'dull, dark, and soundless day in the autumn of the year, when the clouds hung oppressively low in the heavens';[60] resolution can come only through the storm and the whirlwind, echoing the other emphasis in Poe on whirlpools and on the Coleridgean depths they might disclose. Perhaps, after all, what might become apparent at the bottom of the maelstrom, if we can summon our courage, is the way back in; back into the womb, or back into some region where we will be no longer becalmed or stuck in the enclosing heat.

But it would not do, as we see, to attempt too unilateral an interpretation of this configuration of motifs: they are obviously ones which concerned Poe intensely, but the lines of significance are muddled, tied in knots. In *A Tale of the Ragged Mountains* (1844), it is 'upon a dim, warm, misty day, towards the close of November, and during the strange *interregnum* of the seasons which in America is termed the Indian Summer'[61] that Bedloe leaves for his walk in the mountains. In the course of that walk, he finds himself unaccountably transposed into someone else; and on the return from it, he finds it impossible to reinhabit his own body, and dies. The enclosure, the womb, terrify Poe but it is also there, as in Blake, that battle has to be engaged. It is only on that terrain that the struggle for individuation can take place, however prematurely blighted its consequences.

I would characterise this whole side of Poe's writing as a series of tales of dark heat. This may seem surprising; for the premature burial theme, for one, is bound up more with images of eternal cold. Yet I see Poe as preoccupied with a dark heat, the heat of prolonged and pointless tumescence, and at the same time the warmth of an environment which proffers simultaneous safety and suffocation, a security unto death. In other words, I believe that Poe makes apparent the point that Hegel underlines about the nature of desire, which is that it is endless. There is very little 'desire *for*' in Poe; the movement towards the loved one is invariably blocked: in the Gothic mode by 'premature' death, whatever that might mean, in the more comic modes by ridicule or accident. Instead there is the endless circling of desire upon itself, the desire to avoid which must at the same time play constantly with the object of its abhorrence, because to be separated from it would indeed be tantamount to death.

I would suggest, on the basis of this, that reading Poe provides us with a singular experience of romantic and narcissistic ambivalence: birth is feared and needed, the act of naming by which we proceed under the domination of language is longed for yet murderous. This ambivalence is best caught, for me, in the motto from Joseph Glanvill which introduces *Ligeia*:

And the will therein lieth, which dieth not. Who knoweth the mysteries of the will, with its vigour? For God is but a great will pervading all things by nature of its intentness. Man doth not yield himself to the angels, nor unto death utterly, save only through the weakness of his feeble will.[62]

There are three words which I would call attention to here. First, 'vigour': a significant word, especially when placed alongside the fact that Poe's revenants are for the most part remarkable for their lack of vigour, for the relative failure which attends all these acts of rebirth. The hope is, perhaps, to conjure a new vigour from the depths of abandonment; but this cannot succeed.

Second, 'intentness': it is this that I have been trying to get at in Poe by talking of his moments of intensity, and it is this too which underlies the mechanisms of compulsion and repetition which I have tried to describe earlier in this chapter. There is a longing here to bring all the heterogeneous faculties of the romantics to bear on a single object, lying alongside the concomitant knowledge that, if we do bring our faculties to bear in this way, we run the risk of not consolidating the image but fracturing it, such that the body which we intended to invest with the full weight of our passion lies, abruptly, in scattered fragments at our feet; or, at the least touch, shows the rot which has in reality been attending it throughout its so-called 'life'.

And third, 'lieth'. I have little doubt that Poe would extrapolate this first sentence into a statement about the strength of the will which lies within all of us if only we can grasp it with intensity and focus ourselves on the evasion of death. But this drift deconstructs itself, and becomes its own opposite in a classic discursive *locus* for romanticism. For perhaps that concept also 'lieth' in the other sense, indeed deludes us; perhaps it figures merely as a permanent evasion of the problems with the ego's will as it actually exists, in all its faultiness and fluctuation.

A lie of strength to counteract a lie of weakness, a sought-for reassertion of transcendence by the limited ego; a story woven out of the hopes of survival which turns out to betray the fear of being forever stuck in an unchanging universe, enclosed in the incomprehensible and misty heat which, in the end, prevents transformation while it encourages us to fill in the gaps with our own imaginary narratives of transcendence and success.

PART 5

ROMANTICISM: SOME INTERPRETATIONS

Echo and ruin

What I have been trying to do on the preceding pages is to establish some of the building blocks we need in the attempt to construct a picture of romanticism. But to put it this way, as we have seen, is historically inadequate; because it assumes precisely a severance of subject and object, of the inner and outer, which, as an epistemological supposition or as a critical tenet, is untrue to the structuring and development of our experience as human beings.

We might be better served by some composite drawn from the sciences, in their transformed shape after the intrusion of the uncertainty principle.[1] We have to recognise that, in the privileging of shapes, we as critics and as cultural inheritors play our parts in a process: as the crystalline shape of romanticism begins to emerge for us, those facets which attract our attention are those which are in the light, those over which the beams of our own attention play.

This is not to wipe out history. Rather, it is to attempt to reckon into the equation our historiographical desire, and when we encounter and attempt to interpret this desire, we instantly stumble across that which encumbered the romantics, and which presented itself to them in the guise of obstacle. For that desire has at its heart an image of continuity: a need for a way in which we can prove ourselves the equals of our parents, at least in terms of a fantasised level of independence.

Embedded in this desire for continuity is the image of striation, of fracture: of the always already present fault-line which has beforehand wrecked the simplicity of continuity, whether that continuity be imaged as progress or decline. Thus we find an agitation around the concept of the 'new birth': the birth, as it might be, of a class order, the birth of a set of ideas, of a paradigm. And it is thus that we encounter – on a real historical terrain, not merely as an epistemological presupposition – the difficulty of hiatus, the knowledge that, as we seek to establish the meaning of historical difference, we are faced with an everyday paradox: if that with and in which we live is 'different', how has it come to be born from the ceaseless sameness of the world?

One path through this problem lay for the romantics through the so-called 'philosophies of identity'; and this path directly traversed the principles of logic.[2] Thus dialectical systematisation figures in the scheme as a transcendence of contradiction, indeed; but also as the ground on which a view might be held to which nothing is lost. But here we are directly in the realm of the unconscious, as Coleridge and many others sensed.[3] The trajectory of the dialectic is precisely the outcropping of the paradoxical 'sublation' which the romantics saw as the essential ground of coherence.

And it is worth pondering for a moment on the type of coherence which figures as the rebus of the romantic moment. For it is a coherence which traces an embarrassing path through biography. The question here is not about a literary mode, but about what we might well refer to as a specific mode of interpellation. But in order to get to grips with this problem, we have to establish two facts about the nature of interpellation, as Althusser defines it.[4]

The first is that it is, or should be, a historically manipulable concept. There has been too much work of an idealist nature which has claimed that, within a specific text, it is possible to identify a fixed and unchangeable interpellative moment, such that we have to regard ourselves, as individual, experienced readers, under the sign of our matching up to – or failing – that ideal, and ideally identified, space.[5] This, it appears to me, is not what Althusser really meant by interpellation, although it might be a Machereyan heresy;[6] at all events, it means nothing historically, except in so far as it can be used in the politically useful service of exiling our own feelings and responses as readers of specific past texts in the here-and-now; in other words, in so far as it short-circuits the essential trajectory of the interpretative process.

Second, it needs to be established that interpellation is not an activity which can only be described and experienced in respect of specific texts. It must already be obvious, from recent studies, that interpellation takes place, and may indeed be at its strongest, in the arena where auteurship no longer occupies a privileged position.[7] Advertisements are the cardinal twentieth-century example. But further than this, we need to say that we, as critics, as consumers, as people experiencing culture, and as human beings, are interpellated by romanticism: as a construct, certainly, but then all the cultural artifacts, whatever their order, which interpellate us are artificial, and the question is one of level rather than of kind.

And, indeed, with these two rudimentary points established, we can proceed one stage further. For it is not the case that we experience romanticism *and* we experience readings of specific texts written during the period. What actually happens in the moment of apprehension is that the particular and the general come into relation; we read and experience the text – Shelley's 'Alastor' (1816) or Coleridge's 'Kubla Khan' (1798) – *as* a romantic text, and the apparatus which is brought into play is one which contains within itself an essential process of matching, matching our previous assumptions about a typology with the textual detail in front of us, a matching which can only be performed through the usual ideological processes of foregrounding and deletion and through those no less ordinary processes of criticism which attempt to base themselves on a relationship to this ideological thrust.

Therefore, we are interpellated by the construct which I am continuing to name 'romanticism'; and I suggest that as we are thus interpellated, we find brought to the surface a complex interplay between repetition and novelty. We are made to feel, in essence, the ambiguous force of a reverberation. We can identify the substance of this quite simply: in, as a cardinal example, the complex and contradictory troping of Milton which contributes to the setting up of the whole romantic field.

But it is precisely around repetition and novelty that many of the principal issues of psychic development hinge. It is because they are lost in exactly these mazes that the attributions of origin and source assume their irrecoverable guise: because, when we peer round the next hedge, we become increasingly unclear as to whether we have been here before or not. The wanderers and sufferers of early romanticism, the sacrificial victims of incomprehensible gods, suffer – as Poe suffers – both ways. As they enter into their explanations of a mystical sense, they find themselves performing, perhaps in a differentiated context, a task which they have taken on a thousand times before.

We are thus returned to a duality of consciousness: a relevant image is that of the contemporary cultural identity of the US, where feelings of hosting – the nation which welcomes immigrants – can be grafted seamlessly onto feelings about being the welcomed guest – a country of opportunity although it is not available by birthright. This immediately sets us off in two directions.

Inwardly, it moves us towards a concept of romanticism as host and guest, and here Coleridge's wedding guest and the much-abused hospitality of the owners of all those Southern European castles of Gothic fiction are the inverse sides of the same coin. The romantic hero experiences a desire for at-home-ness; but the very thought of being at home is enough to drive him into paroxysms of adolescent resentment. Home is where the heart is; but also, home is where the hate is, and where we experience the warm claustrophobia which denies us our potential for transcendence. This in turn can be connected with problems of patriarchy and problems of mysticism.[8]

The other direction in which we are spun is towards empire and slavery. It was no secret from the economists and political theorists of the late eighteenth century – nor was it a secret from the poets – that between the concepts of production and consumption, as they were retailed through the commanding economic theories of the day, there existed a gap, a hiatus; and that gap was filled only by the notion of the foreign market. There was thus an assumed overseas passivity built into the system; we can find it represented in Gothic exoticism, as we can find it in the earlier orientalist strains which seep into the romantic masterworks.

This, then, is one of the Ur-gaps which need to be filled; and it would be no exaggeration to say that romanticism is the collection of motifs of the hiatus, and at the same time a representation of the travails of the ego as it seeks to encompass – *while denying* – the existence of that hiatus. It is this admixture of encompassment and denial which permeates the texts we have considered. How do you embrace that which you deny, how do you establish a new 'family' when you are denying the existence of its more far-flung members, when you are establishing orphanage as a necessary site of international process?

One way, of course, of managing this contradiction is by manipulating the notion of 'life', as Coleridge tries to do in his *Theory of Life* (1848), and Hegel in his versions of a philosophy of nature.[9] It is possible to maintain the encompassing and the denial if you effect a differentiation between the body *as animated* and the body in fragments; and this attempt to produce a distinction between 'natural' and 'artificial' bodies runs deep through the texts we have considered, as it runs through most thinking which attempts to perform a transcendence and a disenfranchisement in the same breath.

It is thus, then, that we have the myths of the shattered body, in *Frankenstein* and elsewhere, which continue to absorb us; but we have also to contemplate what the gain is, in terms of psychic energy, from this shattering of the body. In contemplating it under such a guise, we are automatically taking up an old adversarial model. The breaking up of the body, the refusal to accept proofs of parenting, the will to transcend the material: all these fit into place if one accepts a model which demonstrates an Ur-wish on the part of the ego, which is a simultaneous wish for *control*, and for monopoly of reflection.

In this context, there are several problems with mirrors to which Lacan never alludes. The first and most obvious one is that they are, by their very nature, inaccurate. It is not the case that they reflect back to us an image of the perfect body; that, on the contrary, is the *only* thing we can be sure they will not do. They thus become the site of an anxiety of a kind which is supplementary to, but different from, the one which Lacan identifies as the 'heart' ('hate') of the mirror-phase.

The second one is more important, which is that mirrors do not have the capacity to adapt their frame neatly to our body. In other words, they may well reflect some version of our perceived self, some identifiable baby; but that baby (or this one) does not have it within his/her power to affect the backdrop. The second thing we can be sure of about mirrors is that they are, always, reflecting something which is *not* us; and furthermore, they continue to do so, even in the red room, even in the nighted chambers where we can never stalk for fear of realising that the grotesque phantom is this very body, our own, which we have always meant, given time and the opportunity, to disown.

Problems with mirrors, as Wilde noticed, are best dealt with by drapes.[10] Not because they offer mere concealment; it is because they offer the necessary framing, so that we can bring reflection under the sway of the ego. We can choose when they are or are not drawn; we can also choose our audience. And what is true of mirrors is also true of windows, which is why the crucial traumatic scenes in versions of *Dracula* always centre around the inexplicably open window. The window in *Dracula* is perennially a substitute for the mirror which refuses to show the vampire's physical form, refuses to offer us the easy inscription which we would need in order to differentiate between bloodlust and the ordinary processes of aristocratic/élitist and imperialist consumption.

For such demarcations are difficult to draw, and even more difficult to sustain, as we see in Poe's attempt to differentiate between the poet and the neurotic. When should the handling of other people's experience gain kudos from its transmutation under the sign of the aesthetic, when does it succumb – or realise that it has already succumbed – to the commands of primary sadism? Of course, this problem itself is only an effect of an assumption about individuation: it is rifts in the sense of 'speaking-on-behalf of', of representation as we have seen it, which cause difficulties to emerge in the relations between self and other, and thus occasion, for instance, the prodigies of consumption which constitute Keats's epistemology.

And these rifts in the 'speaking-on-behalf-of' are, of course, the polemical substance of romanticism. Behind the afflatus, behind, indeed, the developing rhetoric of the inward, there lies a deep doubt about the reality of communication, a doubt which is connected with market changes but also with the consciousness of a dissenting academy. For there is a narcissistic balance to be struck: a psychic energy scale to be weighted. If nothing is to be heard 'outside', if the echo chamber is fractured, if all we are left with is indeed the squeaking baby trumpet of sedition, then there might emerge a comparable need to increase the echoing propensities of the inward: to increase the volume of the caves, the underground rivers, along which the suppressed words might flow.

In this alternative scenario a great deal is left to the 'immutable' operations of history: a kind of long-distance geography, indeed, is required which might map where Alph will surface – such an operation as that on which we are now engaged. It becomes therefore imperative to ensure that the 'inscription', such as it is, is writ not on water, not even on the visages of the sunken stone gods of the Mediterranean, but on a countenance which will never disappear, even if the guarantee of that has to be the alternative countenance of worldly power sunk deep in the desert; even if the inscription can guarantee an emotional validity only by being set upon the forehead of the ruin.[11]

Locating romanticism

It is thus the echo which brings about the ruin; and vice versa. Too much reverberation in an empty landscape (in this case, a historical scene from which the power of the 'literati' has drained away) eventually shatters the certainties which underlay a certain refracted tradition. Similarly, when this has passed away, an echo is set up which cannot be destroyed, for it is the image of a nostalgia for a primal unity which is (wrongly) figured as one where word was adequate to thing, where the voice had the true and godlike power of naming, where the human chord, if once struck up, could have changed forever the eventualities of the way things are.

What, then, are we left with as an enduring model of group operation? A paradoxical image: a gathering in the twilight, as Coleridge, or perhaps Wordsworth or Burns, recite their discoveries into an increasingly empty and somnolent room; and on the other side (of the Alps), a burgeoning group consciousness which finds its only substance in premature death, for we cannot doubt that the deaths of Keats and Shelley were the imagistic substance of Poe's fears.

What this appears to *mean*, in the history of literature in English, is something about sunburst, about a 'movement' which has always resisted the institutionalisation endemic to the genre, and has yet in the end become precisely the archetypal institution, with an attendant hierarchy and set of modes. So, in one sense, romanticism stands as the site of a final re-cuperation; beyond that point, the 'airy-fairy' arts cannot live, and even there they managed pretty febrilely. The sign of a defeat; although that is not the whole of the story (which we now tell ourselves).

We need, however, to return to the question of narcissism; for here we continue to have the hinge of thought. It is the narcissistic impulse which continues to urge us to build systems. And, indeed, it would be comforting to suppose that interpretation, as an activity, offered us a recourse against the apparently omnipresent forces of narcissism, but of course that is not the case. In suggesting a quarternary structure for interpretation, I have been attempting on occasion to point out that interpretation can work *only* through the processes of narcissism; because it is only through narcissism – that summation of the simplified binary relationship – that the subject can be brought to a condition of interest, *Interesse*, which can begin to sustain the deeper processes which may unravel the knot.[12]

And it is, of course, true that the narcissistic ego can only be brought to this point through pain; and the evidence is that the process of psychoanalysis is only undertaken by persons who have been brought to it in the hope of alleviating the agony of their quotidian experience (or, more rarely, in the hope of enabling others' alleviation, a motive which needs lengthy and careful analysis). And romanticism is an experience of pain, of dislocation, the evidence for which is found in the shattered bodies, the refusal of accommodation with part-objects, as well as in the ambiguous returns to the red room, the wish to escape which also knows, painfully, that the recourse suggested also partakes of death.

But these dilemmas are always with us. The question of development, in its most general sense, is inevitably bound to the problem of dealing with the gap, with the priority, with that which stands just behind the position one has with difficulty carved out for oneself. What, I think, we must conclude about the distinctiveness of romanticism has to be in that curious territory where history and psychology meet: we may refer to this territory as the web of discourses.

For we need to do nothing less than think about what a romantic poem *is* (poem because we deal here with the commanding – *typical* in the strong sense – mode of the period). Peter Thorslev has tried usefully to define romantic poems in this way: 'poems as wholes, or relatively self-contained passages in them, can be viewed as phenomenological exercises in which problems of existence are bracketed so that questions of ontology or of ultimate beliefs need not arise'.[13]

This seems to me a productive definition. On the one hand, it gives us the beginning of a historical specificity: it could not be said that Augustan poetry seeks in this way some method of dealing with a dilemma about 'ultimate beliefs', for, problems though there of course were in the Augustan system, they were not of this shape or dimension. But, more importantly, Thorslev hints here at the doubleness in the romantic system. The face which is apparently turned towards the deepest problems of the human soul is simultaneously averted: the delicate probing is also an evasion.

In one sense, this returns us to the issue of mysticism, in its temporal and spatial dimensions. For mysticism can be seen as the effect of a need to wish away differentiation, to achieve a sudden and instantaneous unity which defies the power of history to sequence experience; and, as we have seen, in one sense this replicates the actual operations of the psyche, and indeed of language. But the more basic question concerns the relation between inwardness and outwardness: and I suggest that romanticism can partly be characterised as the furled flower, where the looking down into the heart is also a peering into a kind of transparency, such that the real world reappears at the centre, albeit in a differently coloured guise. And, the wish goes, if it were possible to inhabit the heart of the flower (and here we touch again upon the rhetorical manipulations of physical size which we encountered in the first chapter), then it would not be that the real world would go away; but there would be a protective film between it and ourselves.

It is because of the insistence of this film in romantic writing (Blake's 'veils'/Vala are a cardinal textual instance, Coleridge's repeated sensing of something 'between' himself and the world a more extended structure of feeling)[14] that we need, indeed, to see the romantic phenomenon in terms of this triplicity: the inward, the outward, and that which exists between. For, in all cases, it will be the shaping of this 'which exists between' which provides us with our evidence of the shapings of the within and the without, as the curtains, the heavy drapes, blow in the winds which appear to prefigure a solving arrival – which, of course, never comes.

And this shaping of the veil, the rim of the world, is another way of referring to the vicissitudes of the ego as it attempts to impose order on the fluctuations of shape and history, to construct a system from the shards of experience. And this immediately plunges us as critics into the heart of the dilemma. For the hard thing is to hold to the realisation that it is this shaping itself, its description and interpretation, which is as far as we can go. We cannot go further, and say that romanticism was, in some well-chosen sentence or phrase, like this or that: for to do so is precisely to immerse ourselves once more in the toils of speculative narcissism, and all we shall come up with is some version which looks suspiciously like the equipment and armour of thought with which we first dived.

What we need to retain instead, as Blake tells us, is the careful description of the garments,[15] for it is these garments which constitute the self, and it is the self which is the outward and visible form of an otherwise undecipherable inward process. In attempting to shine a light *through* the robe, we are indeed engaging in an exercise of curiosity, but one which respects the importance of the veil, the curtain, indeed Saussure's sheet of paper, as the evidence on which interpretation must be grounded. We can, if we like, change the metaphor to Lacan's:

> No better idea of the effects of this function can be given than by comparing it to areas of colour which, when applied here and there to a stencil-plate, can make the stencilled figures, rather forbidding in themselves, more reminiscent of hieroglyphics or of a rebus, look like a figurative painting.[16]

And this transformation of the 'abstract' into the 'representational' is, of course, at the heart of the narratives of the psyche, and simultaneously at the heart of the interpretative.

In connection with the romantics, we can also mention the problem of learning which took place under the impetus of historical change and eventuated, precisely, in the discovery of the unconscious. As Jung says, 'nothing estranges man more from the ground-plan of his instincts than his learning capacity, which turns out to be a genuine drive for progressive transformation of human modes of behaviour'.[17] And the added twist here is that, indeed, it is precisely estrangement which the romantics are learning *about*: thus some of the alarming reflexivity which occurs when they learn that the very capacity to 'master' is that which, as it progresses round the spiral, completes the circuits of alienation which it had been their intention to forestall.

And in this spiral, we can return once again to the issue of the subjective and the objective:

The more power man had over nature, the more his knowledge and skill went to his head, and the deeper became his contempt for the merely natural and accidental, for all irrational data – including the objective psyche, which is everything that consciousness is not. In contrast to the subjectivism of the conscious mind the unconscious is objective, manifesting itself mainly in the form of contrary feelings, fantasies, emotions, impulses, and dreams, none of which one makes oneself but which come upon one objectively.[18]

What one senses to be of particular significance here for romanticism is the ambiguous dealing with the 'accidental' and the 'irrational': because all such dealings in the literary realm pass under the sign of form, with its own ambiguities of extension and appropriation. In Paul de Man's writings on romanticism we can, for example, in a deconstructive way isolate a great deal of use of the notion of 'shelter'; shelter, one may presume, from surrounding forces perceived as destabilising and dangerous, but also shelter precisely from that quality of the accidental which represents both the romantics' apotheosis – the accidentality of nature, of love – and also their fear – the accident which will render all systems not so much useless but revealed as temporary constructs, 'shelters' for the ego isolated on the face of the mountain.

De Man also points up the looping of history within which I have been trying to work:

With romanticism we are not separated from the past by that layer of forgetfulness and that temporal opacity that could awaken in us the illusion of detachment. To interpret romanticism means quite literally to interpret the past as such, *our* past precisely to the extent that we are beings who want to be defined and, as such, interpreted in relation to a totality of experiences that slip into the past. The content of this experience is perhaps less important than the fact that we have experienced it in its passing away, and that it thereby has contributed in an unmediated way (that is, in the form of an act) to the constitution of our own consciousness of temporality.[19]

De Man goes on to seal the loop by pointing out that 'it is precisely this experience of the temporal relation between the act and its interpretation that is one of the main themes of romantic poetry'.[20] At the heart of romanticism, therefore, we may discern a massive uncertainty about the effects of interpretation. On the one hand, these effects are perceived as world-changing, the imagination is given to us as a thoroughly constitutive power; on the other, there is the hovering awareness that interpretation is always already too late to the extent that it seeks a location in history, a location which is always as a supplement to the event. The structuring comes precisely as a series of attempts to 're-present' in discourse that which has already incontrovertibly occurred.

Thus the dilemma of the ego, trying to retain its purchase on the Real while sensing the undermining which is going on all the time as the systems of economy, State, discourse, slip and slide, and as new significations are conjured out of what Blake refers to as the bones of the past, those bones on which the remade flesh sits uneasily if at all. De Man takes the point further in relation to Wordsworth:

> The interpretive reflection begins in the experience of this excess in the moment when the travellers come to recognise that they are in error, or in the corresponding moment when Wordsworth feels himself compelled to warn the insurgents of their transgressions. The transition of imagination from the active to the interpretive stage results in a feeling of disorder and confusion ...
>
> The interpretation is possible only from a standpoint that lies on the far side of this failure, and that has escaped destruction thanks to an effort of consciousness to make sure of itself once again. But this consciousness can be had only by one who has very extensively partaken of the danger and failure. Act and interpretation are thus connected in a complex and often contradictory manner. For the interpreter of history, it is never a simple and uniform movement like the ascent of a peak or the installation of a definitive social order. Rather, it appears much more in that twilight in which for Wordsworth the crossing of the Alps was bathed ...[21]

Thus we see some of the ways in which history and the constitution of the self interlock. Romanticism 're-presents' precisely a moment at which the consciousness of this interlocking develops to a point where there is no longer any question of denying the danger, the abyss of the 'unknown' over which the thin curtain is stretched. Narcissus remains poised on the edge of the pool.

NOTES

Part 1

1. Much of the energy of modern fiction, it seems to me, goes into this new set of portrayals: see, e.g., Kurt Vonnegut, *The Sirens of Titan* (1959), or Thomas Pynchon, *Gravity's Rainbow* (1973). And at root it is a matter of a shift in scientific, technological and imaginative paradigms: see, e.g., D.R. Hofstadter, *Gödel, Escher, Bach: An Eternal Golden Braid* (Brighton, 1979); and the multitude of works on the 'new paradigm' in scientific thinking.
2. See Freud, *The Interpretation of Dreams* (1900), Part 2, in *The Standard Edition of the Complete Psychological Works of Sigmund Freud*, ed. J. Strachey *et al.* (24 vols, London, 1953–74), V, p. 536. Freud is here following G.T. Fechner, *Elemente der Psychophysik* (Leipzig, 1860).
3. Jung, 'The Undiscovered Self (Present and Future)' (1957), in *The Collected Works of C.G. Jung*, ed. Herbert Read *et al.* (20 vols, London, 1953–79), X, p. 250.
4. I shall be referring at various points to the two John Berryman poems given above on p. v, 'The Song of the Demented Priest' and Sonnet 12. They can be found in context in Berryman, *Selected Poems 1938–1968* (London, 1972), pp. 20, 37.
5. Jacques Lacan, 'The Direction of the Treatment and the Principles of its Power' (1958), in *Ecrits*, trans. A. Sheridan (London, 1977), p. 233.
6. Lacan, 'Aggressivity in Psycho-analysis' (1948), in *Ecrits*, p. 20. But the question whether, and in what way, interpretation is justly described as a delusion is one which I hope to keep in play.
7. See below, pp. 118–21.
8. Lacan, 'The Mirror Stage as Formative of the Function of the I' (1949), in *Ecrits*, pp. 4–5.
9. *Ibid.*, p. 5.
10. See my *Literature of Terror: A History of Gothic Fictions from 1765 to the Present Day* (London, 1980), pp. 348–9. I am here seeing psychoanalysis itself as structured in terms of the danger from which the delusions of the ego as hunter seek to protect us.
11. Lacan, 'The Function and Field of Speech and Language in Psychoanalysis' (1953), in *Ecrits*, p. 50.
12. Jung, *Psychology and Alchemy* (1944), in *Collected Works*, XII, p. 4.
13. Jung, *ibid.*, p. 24.
14. Lacan, 'Function and Field', p. 83; and, here and throughout, Paul de Man, 'Autobiography as De-Facement', in *The Rhetoric of Romanticism* (New York, 1984), pp. 67–81.
15. See *ibid.*, p. 87.
16. Lacan, 'Direction of the Treatment', in *Ecrits*, p. 234.

17. See, e.g., James Hillman, *The Myth of Analysis: Three Essays in Archetypal Psychology* (Evanston, 1972), pp. 117 ff.
18. Jung, 'The Undiscovered Self', p. 286.
19. See Jung, 'Answer to Job' (1952), in *Collected Works*, XI, pp. 461–70.
20. See, e.g., Jung, *Psychology and Alchemy*, pp. 39–214.
21.

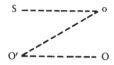

This scheme signifies that the condition of the subject S (neurosis or psychosis) is dependent on what is being unfolded in the Other O. What is being unfolded there is articulated like a discourse (the unconscious is the discourse of the Other), whose syntax Freud first sought to define for those bits that come to us in certain privileged moments, in dreams, in slips of the tongue or pen, in flashes of wit.

Why would the subject be interested in this discourse, if he were not taking part in it? He is, indeed, a participator, in that he is stretched over the four corners of the schema: namely, S, his ineffable, stupid existence, o, his objects, O′, his ego, that is, that which is reflected of his form in his objects, and O, the locus from which the question of his existence may be presented to him.

(Lacan, 'On a Question Preliminary to any Possible Treatment of Psychosis' (1956), in *Ecrits*, 193–4)

22. I am referring to the Kings of Buddhist mythology; see, e.g., *New Larousse Encyclopaedia of Mythology*, introd. Robert Graves (London, 1968), p. 390, on the way in which these images have evolved to fill all available subject-positions.
23. W.R. Bion, *Experiences in Groups and Other Papers* (London, 1961), pp. 142–3.
24. See, e.g., A.F. Klein, *Effective Groupwork: An Introduction to Principle and Method* (New York, 1972), pp. 44, 72 etc.
25. This quotation, the next two, and the one on 'literature' which heads the next section are from Jean Baudrillard, *Le système des objets* (1968).
26. Michael Foucault, *Language, Counter-Memory, Practice*, trans. D.F. Bouchard and S. Simon (Oxford, 1977), p. 162; quoted in Christopher Norris, *Deconstruction: Theory and Practice* (London, 1982), pp. 85–6. Cf. here, and elsewhere, Harold Bloom, *Agon: Towards a Theory of Revisionism* (New York, 1982), e.g. pp. 119–44.
27. I am referring to Wells, *The Island of Doctor Moreau* (1896), which seems to me to be an emblematic study of domination and contamination.
28. Norris, p. 16.
29. See J. Krishnamurti, *The Penguin Krishnamurti Reader*, ed. M. Lutyens (Harmondsworth, 1970), e.g. pp. 91–165.
30. I am thinking here of the cultural and commercial *purposes* of literary study and criticism, especially in English: see, e.g., P. Parrinder, *Authors and Authority: A Study of English Literary Criticism and its Relation to Culture 1750–1900* (London, 1977).
31. I am thinking particularly here of Marge Piercy, *Woman on the Edge of Time* (1976).
32. This, it appears to me, is the nub of the arguments advanced in *The Decade of Disillusion: British Politics in the Sixties*, ed. D. McKie and C. Cook (London, 1972); cf. R.W. Johnson, *The Politics of Recession* (London, 1985).
33. Norris, p. 63.
34. See Jacques Derrida, *Speech and Phenomena, and Other Essays on Husserl's Theory of Signs*, trans. D.B. Allison (Evanston, 1973); and *Edmund Husserl's Origin of Geometry: An Introduction*, trans. J.P. Leavey, Jr (Stony Brook, New York, 1978).
35. See McFarland, *Coleridge and the Pantheist Tradition* (Oxford, 1969), e.g., pp. 53–106.

Part 2

1. For the principal theories of narcissism see Freud, *On Narcissism: An Introduction* (1914), in *Standard Edition*, XIV, pp. 67–102; Heinz Kohut, *The Restoration of the Self* (New York, 1977). See also Malcolm Pines, 'Reflections on Mirroring', *Group Analysis*, XV, p. 2 (1982), Supp. 1–26; D. Westen, *Self and Society: Narcissism, Collectivism, and the Development of Morals* (Cambridge, 1985).
2. See Freud, e.g. *Jokes and their Relation to the Unconscious* (1905), in *Standard Edition*, VIII, 159 ff.
3. Crucial examples here would include, of course, Wordsworth's *Prelude* and Shelley's various aborted attempts, most interestingly perhaps 'The Triumph of Life' (1822); see on the problem of the philosophical poem Graham Hough, *The Romantic Poets* (London, 1953) and Herbert Read, *The True Voice of Feeling: Studies in English Romantic Poetry* (London, 1953).
4. See, particularly, Shelley, 'Julian and Maddalo' (1818), in *Poetical Works*, ed. T. Hutchinson (London, 1943), pp. 190–203; Coleridge, 'Dejection: an Ode' (1802), in *Poetical Works*, ed. E.H. Coleridge (London, 1967), pp. 362–8; Keats, 'La Belle Dame sans Merci' (1820), in *The Poems and Verses of John Keats*, ed. J. Middleton Murry (London, 1949), pp. 351–2. For two different views of this insistent concern with system, see H.W. Piper, *The Active Universe* (London, 1962) and C.J. Rzepka, *The Self as Mind: Vision and Identity in Wordsworth, Coleridge, and Keats* (Cambridge, Mass., 1986).
5. Cf., e.g., Rzepka, pp. 1–30; Antony Easthope, *Poetry as Discourse* (London, 1983), pp. 120–33.
6. See Coleridge, *Poetical Works*, pp. 213–36.
7. 'Christabel', 118–19, *ibid.*, p. 220.
8. 'Christabel', 149, *ibid.*, p. 221.
9. 'Christabel', 171, *ibid.*, p. 221.
10. Emblematically, of course, this is the case with 'Kubla Khan' (1798); but the pressure runs throughout Coleridge's massive corpus, with its vaunting ambitions, breaks and hiatuses.
11. 'Christabel', 239, 242, in Coleridge, *Poetical Works*, p. 223.
12. 'Christabel', 250–6, *ibid.*, p. 224.
13. The original paper on which these sections are based was developed collaboratively with David Aers, Robert Clark, Jonathan Cook, Thomas Elsasser; see Aers *et al.*, 'Strategies for Representing Revolution', in *1789: Reading Writing Revolution*, ed. F. Barker *et al.* (Colchester, 1982), pp. 81–100.
14. See Coleridge, *Poetical Works*, pp. 64–6.
15. See *British War Poetry in the Age of Romanticism: 1793–1815*, ed. B.T. Bennett (New York and London, 1976), pp. 261–2. I have used a great deal of the material collected by Bennett in ensuing pages.
16. The most significant text in question is, of course, Edmund Burke, *A Philosophical Enquiry into the Origin of Our Ideas of the Sublime and Beautiful* (1756).
17. See William Cowper, *Poetical Works*, ed. H.S. Milford (London, 1934), pp. 337–8.
18. Cf. Freud, *Interpretation of Dreams*, Part 2, in *Standard Edition*, V, p. 340.
19. See Blake, 'The First Book of Urizen' (1794), 10:15–18, in *Complete Writings*, ed. G. Keynes (London, 1966), p. 227.
20. See, e.g., J. Berger *et al.*, *Ways of Seeing* (London, 1972), and J. Williamson, *Decoding Advertisements: Ideology and Meaning in Advertising* (London, 1978) on the provision of desired subject-positions. Cf. also below, p. 163–4, on the concept of interpellation.
21. See H. Trevor-Roper, 'Thomas Carlyle's Historical Philosophy', *Times Literary Supplement* (26 June 1981), p. 732.
22. See, e.g., *Jerusalem* (1804–20), 40:58–60, in Blake, *Complete Writings*, p. 668.

23. Roy Fisher, 'Timelessness of Desire', in *Poems 1955–1980* (Oxford, 1980), pp. 106–7.
24. Fredric Jameson, *The Political Unconscious: Narrative as a Socially Symbolic Act* (Ithaca, New York, 1981), p. 68.
25. See above, p. v.
26. See Paul de Man, *The Rhetoric of Romanticism* (New York, 1984), pp. 86 ff.
27. I am using 1789 here as shorthand, although of course the Revolution cannot be described as occurring within a single year: see, e.g., G. Lefebvre, *The French Revolution from its Origins to 1793*, trans. E.M. Evanson (London, 1962), pp. 97 ff.; and D.G. Wright, *Revolution and Terror in France 1789–1795* (London, 1974), pp. 19 ff. On the concept of group narcissism, see the rather ambiguous series of hints in Freud, *Group Psychology and the Analysis of the Ego* (1921), in *Standard Edition*, XVIII, pp. 69–143; and Kohut, pp. 129–31.
28. See Isaac Kramnick, *The Rage of Edmund Burke: Portrait of an Ambivalent Conservative* (New York, 1977), pp. 143–68.
29. *Ibid.*, p. 153.
30. See Burke, *Reflections on the Revolution in France*, ed. C.C. O'Brien (Harmondsworth, 1968), pp. 163–5.
31. *Ibid.*, p. 154.
32. Kramnick, p. 152.
33. *Ibid.*, p. 156.
34. *Ibid.*, p. 157.
35. Burke, 'Letter to a Member of the National Assembly' (1791), in *Works* (16 vols, London, 1826–7), VI, p. 38.
36. See Part 1, note 21.
37. Coleridge, *Poetical Works*, p. 31.
38. See, e.g., *Milton* (1804–08), 25–7, in Blake, *Complete Writings*, pp. 510–14.
39. Bennett, p. 255.
40. Byron, *Poetical Works*, ed. F. Page (Oxford, 1970), p. 73.
41. Matthew Lewis, *The Monk* (London, 1973), pp. 280–1.
42. *Ibid.*, p. 297.
43. Wordsworth, letter to Charles James Fox (14 January 1801), in *The Early Letters of William and Dorothy Wordsworth*, ed. E. de Selincourt (Oxford, 1935), p. 260.
44. *Ibid.*, pp. 261–2.
45. Family disruption is signalled especially by Blake, in, e.g., *Tiriel* (c. 1789), in *Complete Writings*, pp. 99–110; and by Ann Radcliffe in, e.g., *The Mysteries of Udolpho* (1794); see also my *Literature of Terror*, pp. 61–97.
46. M.I. Thomis and P. Holt, *Threats of Revolution in Britain 1789–1848* (London, 1977), p. 130.
47. See E.P. Thompson, *The Making of the English Working Class* (Harmondsworth, 1968), especially towards the end.
48. John Moore, *Zeluco: Various Views of Human Nature, taken from Life and Manners, Foreign and Domestic* (2 vols, London, 1820), I, p. 2.
49. *Ibid.*, I, v.
50. See in addition here Jung, *Memories, Dreams, Reflections*, ed. A. Jaffé (New York, 1962), pp. 220–3.
51. My adaptation of Greimas will be similar to that made by Jameson (see, e.g., pp. 167, 256); although, as will be seen, I prefer a slightly different topography.
52. Coleridge, *Poetical Works*, p. 65.
53. I believe Hephaestos to be the god under whose aegis this work goes on: see above, p. x, and also Jung, e.g., *The Archetypes and the Collective Unconscious* (1968), in *Collected Works*, IX: i, p. 374, where he establishes Hephaestos as one of the 'four archetypal figures belonging ... to the periphery of the self', and as the opposite of the Wise Old Man and thus of the relentless search for omnipotent and unproductive meaning.

54. Coleridge, *Poetical Works*, pp. 65–6.
55. There are many examples of this in Bennett; several of them imply a close connection between the imagery of the French queen and suffering England on the one hand, and the construction of the Gothic heroine on the other.
56. See, e.g., 'The Genius of France' (1792), in Bennett, p. 98.
57. Jonathan Cook, 'The Myth of Revolution: Coup or Consensus?' (unpublished paper, January 1981), p. 2.
58. *Ibid.*, pp. 2–3.
59. The reference, of course, is to Norman Mailer, *Advertisements for Myself* (London, 1961). See for example pp. 281 ff.
60. See Blake, 'Visions of the Daughters of Albion' (1793), 7:24, in *Complete Writings*, p. 194, and Hazlitt, e.g., 'Simple Girls' (1821), in *Selected Writings*, ed. R. Blythe (Harmondsworth, 1970), pp. 454–7.
61. Cowper, *Poetical Works*, p. 412.
62. Cf., e.g., Mario Praz, *The Romantic Agony*, trans. A. Davidson (London, 1951); and Erich Heller, *The Artist's Journey into the Interior, and Other Essays* (London, 1966).
63. The reference is to Blake, e.g., *Jerusalem*, 3:2, in *Complete Writings*, p. 620.
64. See Erdman, *Blake, Prophet against Empire* (Princeton, 1954); and, e.g., I.R. Christie, *Wars and Revolutions: Britain 1760–1815* (London, 1982); Arthur Bryant, *Years of Victory 1802–1812* (London, 1944).
65. See, e.g., D.A. Low, *That Sunny Dome: A Portrait of Regency Britain* (London, 1977), p. 173.
66. See Blake, e.g., 'Book of Urizen', 19:17–46, in *Complete Writings*, p. 232.
67. See, e.g., Coleridge, 'Monody on the Death of Chatterton' (1790), in *Poetical Works*, pp. 13–15; Byron, especially the dramas, e.g., *Manfred*, in *Poetical Works*, pp. 390–406; Shelley, 'Feelings of a Republican on the Fall of Bonaparte' (1815), in *Poetical Works*, pp. 526–7; W.S. Landor, especially the 1830s dialogues: see, e.g., 'Walter Tyrrel and William Rufus', 'Henry the Eighth and Anne Boleyn', in *Poems*, ed. G. Grigson (London, 1964), pp. 102–7, 112–15.
68. See, most significantly, Bloomfield, 'The Farmer's Boy' (1800).
69. Bennett, p. 24.
70. *Ibid.*, pp. 366–8.
71. 'The Farmer and Labourer' (1794), in Bennett, p. 119.
72. *Ibid.*, p. 301.
73. *Ibid.*, pp. 120–1.
74. *Ibid.*, pp. 239–40.
75. *Ibid.*, pp. 266–7.
76. *Ibid.*, pp. 438–9.
77. *Ibid.*, p. 457.
78. The reference is to Blake, e.g., 'The Book of Ahania' (1795), 4:6, in *Complete Writings*, p. 252.
79. This connects again with the presiding presence of Hephaestos. Cf., e.g., W.H. Auden, 'The Shield of Achilles', in *Collected Shorter Poems* (London, 1966), pp. 294–5; also Marion Milner, 'Psychoanalysis and Art' (1956), in *The Suppressed Madness of Sane Men* (London, 1987), pp. 208–9.
80. Keats, *Poems and Verses*, p. 388.
81. *Ibid.*, p. 391.
82. The references are to Keats, 'Ode on Melancholy' (1819), *ibid.*, p. 361.
83. 'Hyperion' (1819), *ibid.*, p. 298.
84. Keats, *ibid.*, p. 310.
85. 'Isabella, or, The Pot of Basil' (1818), *ibid.*, p. 247.
86. I take this to be part of the implication behind Bion's discussion of messianism in basic assumption groups: see Bion, pp. 150 ff.
87. Keats, *Poems and Verses*, p. 223.

88. *Ibid.*, p. 188.
89. Coleridge, 'Kubla Khan', 25, in *Poetical Works*, p. 297.
90. Keats, 'Endymion', in *Poems and Verses*, pp. 188–9.
91. See Auden, 'Culture', in *Collected Shorter Poems, 1930–1944* (London, 1950), p. 62; and Keats, 'Ode on Melancholy', in *Poems and Verses*, p. 361.
92. Cf. Douglas Bush, *Mythology and the Romantic Tradition in English Poetry* (Cambridge, Mass. 1969), p. 84; and for some analogous images, D. Lynch, *Yeats: The Poetics of the Self* (Chicago, 1979).
93. See M.R. James, e.g., 'Mr Humphreys and his Inheritance' (1911), in *The Ghost Stories of M.R. James* (London, 1974), pp. 318–58.
94. The crucial instance here, of course, is the foreshortening of the central definitions of imagination and fancy; see Coleridge, *Biographia Literaria* (1817), ed. G. Watson (London, 1956), pp. 161–7.
95. Wordsworth, 'Guilt and Sorrow' (1791–94), 424–32, in *The Poems*, ed. J.O. Hayden (2 vols, Harmondsworth, 1977), I, p. 133.
96. Wordsworth, 'The Fountain' (1799), 21–32, *ibid.*, I, p. 384.
97. Wordsworth, 'Ode: 1815', 57–86, *ibid.*, II, p. 339.

Part 3

1. See Blake, e.g., 'A Vision of the Last Judgment' (1810), 85, in *Complete Writings*, p. 613. Among critics, see for various positions e.g., Aers, 'William Blake and the Dialectics of Sex', *ELH*, XL (1977), pp. 500–14; J. Lindsay, *William Blake: His Life and Work* (London, 1978), pp. 69–74, 83–5, 90–1, 186; C. Gallant, *Blake and the Assimilation of Chaos* (Princeton, 1978), pp. 172–3; and the revised version of Aers' essay, 'Blake: Sex, Society and Ideology', in Aers, Cook, Punter, *Romanticism and Ideology* (London, 1981), pp. 27–43.
2. See A. Gilchrist, *Life of William Blake* (London, 1942), pp. 96–7. A curious argument is appended:

> The incident of the garden illustrates forcibly the strength of her [Catherine Blake's] husband's influence over her, and the unquestioning manner in which she fell in with all he did or said. When assured by him that she (for the time) was Eve, she would not dream of contradiction — nay, she in a sense believed it. If therefore the anecdote argues madness in one, it argues it in both.

Presumably this laboured piece of interpretation performs the symbolic act of reassuring a Victorian audience of the old, male-supremacist certainties.
3. See J. Lindsay, p. 73; and T. Frosch, *The Awakening of Albion: The Renovation of the Body in the Poetry of William Blake* (Ithaca, New York, 1974), e.g., pp. 25–6.
4. Fielding, *Joseph Andrews*, ed. M.C. Battestin (Oxford, 1967), pp. 299–301.
5. This discourse limited to binary extremes looks forward to processes of psychotic self-identification; it is also the ideological form parodically de-inverted in Blake's usage of 'Angels' and 'Devils'. See, e.g., *The Marriage of Heaven and Hell* (c. 1790–93) and the implications for splitting of the subject in, particularly, Plates 21–4; the preceding images of the monstrous ('spiders' and 'Leviathan') in Plate 18 refer us to the stripes of the 'Tyger', standing over against and interrogating a forbidden unity of agency. See Blake, *Complete Writings*, pp. 156, 157–8.
6. See Ian Watt, *The Rise of the Novel: Studies in Defoe, Richardson and Fielding* (London, 1957), pp. 230–4; and my *Literature of Terror*, pp. 81 ff.
7. Lewis, p. 300.

8. *Ibid.*, p. 301.
9. *Ibid.*, p. 301. The interest of this 'instruction' discourse lies precisely in its revelation of the real connections between a concept of education and the forces of sexual and social reproduction. See in this connection P. Bourdieu and J.-C. Passeron, *Reproduction in Education, Society and Culture*, trans. R. Nice (London and Beverly Hills, 1977).
10. The immediate reference here is to Elizabeth Wilson, *Adorned in Dreams: Fashion and Modernity* (London, 1985), which seems to me relevant to this Pandora-based myth.
11. Blake, *Complete Writings*, p. 40.
12. The most important commentaries are J. Hyppolite, *Studies on Marx and Hegel*, trans. J. O'Neill (New York, 1969), pp. 158–64; and more particularly A. Kojève, *An Introduction to the Reading of Hegel*, ed. A. Bloom, trans. J.H. Nichols, Jr, (Ithaca, New York, 1969), *passim*.
13. See Freud, e.g., *Introductory Lectures on Psychoanalysis* (1916–7), in *Standard Edition*, XV, pp. 208–10; 317–19.
14. Blake, *Complete Writings*, pp. 42–3.
15. This is the major concern of, to take just one instance, M. Rudd, *Organiz'd Innocence: The Story of Blake's Prophetic Books* (London, 1956).
16. It is worth emphasising that this is not an ahistorical point; see Aers, 'Blake: Sex, Society and Ideology', *passim*, and Erdman, *Prophet*, pp. 252–5.
17. *Poetical Sketches*, in Blake, *Complete Writings*, p. 6.
18. J. Laplanche and J.-B. Pontalis, *The Language of Psycho-Analysis*, trans. D. Nicholson-Smith (London, 1980), p. 465.
19. Blake, *Complete Writings*, pp. 189–90.
20. See in this connection Lacan, 'The Signification of the Phallus' (1958), in *Ecrits*, pp. 281–91.
21. Blake, *Complete Writings*, p. 190.
22. *Ibid.*, p. 190.
23. My interpretation of this distinction is based not only on *Daughters of Albion*, but also on passages from the later Prophetic Books. See, e.g., *Milton*, 27:30–41, and *Jerusalem*, 78:1–11, in Blake, *Complete Writings*, pp. 513–14, 718–19.
24. See, e.g., Lovecraft, 'The Dream-Quest of Unknown Kadath', in *At the Mountains of Madness, and Other Novels of Terror* (London, 1966), pp. 155–252.
25. Laplanche and Pontalis, p. 466.
26. See, e.g., *The Book of Thel* (1789), 6:1–22, and *Tiriel*, 2:5–31 (Blake, *Complete Writings*, pp. 130, 100–1). There are, of course, many other literary moments which record rememorations of the birth of the frozen female subject: I think in particular of Sylvia Plath, *The Bell Jar* (London, 1966), pp. 184–5, and Angela Carter, *Love* (London, 1971), pp. 64–72.
27. 'Explosion' is, for instance, the term used in E. Shorter, 'Illegitimacy, Sexual Revolution, and Social Change in Modern Europe', in *The Family in History: Interdisciplinary Essays*, ed. T.K. Rabb and R.I. Rotberg (New York, 1973), p. 49.
28. See, e.g., Shorter, pp. 63–4; also S. Rowbotham, *Women, Resistance and Revolution* (London, 1972), p. 31.
29. Shorter, p. 68; the argument is about children of both sexes, but it is the supply of an anti-authoritarian model to women which is here germane.
30. See W.J. Goode, 'The Role of the Family in Industrialisation', in *Selected Studies in Marriage and the Family*, ed. R.F. Winch and L.W. Goodman (New York, 1968), p. 69; also P. Branca, *Women in Europe since 1750* (London, 1978), p. 91.
31. See, e.g., Branca, p. 86.
32. *Ibid.*, pp. 26–7, and the evidence to which she alludes.
33. See E. Zaretsky, *Capitalism, the Family, and Personal Life* (London, 1976), p. 62; also D. George, *England in Transition* (Harmondsworth, 1953), p. 103.
34. See, e.g., K.M. Rogers, *The Troublesome Helpmate: A History of Misogyny in*

Literature (Seattle, 1966), pp. 160–225; M.A. Doody, 'George Eliot and the Eighteenth-Century Novel', *Nineteenth-Century Fiction*, XXXV (1980), pp. 260–91; and many passages from E. Moers, *Literary Women: The Great Writers* (Garden City, New York, 1977).

35. See Foucault, *The History of Sexuality*, Vol. I: *An Introduction*, trans. R. Hurley (Harmondsworth, 1981).
36. I have elsewhere, in 'Blake, Marxism and Dialectic', *Literature and History*, No. 6 (1977), pp. 229–34, tried to provide some distinctions within this constellation of radicalism.
37. See Foucault, *Power/Knowledge: Selected Interviews and Other Writings, 1972–1977*, ed. Colin Gordon (Brighton, 1980), pp. 118–19.
38. We can find examples of each of these stances in the history of Blake criticism: see, e.g., Rudd, pp. 3–6, 259–60; John Beer, *Blake's Humanism* (Manchester, 1958), pp. 1–22; Max Plowman, *An Introduction to the Study of Blake* (London, 1967), pp. 13–23.
39. *On Virgil* (*c.* 1820), in Blake, *Complete Writings*, p. 778.
40. See Edward Young, *Night Thoughts* (1742–45), I, pp. 68–154 and elsewhere; in, e.g., *The Poetical Works* (2 vols, London, 1844).
41. On the significance of the gaze, see Lacan, *The Four Fundamental Concepts of Psycho-analysis*, ed. Jacques-Alain Miller (London, 1977), pp. 67–119.
42. Cf. my *Literature of Terror*, pp. 36–45.
43. See, e.g., the 'nearly endless depths' referred to in *Blake's Sublime Allegory: Essays on 'The Four Zoas', 'Milton', Jerusalem'*, ed. S. Curran and J.A. Wittreich (Madison, 1973), p. xiv.
44. 'The Keys of the Gates' (*c.* 1818), 19–24, in Blake, *Complete Writings*, p. 771.
45. 'For the Sexes: The Gates of Paradise' (*c.* 1818), 7, *ibid.*, p. 765.
46. See T.J.J. Altizer, *The New Apocalypse: The Radical Christian Vision of William Blake* (East Lansing, Michigan, 1967), pp. xi–xii; M. Schorer, *William Blake: The Politics of Vision* (Gloucester, Mass., 1975), pp. 142–5; P.L. Thorslev, Jr, 'Some Dangers of Dialectic Thinking', in *Romantic and Victorian: Essays in Memory of William H. Marshall*, ed. W.P. Elledge and R.L. Hoffman (Rutherford, New Jersey, 1971), p. 44; and my *Blake, Hegel and Dialectic* (Amsterdam, 1982), e.g., pp. 73–176.
47. I am relying on my understanding of the versions of gender strategy developed in, e.g., Dale Spender, *Man Made Language* (London, 1976); on incorporation, see also, apart from the standard psychoanalytic texts, C. Miller and K. Swift, *Words and Women* (Garden City, New York, 1977), pp. 112–23.
48. Altizer, p. xii.
49. *Marriage of Heaven and Hell*, 11, in Blake, *Complete Writings*, p. 153.
50. Hegel, *On Christianity: Early Theological Writings*, trans. T.M. Knox and R. Kroner (Chicago, 1948), p. 145.
51. *Marriage of Heaven and Hell*, 11, in Blake, *Complete Writings*, p. 153.
52. Hegel, *On Christianity*, p. 133.
53. *Ibid.*, p. 88.
54. *Daughters of Albion*, 5:17–20, in Blake, *Complete Writings*, p. 193.
55. For illustration of the theory here, see Melanie Klein, *The Psycho-analysis of Children*, trans. A. Strachey (London, 1932), pp. 221–4; Klein, 'On Identification', in *New Directions in Psycho-Analysis: The Significance of Infant Conflict in the Pattern of Adult Behaviour*, ed. Klein, P. Heimann and R.E. Money-Kyrle (London, 1955), pp. 330–3; Hanna Segal, 'A Psycho-analytical Approach to Aesthetics', in Klein *et al.*, pp. 391–2; Klein, *Narrative of a Child Analysis: The Conduct of the Psycho-Analysis of Children as Seen in the Treatment of a Ten-year-old Boy* (London, 1961), *passim*.
56. Hegel, *On Christianity*, p. 167.
57. M. Nurmi, *William Blake* (London, 1975), p. 78.
58. See Lacan, *Four Fundamental Concepts*, pp. 34, 113, 281–2; and *Ecrits*, pp. 179–225.

59. J.M.E. McTaggart, *Studies in Hegelian Cosmology* (Cambridge, 1901), pp. 93–4.
60. The references are to Freud, *Totem and Taboo* (1913), in *Standard Edition*, XIII, e.g., pp. 141–6; and Hegel, *Philosophy of Right*, trans. Knox (Oxford, 1942), p. 14.
61. It seems to me to be this 'abrasive' quality, as Barthes might have put it, which also subverts Diana Hume George's attempt at a commentary on the gendered shape of Blake criticism, in *Blake and Freud* (Ithaca, New York, 1980), pp. 244–7; she falls back into moralistic arguments about 'justifying Blake's position'.
62. Cf. Hélène Cixous, 'The Character of ''Character''', trans. K. Cohen, *New Literary History*, V (1974), pp. 383–402; and 'The Laugh of the Medusa', trans. K. and P. Cohen, in *New French Feminisms: An Anthology*, ed. E. Marks and I. de Courtivron (Amherst, Mass., 1980), pp. 245–64.
63. See, e.g. *Milton*, 19:32, and *Jerusalem*, 89:3–4, in Blake, *Complete Writings*, pp. 501, 734.
64. *Milton*, 20:32–40, *ibid.*, p. 502.
65. *Marriage of Heaven and Hell*, 15, *ibid.*, p. 154.
66. *The Introduction to Hegel's 'Philosophy of Fine Art'*, trans. B. Bosanquet (London, 1886), pp. 22–3.
67. *Marriage of Heaven and Hell*, 9:11, in Blake, *Complete Writings*, p. 152.
68. Hegel, *The Phenomenology of Spirit*, trans. A.V. Miller (Oxford, 1977), p. 32.
69. *Marriage of Heaven and Hell*, 10:8, in Blake, *Complete Writings*, p. 152.
70. For some brilliant perceptions about this material and ideological structure, see Andrea Dworkin, *Pornography: Men Possessing Women* (New York, 1981).
71. Hegel, *Aesthetics: Lectures on Fine Art*, trans. Knox (2 vols, Oxford, 1975), p. 164.
72. See Foucault, *Madness and Civilisation: A History of Insanity in the Age of Reason*, trans. R. Howard (New York, 1965), pp. 46–64.
73. Cf. my arguments on the two forms of labour in Blake in 'Blake: Creative and Uncreative Labour', *Studies in Romanticism*, XVI (1977), pp. 544–56; and in 'Blake and the Shapes of London', *Criticism*, XXIII (1981), pp. 16–22.
74. See, e.g., *Jerusalem*, 43:22–3 and 91:21–3, in Blake, *Complete Writings*, pp. 672, 738.
75. Kojève, p. 176.
76. See here, e.g., B. Wilkie and M.L. Johnson, *Blake's 'Four Zoas': The Design of a Dream* (Cambridge, Mass., 1978), pp. 58–60; L. Damrosch, Jr, *Symbol and Truth in Blake's Myth* (Princeton, 1980), pp. 182 ff.; George, pp. 190–201; Aers, 'Dialectics', *passim*.
77. See particularly Hegel, *Lectures on the History of Philosophy*, trans. E.S. Haldane and F.H. Simson (3 vols, London, 1896), III, pp. 431–48.
78. There are parallels here with Tillie Olsen, *Silences* (New York, 1978), especially pp. 22–46.
79. On Hegel see, e.g., J. Glenn Gray, *Hegel and Greek Thought* (New York and Evanston, 1968), p. 92; Hyppolite, pp. 36, 154, 176–7; W.H. Walsh, *Hegelian Ethics* (London, 1969), pp. 31–2; G.R.G. Mure, *The Philosophy of Hegel* (London, 1965), p. 63; F. Engels, *Socialism, Utopian and Scientific*, in Marx and Engels, *Selected Works* (London, 1968), pp. 413–14.
80. Marx, *Capital: A Critique of Political Economy*, ed. Engels (3 vols, New York, 1967), I, p. 20.
81. *Marriage of Heaven and Hell*, 16, in Blake, *Complete Writings*, p. 155.
82. Not, in fact, a phrase of Blake or Hegel, but from their major common source: see Jacob Boehme, *Six Theosophic Points and Other Writings*, trans. J.R. Earle (Ann Arbor, 1958), p. 36. See also Hegel, *History of Philosophy*, III, pp. 188–216.
83. See J. Breuer and Freud, *Studies on Hysteria* (1893–5), in *Standard Edition*, II, especially pp. 37–47, 123–4, 222–39.
84. See, e.g., Moers, pp. 137–67.
85. 'The Mental Traveller' (*c.* 1803), 45–52, in Blake, *Complete Writings*, pp. 425–6.
86. 'Mental Traveller', 53, 55–6, *ibid.*, p. 426.

87. *Daughters of Albion*, 7:24, *ibid.*, p. 194.
88. *Vala, or, The Four Zoas* (1795–1804), Night the Third, 72–6, *ibid.*, p. 293.
89. *Four Zoas*, Night the Ninth, 414–17, *ibid.*, p. 368.
90. *Four Zoas*, Night the Ninth, 849–51, *ibid.*, p. 379.
91. *Jerusalem*, 56:3–9, *ibid.*, p. 688.
92. *Daughters of Albion*, 4:23–4, *ibid.*, p. 192.
93. One of the most resonant reworkings of this area of myth comes in David Lindsay, *A Voyage to Arcturus* (1920), with its hermaphrodites, symbolic representations of sensuous anomaly, and 'shaping' divinities. See below pp. 109–10.
94. *Four Zoas*, Night the Eighth, 92–5, in Blake, *Complete Writings*, p. 343.
95. *Four Zoas*, Night the Eighth, 102–6, *ibid.*, p. 343.
96. *Four Zoas*, Night the Ninth, 830–3, *ibid.*, p. 379.
97. See especially Freud, 'Some Psychical Consequences of the Anatomical Distinction between the Sexes' (1925), in *Standard Edition*, XIX, pp. 249–51, 255.
98. 'The Human Abstract', 24, in Blake, *Complete Writings*, p. 217.
99. See *Four Zoas*, Night the First, 47–58, *ibid.*, p. 265.
100. See, e.g., *Jerusalem*, 85:14–86:13, *ibid.*, pp. 730–31.
101. *Marriage of Heaven and Hell*, 9:5, *ibid.*, p. 152.
102. Hegel, *Phenomenology*, pp. 5–6.
103. See, e.g., Meister Eckhart, 'Talks of Instruction', in *Selected Writings*, ed. J.M. Clark and J.V. Skinner (London, 1958), p. 95.
104. See, e.g., D. MacKinnon, 'Some Epistemological Reflections on Mystical Experience', in *Mysticism and Philosophical Analysis*, ed. S.T. Katz (London, 1978), pp. 132–40.
105. *America*, cancelled plate b:10–14, in Blake, *Complete Writings*, p. 204. The other reference occurs in *Jerusalem*, 53:24, *ibid.*, p. 684.
106. See, e.g., Hans Lassen Martensen, *Jakob Boehme 1575–1624: Studies in his Life and Teaching*, ed. S. Hobhouse (London, 1949), p. 45.
107. See Altizer, *passim*; also Altizer and W. Hamilton, *Radical Theology and the Death of God* (Harmondsworth, 1968), and Jerry Gill, *On Knowing God* (Philadelphia, 1981).
108. This is the Oxford English Dictionary definition.
109. Philippians 2:6–7 (Knox translation).
110. *Milton*, 15:21–7, in Blake, *Complete Writings*, p. 497.
111. Broadbent, 'Darkness', in *Exploring Individual and Organisational Boundaries*, ed. W.G. Lawrence (Chichester, 1979), pp. 193–203.
112. Conrad, *Heart of Darkness* (Harmondsworth, 1973), pp. 50–1.
113. *Ibid.*, p. 8.
114. See, e.g., *Jerusalem*, 43:12–79, in Blake, *Complete Writings*, pp. 672–3.
115. Significantly, in this context, the four heralds of *America*, cancelled plate c:14, *ibid.*, p. 205, and elsewhere; and the four harps of *The Song of Los* (1795), 3:2, *ibid.*, p. 245.
116. Conrad, p. 100.
117. See Algernon Blackwood, *The Human Chord* (London, 1910), especially pp. 283–307.
118. See, e.g., *Jerusalem*, 30:1–8, in Blake, *Complete Writings*, p. 655.
119. D. Lindsay, *Voyage to Arcturus* (London, 1972), p. 197.
120. The references are to *America*, 1:4; *Four Zoas*, Night the Seventh (b), 142, and Night the Eighth, 481; *Europe*, 1:1; *Four Zoas*, Night the Seventh (b), 145, and Night the Eighth, 479; *Four Zoas*, Night the Seventh (b), 125; *Milton*, 34:27. See Blake, *Complete Writings*, pp. 195, 238, 336, 353, 524. Although these references are only a part of Blake's dealings with the 'shadowy female', they nonetheless constitute a sub-narrative of their own.
121. A.C. Swinburne, 'Hertha', in *Collected Poetical Works* (2 vols, London, 1924), I, p. 735.
122. See Tacitus, *De Origine et Situ Germanorum*, ed. J.G.C. Anderson (Oxford, 1938), p. 26.

123. See S. Payne, 'The Christian Character of Christian Mystical Experiences', *Religious Studies*, XX (1984), pp. 417–27.
124. Cf. W.T. Stace, *Mysticism and Philosophy* (London, 1960), pp. 102–3.
125. See, e.g., *Milton*, 42–7, in Blake, *Complete Writings*, pp. 534–5.
126. Samuel Beckett, *The Unnamable* (London, 1975), p. 67.
127. See, e.g., *Book of Urizen*, 5:19–7:9, in Blake, *Complete Writings*, pp. 225–6.
128. See, e.g., *Four Zoas*, Night the Seventh, 370–499, *ibid.*, pp. 329–32.
129. See Brentano, *Psychology from an Empirical Standpoint*, ed. O. Kraus and L.L. McAlister (London, 1973), pp. 88–91.
130. Beckett, p. 128.
131. Toukaram, *Psaumes du pèlerin*, trans. G.-A. Deleury (Paris, 1956), p. 160; but the translation here is that of Ben-Ami Scharfstein, *Mystical Experience* (Oxford, 1974), pp. 155–6, whose argument I am here following closely.
132. Scharfstein, p. 134.
133. *Ibid.*, p. 134.
134. See, e.g., Jakobson, 'Linguistics and Poetics', in *Style in Language*, ed. T.A. Sebeok (Boston, 1960), pp. 350–77.
135. See, e.g., Boehme, *The Signature of All Things*, ed. C. Bax (London, 1969).
136. C. Landis, *Varieties of Psychopathological Experience* (New York, 1964), pp. 283–4.
137. See above, p. v.
138. Cf. Freud, 'Psycho-Analytic Notes on an Autobiographical Account of a Case of Paranoia' (1911), in *Standard Edition*, XII, pp. 1–82.
139. *Four Zoas*, Night the First, 76–81, in Blake, *Complete Writings*, p. 266.
140. W.S. Graham, 'The Dark Dialogues', in *Collected Poems 1942–1977* (London, 1979), p. 159.
141. *Ibid.*, p. 165.

Part 4

1. I am thinking of essays like, for instance, 'Function and Field', in *Ecrits*, pp. 30–113.
2. See, e.g., S. Ferenczi, *Final Contributions to the Problems and Methods of Psychoanalysis*, ed. M. Balint (London, 1955), p. 246.
3. For a description of psychoanalytic stance as I mean it here, see E. Levenson, *The Fallacy of Understanding* (New York, 1972), pp. 211 ff.; and for a close parallel, Krishnamurti, pp. 21 ff.
4. See J. Strachey, 'The Nature of the Therapeutic Action of Psychoanalysis', *International Journal of Psycho-Analysis* (1969). For this reference and those in the previous note, I am indebted to Barry Palmer and his unpublished paper, 'Interpretation and the Consultant Role' (1984).
5. See, e.g., E.B. Gose, *Imagination Indulged: The Irrational in the Nineteenth-Century Novel* (Montreal and London, 1972), pp. 27 ff.; E. MacAndrew, *The Gothic Tradition in Fiction* (New York, 1979), pp. 241 ff.
6. See my *Literature of Terror*, pp. 56–9.
7. See, e.g., E.K. Sedgwick, *Between Men: English Literature and Homosocial Desire* (New York, 1985).
8. On alienation, it is particularly interesting to look at M. Franklin, 'On Hegel's Theory of Alienation and its Historic Force', *Tulane Studies in Philosophy*, IX (1960), pp. 50–100.
9. See Coleridge, *Miscellaneous Criticism*, ed. T.M. Raysor (London, 1936), pp. 355–82.
10. Or 'hermeneutic code'; see Barthes, *S/Z*, trans. R. Miller (London, 1975), p. 19.

11. See particularly Marcuse, *Eros and Civilisation: A Philosophical Inquiry into Freud* (Boston, 1966); Brown, *Life Against Death: the Psychoanalytical Meaning of History* (London, 1959); Reich, *Sex-Pol: Essays 1929-1934*, ed. L. Baxandall (New York, 1972).

12. The most illuminating perspectives on expectancy, I believe, are offered by the group analysts; see, e.g., Bion, pp. 150-2.

13. The most useful book about Klein is Segal, *Klein* (Brighton, 1979). See also M. Rustin, 'A Socialist Consideration of Kleinian Psychoanalysis', *New Left Review*, No. 131 (1982), pp. 71-96. See also *Feminine Sexuality: Jacques Lacan and the 'Ecole Freudienne'*, ed. J. Mitchell and J. Rose (London, 1982), *passim*.

14. See particularly Klein, 'On the Theory of Anxiety and Guilt', in *Envy and Gratitude, and Other Works 1946-1963* (London, 1975), pp. 25-42; 'A Contribution to the Psychogenesis of Manic-Depressive States', in *Love, Guilt and Reparation, and Other Works 1921-1945* (London, 1975), pp. 262-89.

15. See Klein, 'Early Analysis', in *Love, Guilt and Reparation*, pp. 77-105; 'On Observing the Behaviour of Young Infants', in *Envy and Gratitude*, pp. 94-121; and 'The Importance of Symbol-Formation in the Development of the Ego', in *Love, Guilt and Reparation*, pp. 219-32.

16. 'Importance of Symbol-Formation', pp. 219-21.

17. Horace Walpole, *The Castle of Otranto*, ed. W.S. Lewis (London, 1969), pp. xii–xiii.

18. *Ibid.*, pp. 16-17.

19. See, e.g., E. Birkhead, *The Tale of Terror: A Study of the Gothic Romance* (London, 1921), p. 19.

20. See Lacan, especially 'Question Preliminary to any Treatment of Psychosis', pp. 179-225.

21. Mary Shelley, *Frankenstein*, ed. R.E. Dowse and D.J. Palmer (London, 1963), p. 28.

22. *Ibid.*, p. 49.

23. *Ibid.*, p. 51.

24. Cf. Klein, 'Envy and Gratitude', in *Envy and Gratitude*, pp. 176-235.

25. See Lawrence Stone, *The Family, Sex and Marriage in England 1500-1800* (London, 1977); C.C. Harris, *The Family and Industrial Society* (London, 1983).

26. See, e.g., Freud, 'Psycho-analysis' (1923), in *Standard Edition*, XVIII, 245-6.

27. This quotation actually refers to a paper in which one of her colleagues is presenting Klein's views. See Heimann, 'Certain Functions of Introjection and Projection in Early Infancy', in *Developments in Psycho-Analysis*, ed. J. Riviere (London, 1952), pp. 122-68.

28. These themes run throughout Klein's work; but see, e.g., 'Some Theoretical Conclusions Regarding the Emotional Life of the Infant', in *Envy and Gratitude*, pp. 61-93.

29. See Klein, 'Contribution to the Psychogenesis of Manic-Depressive States'; and 'Notes on Some Schizoid Mechanisms', in *Envy and Gratitude*, pp. 1-24.

30. See my *Literature of Terror*, pp. 130-59.

31. See, e.g., Klein, 'On the Theory of Anxiety and Guilt', p. 34.

32. Cf. Freud, e.g., *On Narcissism*, 88-91.

33. See, e.g., R. Douglas, *Land, People and Politics: A History of the Land Question in the United Kingdom, 1878-1952* (London, 1976); G.E. Mingay, *Enclosure and the Small Farmer in the Age of the Industrial Revolution* (London, 1968); P. Deane, *The First Industrial Revolution* (Cambridge, 1979).

34. Shelley, 'Ode to the West Wind', 43-51, in *Poetical Works*, pp. 578-9.

35. 'West Wind', 51-6, *ibid.*, p. 579.

36. 'West Wind', 57-62, *ibid.*, p. 579.

37. 'West Wind', 63-70, *ibid.*, p. 579.

38. The reference is to Poe, 'The Facts in the Case of M. Valdemar' (1845); see *Poetry and Tales*, ed. P.F. Quinn (New York, 1984), pp. 833-42.

39. The references are to Brecht, *The Messingkauf Dialogues*, trans. J. Willett (London, 1965), p. 46; and to Hegel, *Phenomenology*, e.g., p. 356.

40. See Hazlitt, 'On Gusto', in *Selected Writings*, pp. 201–5.
41. There is a whole constellation of evidence within romanticism for this stance towards justice, and it clearly has to do with a dialectic within the self. Rzepka puts it this way:

> The dark underside of this anxious investment of power in the Other to bring the self into being is the poet's feeling that he has to a great extent lost control over the self made manifest in any social situation, and that the Other possesses as great a power to rob him of himself, to distort or misinterpret or paralyse the true self, as to bring it to life.
>
> (Rzepka, p. 27)

42. See G. Vico, *The New Science* (1725), trans. T.G. Bergin and M.H. Fisch (Ithaca, New York, 1970), e.g., p. 5.
43. Much of the theory here can be found in the journal *Human Relations*; see in particular the many articles by J.P. Gustafson *et al.*
44. Coleridge, *Poetical Works*, p. 186.
45. See Aers, Cook, Punter, 'Coleridge: Individual, Community and Social Agency', in Aers, Cook, Punter, pp. 82–102.
46. The reference is to Henry James, 'The Lesson of the Master' (1888), which, like 'The Real Thing' (1892), also poses interesting questions about where mastery really lies, and about the relation between an outer, reflected perfection and a central hollow, held together only by a web of commercialised expectation and need.
47. See Jung, e.g. *Psychology and Alchemy*, p. 22.
48. Cf. my *Literature of Terror*, pp. 256–63.
49. See Klein, *Narrative of a Child Analysis*, e.g., pp. 56–61; 72–7; 146–51.
50. See Poe, pp. 278–97.
51. On puns, see Freud, *Jokes and their Relation to the Unconscious* (1905), in *Standard Edition*, VIII; also *The Psychopathology of Everyday Life* (1901), in *Standard Edition*, VI, pp. 53–105, on 'slips of the tongue'. For *The Cask of Amontillado*, see Poe, pp. 848–54.
52. See here also Norman Holland, *Laughing: A Psychology of Humour* (Ithaca, New York, 1982), pp. 47–60, 88–103; W.H. Martineau, 'A Model of the Social Functions of Humour', in *The Psychology of Humour: Theoretical Perspectives and Empirical Issues*, ed. J.H. Goldstein and P.E. McGhee (New York, 1972), pp. 101–25.
53. Poe, pp. 227–8.
54. See Lacan, 'The Subversion of the Subject and the Dialectic of Desire in the Freudian Unconscious' (1960), in *Ecrits*, pp. 292–325; also Jung, *The Psychology of Dementia Praecox* (1907), and 'The Content of the Psychoses' (1914), in *Collected Works*, III, 1–151 and 153–78.
55. Poe, p. 505.
56. *Ibid.*, p. 221.
57. *Ibid.*, p. 198.
58. *Ibid.*, p. 201.
59. *Ibid.*, p. 159.
60. *Ibid.*, p. 317.
61. *Ibid.*, p. 657
62. *Ibid.*, p. 262.

Part 5

1. Cf., e.g., F. Capra, *The Tao of Physics* (Berkeley, 1975); P. Feyerabend, *Against Method* (London, 1975); J. Losee, *A Historical Introduction to the Philosophy of Science*

(Oxford, 1980), pp. 189–220, and the major works cited therein.

2. See on this tendency Thorslev, 'Some Dangers'.

3. For Coleridge speaking directly of the unconscious, see N. Fruman's tendentious *Coleridge: The Damaged Archangel* (London, 1971), pp. 201 ff.

4. See Louis Althusser, *Lenin and Philosophy, and Other Essays*, trans. B. Brewster (London, 1971), pp. 162–70.

5. See, e.g., Easthope, pp. 34–47 and elsewhere.

6. See Pierre Macherey, 'Lenin, Critic of Tolstoy' (1964), in *A Theory of Literary Production*, trans. G. Wall (London, 1978), pp. 105–35.

7. See above, p. 31.

8. Briefly, because patriarchy fundamentally inflects our imaginings of home as *space*; and mysticism has centrally to do with our at-home-ness in *time*.

9. See Coleridge, *Hints towards the Formation of a more Comprehensive Theory of Life*, ed. S.B. Watson (London, 1848); and Hegel, *Philosophy of Nature*, ed. M.J. Petry (3 vols, London, 1970), esp. III, p. 102 ff.

10. The reference is to Oscar Wilde, *The Picture of Dorian Gray* (1891). I am assuming that the picture here carries the full weight of the mirror as reflection and concealment; see again Pines, 'Reflections on Mirroring', *passim*.

11. The immediate references are to Shelley, 'Ode to the West Wind' and 'Ozymandias' (1817), in *Poetical Works*, pp. 550, 577–9.

12. The reference is to J.G. Fichte, e.g., *Science of Knowledge* (1794–1802), ed. and trans. P. Heath and J. Lachs (New York, 1970), pp. 14–16; and thus to Jürgen Habermas, *Knowledge and Human Interests*, trans. J.J. Shapiro (Boston, 1971), *passim*.

13. Thorslev, *Romantic Contraries: Freedom versus Destiny* (New Haven, 1984), p. 82.

14. See Blake, e.g., *Marriage of Heaven and Hell*, 4 and 14, in *Complete Writings*, pp. 149 and 154; and Coleridge, 'Dejection', 21–38 and 47–58, in *Poetical Works*, pp. 364, 365.

15. See, e.g., *Jerusalem*, 59:26–55, in Blake, *Complete Writings*, pp. 691–2.

16. Lacan, 'The Agency of the Letter in the Unconscious or Reason since Freud' (1957), in *Ecrits*, p. 161.

17. Jung, 'The Undiscovered Self', p. 288.

18. *Ibid.*, p. 291.

19. De Man, p. 50.

20. *Ibid.*, p. 50.

21. *Ibid.*, p. 58.

BIBLIOGRAPHY OF WORKS AND EDITIONS CITED

Aers, David, 'William Blake and the Dialectics of Sex', *ELH*, XL (1977), 500–14.

Aers, David, Cook, Jonathan and Punter, David, *Romanticism and Ideology: Studies in English Writing 1765–1830* (Routledge and Kegan Paul: London, 1981).

Aers, David, Clark, Robert, Cook, Jonathan, Glasser, Thomas, and Punter, David, 'Strategies for Representing Revolution', in *1789: Reading Writing Revolution*, ed. F. Barker *et al.* (Essex University: Colchester, 1982).

Althusser, Louis, *Lenin and Philosophy, and Other Essays*, trans. B. Brewster (New Left Books: London, 1971).

Altizer, T. J. J., *The New Apocalypse: The Radical Christian Vision of William Blake* (Michigan University Press: East Lansing, Mich., 1967).

Altizer, T. J. J. and Hamilton, W., *Radical Theology and the Death of God* (Penguin: Harmondsworth, Middx., 1968).

Auden, W. H., *Collected Shorter Poems*, (Faber & Faber: London, 1966).

Auden, W. H., *Collected Shorter Poems 1930–1944* (Faber & Faber: London, 1950).

Austen, Jane, *Emma* (1816), ed. R. Blythe (Penguin: Harmondsworth, Middx., 1966).

Austen, Jane, *Northanger Abbey* (1818), ed. A. H. Ehrenpreis (Penguin: Harmondsworth, Middx., 1972).

Barthes, Roland, *S/Z*, trans. R. Miller (Cape: London, 1975).

Baudrillard, Jean, *Le système des objets* (Gallimard: Paris, 1968).

Beckett, Samuel, *The Unnamable* (1953) (Pbk edn, Calder and Boyars: London, 1975).

Beer, John, *Blake's Humanism* (Manchester University Press: Manchester, 1958).

Bennett, Betty, ed., *British War Poetry in the Age of Romanticism: 1793–1815* (Garland: New York and London, 1976).

Berger, John, Blomberg, Sven, Fox, Chris, Dibb, Michael and Hollis, Richard, *Ways of Seeing*, (BBC/Penguin: London, 1972).

Berryman, John, *Selected Poems 1938–1968* (Faber & Faber: London, 1972).

Bion, W. R., *Experiences in Groups and Other Papers* (Tavistock: London, 1961).

Birkhead, Edith, *The Tale of Terror: A Study of the Gothic Romance*, (Constable: London, 1921).

Blackwood, Algernon, *The Human Chord* (Macmillan: London, 1910).

Blake, William, *Complete Writings*, ed. G. Keynes (Oxford University Press:

London, 1966).

Bloom, Harold, *Agon: Towards a Theory of Revisionism* (Oxford University Press: New York, 1982).

Bloomfield, Robert and Nathaniel, '*The Farmer's Boy*', '*Rural Tales*', '*Good Tidings*' *with* '*An Essay on War*', ed. D. H. Reiman (Garland: New York, 1977).

Boehme, Jacob, *The Signature of All Things*, ed. C. Bax, (Dent: London, 1969).

Boehme, Jacob, *Six Theosophic Points and Other Writings*, trans. J. R. Earle (University of Michigan Press: Ann Arbor, Mich., 1958).

Bourdieu, Pierre and Passeron, J.-C., *Reproduction in Education, Society and Culture*, trans. R. Nice (Sage: London and Beverly Hills, 1977).

Branca, Patricia, *Women in Europe since 1750* (Croom Helm: London, 1978).

Brecht, Bertolt, *The Messingkauf Dialogues*, trans. J. Willett (Methuen: London, 1965).

Brentano, Franz, *Psychology from an Empirical Standpoint*, ed. O. Kraus and L. L. McAlister (Routledge and Kegan Paul: London, 1973).

Broadbent, John, 'Darkness', in *Exploring Individual and Organisational Boundaries*, ed. W. G. Lawrence (Wiley: Chichester, 1979).

Brontë, Emily, *Wuthering Heights* (1847), ed. D. Daiches (Penguin: Harmondsworth, Middx., 1968).

Brown, Norman O., *Life Against Death: the Psychoanalytical Meaning of History* (Routledge and Kegan Paul: London, 1959).

Bryant, Arthur, *Years of Victory 1802–1812* (Collins: London, 1944).

Burke, Edmund, *A Philosophical Enquiry into the Origin of Our Ideas of the Sublime and Beautiful* (1756), ed. J. T. Boulton (Routledge and Kegan Paul: London, 1958).

Burke, Edmund, *Reflections on the Revolution in France* (1790), ed. C. C. O'Brien (Penguin: Harmondsworth, Middx., 1968).

Burke, Edmund, *Works*, 16 vols (Rivington: London, 1826–7).

Bush, Douglas, *Mythology and the Romantic Tradition in English Poetry* (Harvard University Press: Cambridge, Mass., 1969).

Byron, Lord, *Poetical Works*, ed. F. Page (Oxford University Press: Oxford, 1970).

Capra, Fritjof, *The Tao of Physics* (Shambhala: Berkeley, Calif., 1975).

Carter, Angela, *Love*, (Hart-Davis: London, 1971).

Christie, I. R., *Wars and Revolutions: Britain 1760–1815* (Edward Arnold: London, 1982).

Cixous, Hélène, 'The Character of "Character"', trans. K. Cohen, *New Literary History*, V (1974), pp. 383–402.

Coleridge, S. T., *Biographia Literaria* (1817), ed. G. Watson (Dent: London, 1956).

Coleridge, S. T., *Hints towards the Formation of a more Comprehensive Theory of Life*, ed. S. B. Watson (John Churchill: London, 1848).

Coleridge, S. T., *Miscellaneous Criticism*, ed. T. M. Raysor (Constable: London, 1936).

Coleridge, S. T., *Poetical Works*, ed. E. H. Coleridge (Oxford University Press: London, 1967).

Conrad, Joseph, *Heart of Darkness* (1902) (Pbk edn, Penguin: Harmondsworth, Middx., 1973).

Cowper, William, *Poetical Works*, ed. H. S. Milford (Oxford University Press:

London, 1934).

Curran, Stewart and Wittreich, J. A., eds, *Blake's Sublime Allegory: Essays on 'The Four Zoas', 'Milton', 'Jerusalem'* (University of Wisconsin Press: Madison, Wisc., 1973).

Damrosch, Leopold, Jr, *Symbol and Truth in Blake's Myth* (Princeton University Press: Princeton, N.J., 1980).

Deane, Phyllis, *The First Industrial Revolution* (Cambridge University Press: Cambridge, 1979).

De Man, Paul, *The Rhetoric of Romanticism* (Columbia University Press: New York, 1984).

Derrida, Jacques, *Edmund Husserl's Origin of Geometry: An Introduction*, trans. J. P. Leavey, Jr (N. Hays: Stony Brook, N.Y., 1978).

Derrida, Jacques, *Speech and Phenomena, and Other Essays on Husserl's Theory of Signs*, trans. D. B. Allison (Northwestern University Press: Evanston, Ill., 1973).

Doody, M. A., 'George Eliot and the Eighteenth-Century Novel', *Nineteenth-Century Fiction*, **XXXV** (1980), pp. 260–91.

Douglas, Roy, *Land, People and Politics: A History of the Land Question in the United Kingdom 1878–1952* (Allison and Busby: London, 1976).

Dworkin, Andrea, *Pornography: Men Possessing Women* (The Women's Press: New York, 1981).

Easthope, Antony, *Poetry as Discourse* (Methuen: London, 1983).

Eckhart, Meister, *Selected Writings*, ed. J. M. Clark and J. V. Skinner (Faber & Faber: London, 1958).

Erdman, D. V., *Blake: Prophet against Empire* (Princeton: Princeton University Press, N.J., 1954).

Fechner, G. T., *Elemente der Psychophysik* (Leipzig, 1860).

Ferenczi, Sándor, *Final Contribution to the Problems and Methods of Psychoanalysis*, ed. M. Balint (Hogarth: London, 1955).

Feyerabend, Paul, *Against Method* (New Left Books: London, 1975).

Fichte, J. G., *Science of Knowledge*, (1794–1802), ed. and trans. P. Heath and J. Lachs (Appleton-Century-Crofts: New York, 1970).

Fielding, Henry, *The History of the Adventures of Joseph Andrews* (1742), ed. A. R. Humphreys (Dent: London, 1968).

Fisher, Roy, *Poems 1955–1980* (Oxford University Press: Oxford, 1980).

Foucault, Michel, *The History of Sexuality*, Vol. I, *An Introduction*, trans. R. Hurley, (Penguin: Harmondsworth, Middx., 1981).

Foucault, Michel, *Language, Counter-Memory, Practice*, trans. D. F. Bouchard and S. Simon (Blackwell: Oxford, 1977).

Foucault, Michel, *Madness and Civilisation: A History of Insanity in the Age of Reason*, trans. R. Howard (Tavistock: New York, 1965).

Foucault, Michel, *Power/Knowledge: Selected Interviews and Other Writings, 1972–1977*, ed. Colin Gordon, (Harvester: Brighton, 1980).

Franklin, Mitchell, 'On Hegel's Theory of Alienation and its Historic Force', *Tulane Studies in Philosophy*, **IX** (1960), 50–100.

Freud, Sigmund, *The Standard Edition of the Complete Psychological Works of Sigmund Freud*, ed. James Strachey in collaboration with Anna Freud, assisted by Alix Strachey and Alan Tyson, 24 vols, (Hogarth: London, 1953–74).

Frosch, Thomas, *The Awakening of Albion: The Renovation of the Body in the*

Poetry of William Blake (Cornell University Press: Ithaca, N.Y., 1974).

Fruman, Norman, *Coleridge. The Damaged Archangel* (Allen and Unwin: London, 1971).

Gallant, Christine, *Blake and the Assimilation of Chaos* (Princeton University Press: Princeton, N.J., 1978).

George, Diana Hume, *Blake and Freud* (Cornell University Press: Ithaca, N.Y., 1980).

George, Dorothy, *England in Transition* (Penguin: Harmondsworth, Middx., 1953).

Gilchrist, Alexander, *Life of William Blake* (1863), ed. Ruthven Todd (Dent: 1942).

London, Gill, Jerry, *On Knowing God* (Westminster Press: Philadelphia, Pa., 1981).

Godwin, William, *The Adventures of Caleb Williams: or, Things as They Are* (1794), ed. H. von Thal, introd. W. Allen (Cassell: London, 1966).

Goldstein, J. H. and McGhee, P. E., eds, *The Psychology of Humour: Theoretical Perspectives and Empirical Issues* (Academic Press: New York, 1972).

Gose, E. B., *Imagination Indulged: The Irrational in the Nineteenth-Century Novel* (McGill-Queen's University Press: Montreal and London, 1972).

Graham, W. S., *Collected Poems 1942-1977* (Faber & Faber: London 1979).

Gray, J. Glenn, *Hegel and Greek Thought* (Harper and Row: New York and Evanston, Ill., 1968).

Habermas, Jürgen, *Knowledge and Human Interests*, trans. J. J. Shapiro (Beacon: Boston, Mass., 1971).

Harris, C. C., *The Family and Industrial Society* (Allen and Unwin: London, 1983).

Hazlitt, William, *Selected Writings*, ed. R. Blythe (Penguin: Harmondsworth, Middx., 1970).

Hegel, G. W. F., *Aesthetics: Lectures on Fine Art*, trans. T. M. Knox, 2 vols (Clarendon: Oxford, 1975).

Hegel, G. W. F., *The Introduction to Hegel's 'Philosophy of Fine Art'*, trans. B. Bosanquet (Kegan Paul: London, 1886).

Hegel, G. W. F., *Lectures on the History of Philosophy*, trans. E. S. Haldane and F. H. Simson, 3 vols (Kegan Paul, Trench, Trubner: London, 1896).

Hegel, G. W. F., *On Christianity: Early Theological Writings*, trans. T. M. Knox and R. Kroner (University of Chicago Press: Chicago, 1948).

Hegel, G. W. F., *The Phenomenology of Spirit* (1807), trans. A. V. Miller (Clarendon: Oxford, 1977).

Hegel, G. W. F., *Philosophy of Nature*, ed. M. J. Petry, 3 vols (Allen and Unwin: London, 1970).

Hegel, G. W. F., *Philosophy of Right* (1821), trans. T. M. Knox (Clarendon: Oxford, 1942).

Heller, Erich, *The Artist's Journey into the Interior, and Other Essays* (Secker and Warburg: London, 1966).

Hillman, James, *The Myth of Analysis: Three Essays in Archetypal Psychology* (Northwestern University Press: Evanston, Ill., 1972).

Hoban, Russell, *Riddley Walker* (Cape: London, 1980).

Hofstadter, D. R., *Gödel, Escher, Bach: An Eternal Golden Braid* (Harvester:

Brighton, 1979).

Hogg, James, *The Private Memoirs and Confessions of a Justified Sinner* (1824), ed. J. Carey (Oxford University Press: London, 1970).

Holland, Norman, *Laughing: A Psychology of Humour* (Cornell University Press: Ithaca, N.Y., 1982).

Hough, Graham, *The Romantic Poets* (Hutchinson: London, 1953).

Hyppolite, Jean, *Studies on Marx and Hegel*, trans. J. O'Neill (Heinemann: New York, 1969).

Jakobson, Roman, 'Linguistics and Poetics', in *Style in Language*, ed. T. A. Sebeok (M.I.T. Press: Boston, 1960).

James, M. R., *The Ghost Stories of M. R. James* (Edward Arnold: London, 1974).

Jameson, Fredric, *The Political Unconscious: Narrative as a Socially Symbolic Act* (Cornell University Press: Ithaca, New York, 1981).

Johnson, R. W., *The Politics of Recession* (Macmillan: London, 1985).

Jung, C. G., *The Collected Works of C. G. Jung*, ed. Herbert Read, Michael Fordham, Gerhard Adler, 20 vols (Routledge and Kegan Paul: London, 1953-79).

Jung, C. G. *Memories, Dreams, Reflections*, ed. A. Jaffé (Pantheon: New York, 1962).

Katz, S. T., ed., *Mysticism and Philosophical Analysis* (Sheldon Press: London, 1978).

Keats, John, *The Poems and Verses of John Keats*, ed. J. Middleton Murry (Peter Nevill: London, 1949).

Klein, A. F., *Effective Groupwork: An Introduction to Principle and Method* (Association Press: New York, 1972).

Klein, Melanie, *Envy and Gratitude, and Other works 1946-1963* (Hogarth: London, 1975).

Klein, Melanie, *Love, Guilt and Reparation, and Other Works 1921-1945* (Hogarth: London, 1975).

Klein, Melanie, *Narrative of a Child Analysis: The Conduct of the Psycho-Analysis of Children as seen in the Treatment of a Ten-year-old Boy* (Hogarth: London, 1961).

Klein, Melanie, *The Psychoanalysis of Children*, trans. A. Strachey (Hogarth: London, 1932).

Klein, Melanie, Heinmann P. and Money-Kyrle, R. E., eds., *New Directions in Psycho-Analysis: The Significance of Infant Conflict in the Pattern of Adult Behaviour* (Tavistock: London, 1955).

Kohut, Heinz, *The Restoration of the Self* (International Universities Press: New York, 1977).

Kojève, Alexandre, *An Introduction to the Reading of Hegel*, ed. A. Bloom, trans. J. H. Nichols, Jr (Cornell University Press: Ithaca, New York, 1969).

Kramnick, Isaac, *The Rage of Edmund Burke: Portrait of an Ambivalent Conservative* (Basic Books: New York, 1977).

Krishnamurti, J., *The Penguin Krishnamurti Reader*, ed. M. Lutyens (Penguin: Harmondsworth, Middx., 1970).

Lacan, Jacques, *Ecrits*, trans. A. Sheridan (Tavistock: London, 1977).

Lacan, Jacques, *The Four Fundamental Concepts of Psycho-Analysis*, ed. J.-A. Miller (Hogarth: London, 1977).

Landis, Carney, *Varieties of Psychopathological Experience* (Holt, Rinehart and Winston: New York, 1964).

Landor, W. S., *Poems*, ed. G. Grigson, (Centaur Press: London, 1964).

Laplanche, Jean and J.-B. Pontalis, *The Language of Psycho-Analysis*, trans. D. Nicholson-Smith (Hogarth: London, 1980).

Lee, Sophia, *The Recess, or, A Tale of Other Times*, 3 vols (London, 1785).

LeFanu, Joseph Sheridan, *Uncle Silas: A Tale of Bartram-Haugh* (1864), ed. F. Shroyer (Dover: New York, 1966).

Lefebvre, G., *The French Revolution from its Origins to 1793*, trans. F. M. Evanson (Routledge and Kegan Paul: London, 1962).

Levenson, Edgar, *The Fallacy of Understanding* (Basic Books: New York, 1972).

Lewis, Matthew, *The Monk* (1796), (pbk edn, New English Library: London, 1973).

Lindsay, David, *A Voyage to Arcturus* (1920) (pbk edn, Sphere: London, 1972).

Lindsay, Jack, *William Blake: His Life and Work* (Constable: London, 1978).

Losee, John , *A Historical Introduction to the Philosophy of Science* (Oxford University Press: Oxford, 1980).

Lovecraft, H. P., *At the Mountains of Madness, and Other Novels of Terror* (Panther: London, 1966).

Low, D. A., *The Sunny Dome: A Portrait of Regency Britain* (Dent: London, 1977).

Lynch, David, *Yeats: The Poetics of the Self* (University of Chicago Press: Chicago 1979).

MacAndrew, Elizabeth, *The Gothic Tradition in Fiction* (Columbia University Press: New York, 1979).

Macherey, Pierre, *A Theory of Literary Production*, trans. G. Wall (Routledge and Kegan Paul: London, 1978).

Mailer, Norman, *Advertisements for Myself* (Deutsch: London, 1961).

Marcuse, Herbert, *Eros and Civilisation: A Philosophical Inquiry into Freud* (Beacon: Boston, Mass., 1966).

Marks, Elaine and de Courtivron, I., eds, *New French Feminisms: An Anthology* (University of Massachusetts Press, Amherst, Mass., 1980).

Martensen, Hans Lassen, *Jacob Boehme 1575–1624: Studies in his Life and Teaching*, ed. S. Hobhouse (Rockliff: London, 1949).

Marx, Karl, *Capital: A Critique of Political Economy*, ed. F. Engels, 3 vols (International Publishers: New York, 1967).

Marx, Karl and Engels, Friedrich, *Selected Works* (Lawrence and Wishart: London, 1968).

McFarland, Thomas, *Coleridge and the Pantheist Tradition* (Clarendon: Oxford, 1969).

McKie, David and Cook, Chris, eds, *The Decade of Disillusion: British Politics in the Sixties* (Macmillan: London, 1972).

McTaggart, J. M. E., *Studies in Hegelian Cosmology* (Cambridge University Press: Cambridge 1901).

Miller, Casey and Swift, Kate, *Words and Women* (Anchor: Garden City, N.Y., 1977).

Milner, Marion, *The Suppressed Madness of Sane Men* (Tavistock: London, 1987).

Mingay, G. E., *Enclosure and the Small Farmer in the Age of the Industrial Revolution* (Macmillan: London, 1968).

Mitchell, Juliet and Rose, J., eds., *Feminine Sexuality: Jacques Lacan and the 'Ecole Freudienne'* (Macmillan: London, 1982).

Moers, Ellen, *Literary Women: The Great Writers* (Doubleday: Garden City, N.Y., 1977).

Moore, John, *Zeluco: Various Views of Human Nature, taken from Life and Manners, Foreign and Domestic*, 2 vols (A. Strahan and T. Cadell: London, 1820).

Mure, G. R. C., *The Philosophy of Hegel* (Oxford University Press: London, 1965).

Norris, Christopher, *Deconstruction: Theory and Practice* (Methuen: London, 1982).

Nurmi, Martin, *William Blake* (Hutchinson: London, 1975).

Olsen, Tillie, *Silences* (Delacapte: New York: 1978).

Parrinder, Patrick, *Authors and Authority: A Study of English Literary Criticism and its Relation to Culture 1750–1900* (Routledge and Kegan Paul: London, 1977).

Payne, Steven, 'The Christian Character of Christian Mystical Experience', *Religious Studies*, XX (1984), 417–27.

Piercy, Marge, *Woman on the Edge of Time* (Knopf: New York, 1976).

Pines, Malcolm, 'Reflections on Mirroring', *Group Analysis*, XV, 2 (1982), Supp. 1–26.

Piper, H. W., *The Active Universe* (Athlome Press: London, 1962).

Plath, Sylvia, *The Bell Jar* (Faber & Faber: London, 1966).

Plowman, Max, *An Introduction to the Study of Blake* (Gollancz: London, 1967).

Poe, Edgar Allan, *Poetry and Tales*, ed. P. F. Quinn (Cambridge University Press: New York, 1984).

Praz, Mario, *The Romantic Agony*, trans. A. Davidson (Oxford University Press: London, 1951).

Punter, David, 'Blake and the Shapes of London', *Criticism*, XXIII (1981), 16–22.

Punter, David, 'Blake: Creative and Uncreative Labour', *Studies in Romanticism*, XVI (1977), 544–56.

Punter, David, *Blake, Hegel and Dialectic* (Rodopi: Amsterdam: 1982).

Punter, David, 'Blake, Marxism and Dialectic', *Literature and History*, 6 (1977), 229–34.

Punter, David, *The Literature of Terror: A History of Gothic Fictions from 1765 to the Present Day* (Longmans: London, 1980).

Pynchon, Thomas, *Gravity's Rainbow* (Cape: New York and London, 1973).

Rabb, T. K. and R. I. Rotberg, eds, *The Family in History: Interdisciplinary Essays* (Harper and Row: New York, 1973).

Radcliffe, Ann, *The Italian: or The Confessional of the Black Penitents* (1797), ed. F. Garber (Oxford University Press: London, 1971).

Radcliffe, Ann, *The Mysteries of Udolpho* (1794), ed. Bonamy Dobrée (Oxford University Press: London, 1970).

Read, Herbert, *The True Voice of Feeling: Studies in English Romantic Poetry* (Faber & Faber: London, 1953).

Reich, Wilhelm, *Sex-Pol: Essays 1929–1934*, ed. L. Baxendall (Random House: New York, 1972).

Riviere, J., ed., *Developments in Psycho-Analysis* (Hogarth: London, 1952).

Rogers, K. M., *The Troublesome Helpmate: A History of Misogyny in Literature*

(University of Washington Press: Seattle, 1966).

Rowbotham, Sheila, *Women, Resistance and Revolution* (Allen Lane: London, 1972).

Rudd, Margaret, *Organiz'd Innocence: The Story of Blake's Prophetic Books* (Routledge and Kegan Paul: London, 1956).

Rustin, Michael, 'A Socialist Consideration of Kleinian Psychoanalysis', *New Left Review*, **131** (1982), 71–96.

Rzepka, C. J., *The Self as Mind: Vision and Identity in Wordsworth, Coleridge and Keats* (Harvard University Press: Cambridge, Mass., 1986).

Scharfstein, Ben-Ami, *Mystical Experience* (Blackwell: Oxford, 1974).

Schorer, Mark, *William Blake: The Politics of Vision* (Peter Smith: Gloucester, Mass., 1975).

Sedgwick, E. K., *Between Men: English Literature and Homosocial Desire* (Columbia University Press: New York, 1985).

Segal, Hanna, *Klein* (Harvester: Brighton, 1979).

Shelley, Mary, *Frankenstein* (1818), ed. R. E. Dowse and D. J. Palmer (Dent: London, 1963).

Shelley, P. B., *Poetical Works*, ed. T. Hutchinson (Oxford University Press: London, 1943).

Spender, Dale, *Man Made Language* (Routledge and Kegan Paul: London, 1976).

Stace, W. T., *Mysticism and Philosophy* (Macmillan: London, 1960).

Sterne, Laurence, *A Sentimental Journey through France and Italy* (1768), ed. G. Petrie, introd. A. Alvarez (Penguin: Harmondsworth, Middx., 1967).

Sterne, Laurence, *Tristram Shandy* (1759–67), ed. G. Petrie (Penguin: Harmondsworth, Middx., 1967).

Stoker, Bram, *Dracula* (1897) (pbk edn, New American Library: New York, 1965).

Stone, Lawrence, *The Family, Sex and Marriage in England 1500–1800* (Weidenfeld and Nicolson: London, 1977).

Swinburne, A. C., *Collected Poetical Works*, 2 vols (Heinemann: London, 1924).

Tacitus, *De Origine et Situ Germanorum*, ed. J. G. C. Anderson (Clarendon: Oxford, 1938).

Thomis, M. I. and Holt, P., *Threats of Revolution in Britain 1789–1848* (Macmillan: London, 1977).

Thompson, E. P., *The Making of the English Working Class* (Penguin: Harmondsworth, Middx., 1968).

Thorslev, P. L., Jr, *Romantic Contraries: Freedom versus Destiny* (Yale University Press: New Haven, 1984).

Thorslev, P. L., Jr, 'Some Dangers of Dialectic Thinking', in *Romantic and Victorian: Essays in Memory of William H. Marshall*, ed. W. P. Elledge and R. L. Hoffman (Fairleigh Dickinson University Press: Rutherford, N.J., 1971).

Toukaram, *Psaumes de pèlerin*, trans. G.-A. Deleury (Gallimard: Paris, 1956).

Trevor-Roper, Hugh, 'Thomas Carlyle's Historical Philosophy', *Times Literary Supplement* (26th June 1981), p. 732.

Vico, Giambattista, *The New Science* (1775), trans. T. G. Bergin and M. H. Fisch (Cornell University Press: Ithaca, N.Y., 1970).

Vonnegut, Kurt, *The Sirens of Titan* (Delacorte: New York, 1959).

Walpole, Horace, *The Castle of Otranto* (1764), ed. W. S. Lewis (Oxford University Press: London, 1969).

Walsh, W. H., *Hegelian Ethics* (Macmillan: London, 1969).

Watt, Ian, *The Rise of the Novel: Studies in Defoe, Richardson and Fielding* (Chatto and Windus: London, 1957).

Wells, H. G., *The Island of Doctor Moreau* (1896) (pbk edn, New American Library: London, 1973).

Western, Drew, *Self and Society: Narcissism, Collectivism and the Development of Morals* (Cambridge University Press: Cambridge, 1985).

Wilde, Oscar, *The Picture of Dorian Grey* (1891), ed. I. Murray (Oxford University Press: London, 1974).

Wilkie, Brian and Johnson, M. L., *Blake's 'Four Zoas': The Design of a Dream* (Harvard University Press: Cambridge, Mass., 1978).

Williamson, Judith, *Decoding Advertisements: Ideology and Meaning in Advertising* (Marion Boyers: London, 1978).

Wilson, Elizabeth, *Adorned in Dreams: Fashion and Modernity* (Virago: London, 1985).

Winch, R. F. and Goodman, L. W., eds, *Selected Studies in Marriage and the Family* (Holt, Rinehart and Winston: New York, 1968).

Wordsworth, William, *The Poems*, ed. J. O. Hayden, 2 vols (Penguin: Harmondsworth, Middx., 1977).

Wordsworth, William and Dorothy, *The Early Letters of William and Dorothy Wordsworth*, ed. F. de Selincourt, (Clarendon: Oxford, 1935).

Wright, D. G., *Revolution and Terror in France 1789–1795* (Longman: London, 1974).

Young, Edward, *The Poetical Works*, 2 vols (William Pickering: London, 1844).

Zaretsky, Eli, *Capitalism, The Family, and Personal Life* (Pluto: London, 1976).

INDEX